# VISUAL, NARRATIVE AND CREATIVE RESEARCH METHODS

Visual research methods are quickly becoming key topics of interest and are now widely recognised as having the potential to evoke emphatic understanding of the ways in which other people experience their worlds. *Visual, Narrative and Creative Research Methods* examines the practices and value of these visual approaches as a qualitative tool in the field of social science and related disciplines.

This book is concerned with the process of applying visual methods as a tool of inquiry from design, to production, to analysis and dissemination. Drawing on research projects which reflect real-world situations, you will be methodically guided through the research process in detail, enabling you to examine and understand the practices and value of visual, narrative and creative approaches as effective qualitative tools.

Key topics include:

- techniques of data production, including collage, mapping, drawing and photographs;
- the practicalities of application;
- the positioning of the researcher;
- interpretation of visual data;
- images and narratives in public spaces;
- evaluative analysis of creative approaches.

*Visual, Narrative and Creative Research Methods* will be an invaluable companion for researchers, postgraduate students and other academics with an interest in visual and creative methods and qualitative research.

**Dawn Mannay** is Lecturer in Social Sciences at Cardiff University, Wales, and she employs participatory, visual, creative and narrative methods in her research with diverse communities.

An essential read for everyone interested in participatory visual and creative methods. Mannay is an experienced guide through the complexities of the research process, and sheds valuable light on their dynamics by considering the broader contexts in which they are embedded.

**Gillian Rose**, *Professor of Cultural Geography,*
The Open University

Mannay offers social scientists – from those in the final years of undergraduate study to qualitative researchers more generally – an insightful guide to visual research. Beautifully written and accessible, the book tackles important debates concerning the generation, analysis and dissemination of visual material, drawing on classic and contemporary literature to offer insights that look beneath the gloss of the visual.

**Helen Lomax**, *Professor in Health and Wellbeing,*
University of Northampton

This is an engaging and insightful book that I would highly recommend to students, lecturers and researchers. With its exemplary attention to questions of theory, methodology, ethics and dissemination, it offers a creatively accessible guide to the possibilities and challenges of working with the visual across the social sciences.

**Janet Fink**, *Professor of Childhood and Personal Relationships,*
University of Huddersfield

# VISUAL, NARRATIVE AND CREATIVE RESEARCH METHODS

## Application, reflection and ethics

*Dawn Mannay*

Routledge
Taylor & Francis Group

LONDON AND NEW YORK

First published 2016
by Routledge
2 Park Square, Milton Park, Abingdon, Oxon OX14 4RN

and by Routledge
711 Third Avenue, New York, NY 10017

*Routledge is an imprint of the Taylor & Francis Group, an informa business*

*British Library Cataloguing in Publication Data*
A catalogue record for this book is available from the British Library

*Library of Congress Cataloging in Publication Data*
A catalog record for this book has been requested

ISBN: 978-1-138-02431-1 (hbk)
ISBN: 978-1-138-02432-8 (pbk)
ISBN: 978-1-315-77576-0 (ebk)

Typeset in Bembo
by Cenveo Publisher Services

# CONTENTS

# ACKNOWLEDGEMENTS

In completing my book, *Visual, Narrative and Creative Research Methods: Application, Reflection and Ethics*, there are many people who should be thanked and acknowledged, too many perhaps to fit in an *Acknowledgements* section so I apologise in advance to those not named individually. As much of my initial engagement with visual, narrative and creative methods began with my doctoral research project, '*Mothers and Daughters on the Margins: Gender, Generation and Education*', funded by the Economic and Social Research Council (PTA031200600088), I would like to acknowledge all the participants who made this study possible. Also my thanks go to Professor John Fitz, Professor Emma Renold and Professor Bella Dicks for supervising my doctoral research project; and Gill Boden who was my mentor.

My knowledge and understanding of visual and creative methodologies has developed through my teaching, therefore, I would like to thank all my students, particularly those who I have taught in the module '*Issues in Social and Cultural Psychology*'; and all of the students, researchers and practitioners who have attended my workshops. These lectures, seminars and workshops have raised many of the questions, ideas and discussions that feature in the book. I would also like to thank colleagues at Cardiff University, particularly the psychology teaching team, for supporting and contributing to my modules.

In the same way, the research and writing projects that I have been involved with have acted as a vehicle to engage with and reflect on a number of qualitative techniques and I would like to acknowledge all of the participants and some of the people that I have worked with on these projects: Ceri Wilcock at the Open University, Clare O'Connell at the University of South Wales, Victoria Edwards, Ruby Marzella and Dr Aimee Grant at Cardiff University, Ministry of Life, Fostering Network and the Children's Social Care Research and Development Centre (CASCADE), particularly Dr Eleanor Staples and Dr Sophie Hallett.

I am also grateful to a wide range of authors and inspiring speakers and although I cannot name them all individually, much of their work is cited in the book. I have also learned a lot working with my co-conveners in the Childhood and Youth Research Group, Families, Identity and Gender Research Network, and the British Sociological Society's Visual Studies Research Group.

I am grateful to Dr Sara Delamont and Professor Paul Atkinson for their invaluable help and guidance in putting together the initial proposal, and to Professor Gillian Rose for her support and encouragement. I would also like to thank the proposal reviewers for their comments and suggestions; and the editorial team at Routledge for their support, particularly Philip Mudd and Natasha Ellis-Knight, who have had to work with me patiently to attend to permissions, visual image files and all the essential administrative tasks that were necessary to move forward.

Special thanks goes to all the people who read and made comments on and corrections to my chapters: Dr Michael Richardson, Dr Lisa Morriss, Professor Helen Lomax, Professor Janet Fink, Dr Katherine Carroll, Victoria Edwards and Melanie Morgan. I could not have finished this book without your help. I should also mention Dr Rachel Swann, who shares an office with me and had to put up with me moaning about book-related things for too long.

Borrowing a quote from science fiction author Ray Bradbury [1] '*You learn to live with your crazy enthusiasms which nobody else shares, and then you find a few other nuts like yourself, and they're your friends for a lifetime. That's what friends are, the people who share your crazy outlook and protect you from the world, because nobody else is going to give a damn what you're doing, so you need a few other people like yourself*'; I would also like to thank my friends for being there.

Last but certainly not least, with much love, I would like to thank my family – particularly my partner in life and for life, David, who has grown tired of seeing the back of my head as I type on my laptop but made sure that I didn't go hungry, making lots of meals that were a material demonstration of his love and commitment. Also our wonderful children, who are no longer children, Toyah, Jordon and Travis, and their partners Tim, Sherelle and Jamie, for asking how things were going and listening to me complain. I am also grateful to our granddaughter Taya, who, at only one year of age, can forcibly demand that I get off the laptop every time she visits – she has brought a lot of fun and laughter into our lives and will continue to be an absolute pleasure. We are also looking forward to getting to know our newest granddaughter Tilleah who arrived just in time to feature in the Acknowledgements.

## Note

1  Science fiction author Ray Bradbury interviewed in 1972 by two college students driving him to a speaking gig – an animated interview about friendship, fiction, and death-by-driving, available at: http://boingboing.net/2015/04/29/ray-bradbury-animated-interview. html (Accessed 30 March 2015).

# LIST OF FIGURES

# 1

# INTRODUCTION

*Visual, Narrative and Creative Research Methods: Application, Reflection and Ethics* examines the practices and value of visual approaches as a qualitative tool in the field of social science and related disciplines. The book is centred on the use of visual approaches but the use of *narrative* and *creative* in the title are symbolic of the commitment to embed the visual within wider frames, rather than isolating visual studies as somehow existing as a separate entity. The visual images that we study are often surrounded by the existing narrative of an accompanying print press story, the images that we produce form part of a wider narrative that directs their framing, and when we ask participants to create something visual, our understanding of these images is often predicated not just on the image itself but the accompanying elicitation interview.

Visual researchers have worked hard to overcome a pervasive textual bias and the argument that the social sciences are 'a discipline of words' (Mead 1995) in which there is no room for pictures, except as peripheral, supporting illustrations. This work has been recognised and in contemporary social science research there has been an appreciation of the value of visual approaches; where the visual is often positioned as 'an immediate and authentic form, which verbal accounts are unable to fully encompass' (Spencer 2011, p. 32). However, although we are now living in an 'ocularcentric' culture (Mitchell 1994), where images form a vital part of our everyday worlds, we need to be careful not to focus so much on the visual as to suggest that the social sciences become 'a discipline of pictures'. The visual has to be embedded in the narratives of its inception, reception, interpretation and impact.

In the same way, there needs to be an appreciation of creativity. The creation of the visual image itself can be linked with originality, imagination and inspiration, which all form the components of the concept of creativity. However, beyond their making, images themselves are constantly subject to interpretation and re-interpretation. Images never 'contain a singular or true meaning' (Hall 1997) and all readings employ forms of creative analysis. In disseminating visual images, ideas of creativity also hold importance, as emergent forms of dissemination often explore spaces beyond the forceful limitations of traditional academic outputs. Additionally, much creative work is undertaken to achieve projects of social justice by engaging with the emotions of audiences. These creative forms of dissemination and engagement are sometimes enabled with images; but they also rely on narrative accounts, theatre and poems, where, ethically or practically, images cannot be shared or widely circulated.

## Audiences and aims

This book has been written with a wide readership in mind. The text aims to provide an advanced but accessible guide that takes the reader through every aspect of the research process, drawing on planning, ethics, implementations and reflections. It will be a useful framework for students in the later years of social science degrees and postgraduate students, as well as a support for lecturers and researchers with an interest in visual and creative methods; and qualitative research more generally. The term social sciences is seen as an umbrella term for anthropology, sociology, psychology, education and cultural studies; however, this disciplinary positioning does not intend to exclude those working in human geography, health sciences, media studies or the humanities.

It is a book for anyone with an interest in qualitative research methods and their application in academia but also in the projects undertaken by researchers in government agencies, the third sector and other organisations. Later in this chapter, as is common practice, I offer a concise overview of the organisation of the volume for ease of reference and for readers to select their own starting points; for although each chapter links across the volume to build a coherent picture of theoretical, methodological and ethical concerns, each chapter has been written so that it can also stand alone as a source of information for researchers and practitioners, or as a set reading for students with interests in particular facets of visual studies.

In writing this book, I was influenced by my own research journey but equally by my teaching both in relation to teaching third year undergraduate students and facilitating workshops. I have organised and led a number of visual methods workshops, both nationally and internationally, and the diverse audiences have informed the content of the following chapters. These workshops have been embedded in summer schools, attached to Continuing Professional Development events, linked to wider training programmes on qualitative research methods or as standalone activities focusing on particular visual techniques. At all of these workshops, I have learnt new things from my audience and, importantly, gained an insight into 'what visual researchers want to know more about'. These are often issues that have been particularly difficult to access, or gain a comprehensive knowledge about, in their studies of the visual.

I am not claiming that the book is a panacea for all questions about the visual or that it can provide an account that is comprehensive enough to attend to 'what visual researchers want' in its entirety. There will always be new questions and challenges. However, I have been responsive to a widespread interest in moving beyond the gloss of the visual, to present an account of 'the good, the bad and the ugly' of doing research on the ground. I have considered the need for coverage of the highly practical questions about the everyday negotiation of fieldwork; and a reflection on both situated ethics and the complex and controversial landscape of dissemination, representation and visibility, which questions what we 'do' and 'should do' with visual outputs. Additionally, I have been receptive to researchers', and students', desire to explore the interpretation of images and the social power relations that are implicit in who is seen, how they are seen and who is viewing; appreciating that images are never 'innocent' (Rose 2001).

In this way, the book aims to engage with issues of theory, methodology, ethics and dissemination to explore the opportunities and challenges, which shape how qualitative visual research is conducted in a multidisciplinary context. There are, of course, many visual approaches, only some of which are addressed in this book, but all of the approaches discussed consider the relationship between the creative, the visual, and the narrative; combining both verbal, textual and visual data in an integrated way. Here I draw on my own work and collaborations with colleagues, embedding these discussions in reference to the studies of other researchers who work in similar modes of visual research. There is an emphasis on creative, hand-crafted methods such as drawing, mapping, collaging and sandboxing, as well as an interest in working with personal artefacts and temporal narratives. There is also a focus on static media (Reavey 2011) in relation to the use of existing photographic images and their creation in the techniques of photo-elicitation and photovoice. The following section will provide the reader with a sense of my background, which will clarify 'the gravitational centres around which my thinking on research methods revolves' (Banks 2001, x).

## A visual journey

My own interest in the visual as a tool of qualitative inquiry was ignited by a moment of serendipity, not only in relation to the accidental nature of something unexpected, but importantly also the space to draw novel connections and synthesise insights (Fine and Deegan 1996). I had taken a short, twenty-week course at an adult learning centre called 'Basic Counselling Part 2' and as a homework activity we had been asked to make a collage about ourselves to share with others in the class. My collage was very much a representation of the mundane aspects of everyday life, such as housework, and also hobbies, likes and dislikes. However, in the sharing of the collages some of the other students had embraced the task in a different and deeper way, picturing absent fathers and key transitions, junctures and significant events in their life course. Nonetheless, each collage, whether superficial or highly reflexive, acted to tell a different story about the self, one that had not necessarily been engendered in the purely verbal class activities or the informal chatting of the coffee breaks. The visual had achieved something richer and more distinctive.

This chance encounter with the visual introduced me to the power of the visual to generate different accounts, to act as a tool to fight familiarity and engender defamiliarisation (Mannay 2010). It also made me reflect on the ethics of creative techniques. Later as I completed a first degree based in Education and Psychology and a Masters degree in Social Science Research Methods, I remembered this experience of the visual and embedded it in my Master's dissertation, which acted very much as a space to explore, work with and evaluate techniques of visual data production (see Mannay 2008, 2010). For me, this dissertation study reinforced the value of visual approaches and these were again centralised, along with the use of creative narrative work, in my doctoral study *Mothers and Daughters on the Margins: Gender, Generation and Education* (Mannay 2012).

This study explored the intergenerational marginalisation of working-class mothers and their daughters both in terms of education, employment and family relationships; examining social reproduction, and the ways in which gender, place and class act as barriers to educational progression for the participants, and the psychological, physical and practical costs of social mobility (Mannay 2013a). The specific techniques that I employed in this study were mapping, collaging, photovoice and 'possible selves' narratives.

The mapping technique was not a geographically accurate representation of home, rather one that encouraged participants to represent their localised worlds as they imagine them to be through drawings. These participant-directed maps were then used as tools of elicitation as participants talked me through their hand-drawn illustrations to communicate their understandings of home and the surrounding neighbourhood. The collaging and photovoice techniques were presented in the same way and participants could select the mode, or modes, that they wanted to work with from these options, although one chose to be interviewed without taking part in any visual data production. Collages were constructed from everyday objects, magazines, photographs and printed online images, while the photovoice activity was facilitated with disposable cameras.

These techniques engendered in-depth interviews where an understanding of participants' everyday lives was communicated with their visual creations; but to move beyond the everyday and focus on participants' past lives and imagined futures, I also introduced the concept of 'possible selves'. Initially, I was drawn to the work of Markus and Nurius (1986, p. 954) who attempt to provide a conceptual link between cognition and motivation by exploring individuals' possible selves; their 'ideas of what they might become, what they would like to become, and what they are afraid of becoming'. However, their quantitative design offered forced choices presented in questionnaires, which limited participants' responses to the categories offered by the researchers. Accordingly, I developed an approach more compatible with my aims; one that asked participants to create narrative or visual forms to represent their 'possible selves' (Mannay 2014), which again formed the basis for elicitation interviews.

The successes and points of contention from the *Mothers and Daughters on the Margins* project, discussed in detail in the following chapters, informed my further engagement with creative qualitative inquiry. For example, the project, *University Challenge* (Mannay and Edwards 2013) employed the innovative technique of sand-boxing, where participants created sand scenes using objects and miniature figures to represent their educational journeys. I return to this in Chapter 5. More recently, my work with Dr Aimee Grant and Ruby Marzella (2014), explored in Chapter 6, has drawn on participants' everyday artefacts to explore their experiences of breastfeeding and new motherhood; and in a different project, *Negotiating Young Parenthood*, we introduced found images as a photo-elicitation tool.

Therefore, although I have been involved in other forms of data production (for example, see Mannay and Wilcock 2015), overall visual, narrative and creative approaches have remained central in my research work. Additionally, these approaches are embedded in my undergraduate teaching and workshop facilitation, where students and delegates do not simply listen to me talk about the visual but actively create and analyse images in relation to formative and summative assessments and workshop activities. In this way, I am thoroughly located in the visual and the creative; however, this location does not blind me to the problematic nature of visual research, its interpretation and its dissemination. The book aims to draw on these experiences in a critical manner that considers the potentialities, ambiguities and challenges in the field.

## Structure of the book

The book is divided into seven further chapters, which work through different lenses to explore visual, narrative and creative research methods. The following chapter, Chapter 2, '*Mapping images: charting the visual and creative in social science research*' contextualises the topic of visual research methods by providing a concise historical overview of the use of these techniques in the social sciences. Rather than falling into the trap of presenting the visual as something novel the chapter examines how contemporary practice can be linked back to studies in the arts, archeology, history and early anthropology. The chapter argues that rather than constantly reinventing the wheel, it is advantageous to reflect across disciplines and timelines and build on the considerable existing knowledge and best practices examples, which can usefully inform our work.

In this second chapter, I draw on Pauwels' (2011) framework for grouping, sorting and reflecting on visual approaches, and organise my discussion under the categories of found materials, researcher-initiated productions and participatory productions. The category of found materials positions social scientists as image collectors and the chapter reflects on how art historians 'perform the art' (Belton 2002) and what social scientists can learn from this form of interpretation. There is also an exploration of anthropological engagement with found images and artefacts (Banks 2001) and more recent applications such as Gillian Rose's (2010) work around images in the British print press and the 'politics of sentiment'. Researcher-initiated productions, where social scientists act as image-creators, is conceptualised within the documentary tradition and the chapter examines how the pioneering work of anthropologists, such as John Collier Jnr, has been adapted and developed by an ever-growing body of work across disciplines. Lastly, participatory productions are explored in relation to the extent to which the social scientist has been and can be the participatory facilitator in visual research; an issue covered in more depth in Chapter 4.

The third chapter, '*Making the familiar strange: questions we would not think to ask*' builds on earlier work (Mannay 2010). It offers the theoretical basis of defamiliarisation to position the visual as a vehicle for unlocking new understandings for researchers. However, I argue that the potential for defamiliarisation is always a dual process because the creation of visual artefacts also works to make the familiar strange for research participants. They also gain new perspectives on their subjective understandings of their worlds. Focusing on participatory productions, the chapter presents a range of concrete examples, which demonstrate how photographs, maps, drawings and collages can render the familiar setting more perceptible. In this chapter there is a specific focus on defamiliarisation techniques in my own research, as well as the work of Richardson (2015) and Goff *et al.* (2013). In this way, the chapter focuses on the usefulness of visual approaches for making the familiar strange for both researchers and research participants.

Chapter 4, '*Participatory methodologies: questions of power and positionality in visual and narrative research*', returns to the question of the extent to which a social scientist can be the participatory facilitator in visual research. An easy marriage between visual data production and participatory practice is well versed and in vogue within the field of social science and the chapter explores how historically visual artefacts have been employed as a vehicle to 'give voice' to marginalised and politically oppressed communities through cloth work, photography and painting (Bacic 2013; Goggin 2003; Wahl 2014). However, these examples can be positioned as grass-roots movements and forms of individualised political activism demonstrating flexible and decentralised networked forms rather than the more formulised methods of social research.

Participatory research projects have not resolved the goal of 'giving voice', and a recurring issue for researchers is that of whose voice is being spoken and, simultaneously, whose voice is being heard, particularly when research participants are children. Consequently, positionality has been widely debated in terms of power relations, and although participatory techniques offer an opportunity to disrupt power relations it is recognised that they are unable to transcend these hierarchies (Lomax *et al.* 2011; Luttrell and Chalfen 2010). The relationships between participants and researchers have been heavily documented in the field of participatory visual research; however, less attention has been given to wider social relations and their impacts. Accordingly, this chapter argues that we need to reconsider and acknowledge that even when the 'intrusive presence' of the researcher steps out of the site of visual data production this leaves a space that is often filled by the 'intrusive presence' of significant others (Mannay 2013b).

The following chapter, Chapter 5, '*Problematising interpretation: applying auteur theory, disrupting the surface and breaking the frame*', shifts the focus from processes of visual and narrative data production to questions of interpretation, particularly the seeing and reading of images. The chapter explores the difference between vision and visuality and the juxtaposition between the audiences' reading and interpretation and the internal narrative of images, as intended by their creator. Auteur theory rests on the premise that the most salient aspect of an image is what the image maker intended to communicate (Rose 2001). The chapter advocates, therefore, the use of elicitation interviews around the images created in the visual data production stage to centralise the meaning making of and interpretations of participants, the image-creators. In this way, images and narratives are seen as part of a conversation where interpretation needs to be embedded in the contextualised process of the interview, rather than an analysis of de-contextualised and silenced images and stories.

However, the chapter also considers how 'the notion that meaningful interpretation is contingent on knowing its creator's intentions is nonetheless problematic, not least because these are not always available to viewers' (Lomax 2012, p. 228). This is particularly important in relation to the analysis of found images and the chapter considers how we can come to know an image without access to the image-creator. The chapter offers a number of practical suggestions for contextualising found images and four different approaches to knowing the image when it is not possible to ask participants to share their subjective interpretations of their creations. Namely, 'breaking the frame', cultural studies, social representations theory and semiotics. Overall, the chapter emphasises the need to move beyond vision and consider visuality, and the inherent power relations, misinterpretations, silences and subjectivities, which come to bear on both visual and narrative culture.

In understanding the visual, it is always important to have a sense of the mechanisms of production and Chapter 6, '*Visual and narrative data production: time, artistic ability and incongruence*', offers a highly practical guide that engages with the everyday issues of creative research with a series of illustrative, reflexive and reflective tales from the field. The chapter moves from the micro, to the meso and then to the macro to explore key processes in visual and narrative data production. At the micro level there is a consideration of the issues of time, artistic ability and incongruence, which surface in everyday interactions between researchers and participants. The meso perspective begins to consider creative techniques within wider research designs and frameworks, and explores the need to engage with the 'spaces previous to' and 'spaces of reflection' in the 'waiting field' (Mannay and Morgan 2015). Taking a macro perspective, the chapter also draws on Mills and Ratcliffe's (2012, p. 152) sobering account of the impact of the knowledge economy on qualitative research where the push for efficiency potentially narrows the opportunities to engender 'the unpredictable, the tangential and the creative' so that all that remains is 'methodological instrumentalism'. In this way, the chapter speaks to researchers' concerns about their everyday practice in the field, how visual techniques can be located within wider qualitative approaches, and the place of visual researchers and their work within the wider field of academia and its associated funding mechanisms.

The last topic of the book is presented in Chapter 7, '*Ethical concerns: answers to questions we did not want to ask*', which documents how the practicalities of visual research, and the ethics of creative methodologies, raise a number of challenges. In particular, the chapter focuses on the challenges that anonymity and confidentiality raise in visual research, and what it means to 'give voice' in participatory approaches but then silence the voices of participants by making their images invisible or unrecognisable in research outputs. The chapter explores issues of representation in relation to the 'politics of recognition' (Sweetman 2009), 'audiencing' (Lomax and Fink 2010) and the permanence of visual images in a digital society with reference to the concept of 'time immemorial' (Brady and Brown 2013). In response to these debates, the chapter presents strategies for creative dissemination and impact, such as theatre and poetry, which can act as a vehicle to retain the vibrancy and saliency of participants' accounts without employing their visual data. Lastly, the chapter moves beyond the researcher and researched coupling to consider those outside this relationship who are storied into participants' accounts and therefore recorded, analysed and disseminated without their knowledge or informed consent.

Finally, in Chapter 8, '*Conclusion: looking back and moving forward*', I bring together some of the central issues raised in the book and consider the future of visual research. The chapter is focused on emergent writing methodologies and recent debates around the personal, subjective and transformative dimensions of writing up and disseminating research findings; as well as considering how moves towards Open Access publishing can raise new ethical dilemmas for visual researchers. The chapter will also discuss how the field of visual research, and developments within it, become fragmented because of disciplinary boundaries and how the visual community can build better bridges, and share best practice. In this way, the final chapter will reflect on lessons learnt, further opportunities for, and threats to visual approaches in qualitative research. As Harper (2012, p. 7) agues, 'the world has never been more visually aware and visually engaged'. It is, therefore, imperative to think again about application, reflectivity and ethics in visual, narrative and creative research methods.

## References

Bacic, R. (2013) 'Arpilleras: Evolution and Revolution' Keynote Paper and Exhibition, *3rd International Visual Methods Conference*, Victoria University of Wellington, Wellington, New Zealand, 2–6 September 2013. http://www.cain.ulst.ac.uk/quilts/exhibit/followup.html#wellington03091 (Accessed 19 August 2015).

Banks, M. (2001) *Visual Methods in Social Research*. London: Sage.

Belton, R. (2002) *Art: The World of Art from Aboriginal to American Pop, Renaissance Masters to Postmodernism*. London: Flame Tree.

Brady, G. and Brown, G. (2013) 'Rewarding but Let's Talk About the Challenges: Using Arts Based Methods in Research with Young Mothers', *Methodological Innovations Online*, 8 (1): 99–112.

Fine, G. A. and Deegan, J. (1996) 'Three Principles of Serendip: Insight, Chance, and Discovery in Qualitative Eesearch', *Qualitative Studies in Education*, 9 (4): 434–47.

Goggin, D. (2003) 'Introduction', in C. McEwan, 'Building a postcolonial archive? Gender, Collective Memory and Citizenship in Post-Apartheid South Africa', *Journal of Southern African Studies*, 29 (3): 748.

Goff, S., Kleppel, R., Lindenauer, P. and Rothberg, M. (2013) 'Hospital Workers' Perceptions of Waste: a Qualitative Study Involving Photo-elicitation', *BMJ Quality & Safety*, 22: 826–35.

Hall, S. (1997) *Representation: Cultural Representations and Signifying Practices*. Buckingham: Open University Press.

Harper, D. (2012) *Visual Sociology*. London: Routledge.

Lomax, H. (2012) 'Shifting the Focus: Children's Image-making Practices and their Implications for Analysis', *International Journal of Research and Method in Education, Special Issue – Problematising Visual Methods*, 35 (3): 227–34.

Lomax, H. and Fink, J. (2010) 'Interpreting Images of Motherhood: The Contexts and Dynamics of Collective Viewing', *Sociological Research Online*, 15 (3).

Lomax, H., Fink, J., Singh, N. and High, C. (2011) 'The Politics of Performance: Methodological Challenges of Researching Children's Experiences of Childhood through the Lens of Participatory Video', *International Journal of Social Research Methodology*, 14 (3): 231–43.

Luttrell, W. and Chalfen, R. (2010) 'Lifting up the Voices of Participatory Research', *Visual Studies*, 25 (3): 197–200.

Mead, M. (1995) 'Visual Anthropology in a Discipline of Worlds', in P. Hocking (ed.) *Principles of Visual Anthropology*, pp. 3–10. Berlin: Mouton de Gruyter.

Mannay. D. (2008) 'Picture this! An Intergenerational Case Study Involving Participant-directed Visual Data Production', *Cardiff School of Social Sciences Paper 122 Postgraduate Café Papers*. Cardiff: Cardiff University.

Mannay, D. (2010) 'Making the Familiar Strange: Can Visual Research Methods Render the Familiar Setting more Perceptible?', *Qualitative Research*, 10 (1): 91–111.

Mannay, D. (2012) *Mothers and Daughters on the Margins: Gender, Generation and Education*. PhD Thesis, Cardiff University.

Mannay, D. (2013a) 'Keeping Close and Spoiling: Exploring Discourses of Social Reproduction and the Impossibility of Negotiating Change and Maintaining Continuity in Urban South Wales', *Gender and Education*, 25 (1): 91–107.

Mannay, D. (2013b) '"Who put that on there … why why why?" Power Games and Participatory Techniques of Visual Data Production', *Visual Studies*, 28 (2): 136–46.

Mannay, D. (2014) 'Mother and Daughter "Homebirds" and Possible Selves: Generational (Dis)connections to Locality and Spatial Identity in South Wales', in N. Worth and R. Vanderbeck (eds) *Intergenerational Space. Routledge Studies in Human Geography*. London: Routledge.

Mannay, D. and Edwards, V. (2013) 'It's Written in the Sand: Employing Sandboxing to Explore the Experiences of Non-traditional, Mature Students in Higher Education'. Presented at: *Society for Research into Higher Education (SRHE) Annual Research Conference 2013*, Celtic Manor, Newport, Wales, UK, 11–13 December 2013.

Mannay, D., Grant, A. and Marzella, R. (2014) 'Motherhood, Morality and Infant Feeding'. Presented at: *MeSC – Medicine, Science and Culture Event*, Cardiff University, Cardiff, Wales, UK, 15 October 2014.

Mannay, D. and Morgan, M. (2015) 'Doing Ethnography or Applying a Qualitative Technique?: Reflections from the "Waiting Field"', *Qualitative Research*, 15 (2): 166–82.

Mannay, D. and Wilcock, C. (2015) 'What Students Want? Exploring the Role of the Institution in Supporting Successful Learning Journeys in Online Distance Education', *Widening Participation and Lifelong Learning*, 17 (1): 49–63.

Markus, H. and Nurius, P. (1986) 'Possible Selves', *American Psychologist*, 41 (9): 954–69.

Mills, D. and Ratcliffe, R. (2012) 'After Method? Ethnography in the Knowledge Economy', *Qualitative Research*, 12 (2): 147–64.

Mitchell, W. J. T. (1994) *Picture Theory: Essays on Verbal and Visual Representation*. Chicago: University of Chicago Press.

Pauwels, L. (2011) 'An Integrated Conceptual Framework for Visual Social Research', in E. Margolis and L. Pauwels (eds) *The Sage Handbook of Visual Research Methods*, pp. 3–23, London: Sage.

Reavey, P. (2011) 'The Return to Experience: Psychology and the Visual' in P. Reavey (ed.) *Visual Methods in Psychology: Using and Interpreting Images in Qualitative Research*, pp. 1–16. London: Routledge.

Richardson, M. (2015) 'Embodied Intergenerational: Family Position, Place and Masculinity', *Gender, Place and Culture*, 22 (2): 157–71.

Rose, G. (2001) *Visual Methodologies: An Introduction to Researching with Visual Materials*. London: Sage.

Rose, G. (2010) *Doing Family Photography: The Domestic, the Public and the Politics of Sentiment*. Farnham: Ashgate.

Spencer, S. (2011) *Visual Research Methods in the Social Science: Awakening Visions*. London: Routledge.

Sweetman, P. (2009) 'Just Anybody? Images, Ethics and Recognition', in John Gillett (ed.) *Just Anybody. Renja Leino*, pp. 7–9. Winchester: Fotonet/The Winchester Gallery.

Wahl, H. (2014) 'Negotiating Representation in Israel and Palestine', *Visual Studies*, 29 (1): 1–14.

# 2

# MAPPING IMAGES

## Charting the visual and creative in social science research

## Introduction

This chapter contextualises the topic of visual and creative research methods by providing a concise overview of the use of particular techniques and approaches in the social sciences. Rather than falling into the trap of presenting the visual as something novel, the chapter examines the long-held concern with visual and creative works across disciplines such as history, art and archeology. The chapter argues that this body of diverse work constitutes intellectual schools of thought, methodologies, empirical work and techniques of analysis, which should act to inform contemporary applications, but that they are often forgotten. Although it is not always acknowledged, the pioneering work of cross-disciplinary scholars has been adapted and developed by an ever-growing body of work in the social sciences, in a variety of approaches and forms.

Pauwels (2010) offers a useful framework for grouping, sorting and reflecting on visual and creative approaches, in relation to found materials, researcher-initiated productions and participatory productions, which will be drawn on to structure the chapter. Found materials position social scientists as image collectors and refer to the study of existing materials. In considering found materials, analysis and interpretation, rather than creation and production, are often centralised. The following section will reflect on the contribution that studies in the humanities can have in contemporary visual studies, exploring how art historians 'perform the art', and recognising archeology's knowledge of found materials. The chapter illustrates how more recent work maps onto these approaches with reference to Marcus Banks' (2001) social anthropology and Gillian Rose's exploration of mediated images. Importantly, drawing again from Rose and Rachel Hurdley's study of artefacts, the permeability of the category of 'found' is highlighted, where 'found materials' move from being simply found to becoming active within the interview setting.

In relation to researcher-initiated productions, which position social scientists as image-creators, the chapter focuses on the power of photography and its unsavoury history as a tool of authoritative evidence in a hierarchical, colonial form of pseudo-science. The chapter then conceptualises researcher-initiated productions within the documentary tradition and visual ethnography, emphasising the importance of reflexivity in moving beyond the reductive realism that characterised earlier work. The section also presents the pioneering work of anthropologist, John Collier Junior, and explores how his concept of photo-elicitation has been adapted and developed by researchers interested in participatory and collaborative work with, not on, participants and communities.

Participatory productions, then, position the social scientist as the participatory facilitator and this final section of the chapter sets out some of the underlying philosophies that guide researchers' selection of creative forms of participant-led data production. Within these participatory frames participants are seen as active within the research process and there is an attempt to produce research with participants, rather than collect data from them. Studies range from being partially participatory, often at the stage of data production, to those that involve participants in all stages of the research process: design, fieldwork, analysis and dissemination. The participatory nature of research and its connection with the visual will be a key area of discussion in later chapters; and as such this section, and to some extent the chapter as a whole, simply offers the reader an overview of salient concepts, issues and debates, to enable a more nuanced engagement with the research approaches discussed in later chapters.

## Found images and narratives

In considering what can be found, and made the object of social science inquiry, there are a plethora of existing visual and textual sources including print media, film, everyday cultural artefacts, personal communications, advertisements, internet, heritage sites and art works. Found materials position social scientists as image and narrative collectors, who then apply theoretical lenses to interrogate, examine and understand these objects of inquiry. However, these interpretations are often structured and informed by the disciplines that were active before the social sciences emerged; and the classification of the visual and the narrative by historians, art critics and archeologists remains central in framing contemporary social science understandings of found materials.

In the following chapter, I discuss issues of familiarity, interpretation and subjectivity within a social science frame. However, the arts have long recognised the process of sentient engagement and appreciated the migratory aesthetics, which create an active interface between viewer and artwork and are relational, embodied and affective (Bal 2007). In arts theory, these migratory encounters take place in the relational interface, the space of viewing, where the individual is central and the viewer, consumer or spectator in the encounter, cannot be aloof, autonomous, shielded, or in charge of the aesthetic experience. This consideration of subjectivity positions 'artwork to be empty as long as the act of viewing is not inherent to it' (Bethlehem and Harris 2012), where aesthetics is primarily an encounter, the subject body is engaged and we bring our subjectivities to the viewing. The social science conceptualisation of visuality and the overlapping term scopic regime, which refer to the ways in which audiences bring their own ways of seeing and other knowledges to bear on an image (Rose 2001), then, is a recognisable trope that has been well rehearsed in the philosophies of arts theory.

The mechanics of much analysis of found materials can also be linked back to studies in the arts and history where context, form and content are integrated. In relation to interpretation, art historians often encourage their students to 'perform the art', the word perform here is linked with interpretation (Belton 2002). In 'performing the art', there is a recognition of the subjectivity of the viewer but also a focus on creating a statement about the work itself. When 'performing the art', scholars apply the lenses of context, form and content; and all of these categories can be seen as active within social science research, although sometimes with different terms applied. Context simply refers to the circumstances surrounding the production of a work, rather than what can be seen within the work itself. This contextual lens may consider the artist, the circumstances of the commission, temporal and geographical placement, and the philosophy, politics and religion that contribute to the zeitgeist.

The category of form lies in the object of analysis itself and relates to its constitute elements such as light, perspective, medium, technique, arrangement and composition. There is a tendency to move from form to content automatically, blurring the two in any casual viewing; however, in analysis it is useful to attempt to make a distinction. Content, then, refers to what a work can say and the effects it produces in the viewer; and primary content distinguishes the literal level of language and object, while secondary content moves beyond the literal to explore symbolism, metaphor and the duality of meaning.

For example, Lambert (2014) considers the Renaissance period and how large belly and thighs were positioned as erotic. In a time when food was less plentiful, a large stomach signified health and wealth, while large sagging breasts were associated with the old and the poor; and the paintings of the time reflected this preference with large breasts only appearing on images of old, ugly women and evil witches. High fashion offered dresses that minimised the breasts and those who could pay the price farmed their children out to a wet nurse to escape from the enlarged breasts that developed with the instigation and continuance of infant feeding. In this way, the content analysis of Renaissance art can tell us about the embodied symbolism of acceptable femininity; and the socio-historical context that breasts occupied before their positioning as the ultimate symbol of erotica.

In relation to context, the artist or writer has been romantically positioned in idealist philosophy, as a unique individual whose creative, solitary genius generates the invention of their art; however, these creators are individuals who reside in real rather than fictional worlds. Images produce meanings, which are constantly circulated within the social formation and the production of these meanings is inseparable from the production of power. Chadwick (1990, p. 14) explores power in art by focusing on the intersection between women as producers of art and woman in representation, because it is here that we can 'become most aware of what is not represented or spoken, the omissions and silences that reveal the power of cultural ideology'.

Chadwick (1990) charts art history through the lenses of the middle ages, the Renaissance, Modern Art and Postmodernism. Focusing on context, she explores the complexity of attribution and reattribution; and its links to power, gender and value. Chadwick demonstrates the ways in which art history and art critique is closely aligned with art market economies, and argues that ways of seeing are always 'qualified by greed, desire and expectation'. For example, in the case of the sixteenth-century painter Marietta Robusti, the classic piece *Portrait of an Old Man with a Boy* (1585) was attributed to her father Tintoretto, and was considered one of his finest portraits, until Robusti's monogram was discovered in 1920. This focus on context, allows us to consider the circumstances of the production of the work but also its later readings. The reattribution to a woman artist often produces a monetary devaluation. Furthermore, the language of art critique often shifts from one that praises the powerful brush strokes of the master, to one which finds that the 'articulation lacks correctness' or illustrates 'cleverly concealed weaknesses' and 'subtle artifices' (Chadwick 1990, p. 23).

The study of found images then, does not begin with visual studies in the social sciences; and although this is clearly the work of art historians and scholars, we can see how these forms of analysis map onto visual studies in the social sciences. For example, in his analysis of early to mid-twentieth-century postcards, social anthropologist, Banks (2001), argues that with found images we cannot simply look closely but instead we must bring knowledges to bear upon the image. For Banks (2001, p. 3), this involves moving beyond the content and considering the image as an object. Interpreting a postcard picturing a scene from India, he begins by exploring the category of form, thinking about the positioning of the photograph's subjects in relation to the camera. Banks then moves to the content, the subjects, their clothing, the background and the interpretation of these things from a Western gaze. Moving to context, the postcard itself is a photomechanical production rather than a photograph; but there could be an opportunity to trace the company that produced the postcard, then perhaps the image-maker. The message on the back of the photograph provides a narrative to add further context and the writer claims that 'there really are people and places that look like this'. There is a further story about the sender of the postcard, Joe, and the recipient, 'Mary darling', which could be explored further with the use of archival sources.

Banks (2001, p. 7) does not employ the language of art historians directly, rather he suggests that we ask particular questions about found images, 'what the image is of, what is its context?, who took it or made it, when and why?, how do other people come to have it, how do they read it, what do they do with it?'. All of these questions touch upon form, content and context. Importantly, Banks is also careful to consider the effects an image produces in the viewer and the duality of meanings that become visible in the secondary level of content. However, in this social science lens there is perhaps more emphasis on the reader and viewer in the interpretation of the image, not the general or specific 'other', rather the viewing self of the analyst, historian or in this case social anthropologist. Accordingly, it is the researcher's interpretation that needs to be questioned and scrutinized; and in the social sciences it is important to see our initial understandings as pre-scripted and our interpretations as culturally, historically and personally specific.

This requirement to explore and question our own subjectivity is centralised throughout the following chapters, as an essential means of gaining an understanding of found images and narratives. Chapter 5 returns to the subject of found images and their analysis; and here I introduce other forms of interpretation, including 'breaking the frame', cultural studies, social representations theory and semiotics, which provide different tools to interrogate found materials, but which still have resonance with the arts and humanities-based approaches of 'performing the art' (Belton 2002). However, although the classification of materials as 'found' provides a useful starting point, such categories have blurred lines. Found materials are not themselves participatory productions; but they can be utilsed to position the social scientist as the participatory facilitator.

For example, in her book *Doing Family Photography: The Domestic, the Public and the Politics of Sentiment*, Rose (2010) reflects on two of her studies with 'found materials'. One is more clearly situated within the found framework as it examines the reporting by the British print press of the bombs that exploded on the public transport system in 2005, paying particular attention to how the readers of the newspapers were positioned and what they were invited to feel. In analysing these found images, Rose considers how colonial imaginary, gendered discourses and the exclusionary exceptions of who is normatively human were presented in the form of photographs, and their accompanying text, to engender a particular kind of intimate public. For Rose, this intimate public is resonant of a pain alliance where a passive ideal of empathy is constructed from caring based on similarity, which comes 'dangerously close to the appropriation of someone else's experience because we feel for another only insofar as we are positioned as being like that other' (2011, p. 113). In response, Rose calls for ethics in the field of vision where we learn to look again, differently.

The second study moves from the public sphere to the domestic space of family photography. Family photographs have become an unpopular site of exploration, characterised as stereotyped, ubiquitous and having an overwhelming sense of similarity and redundancy. However, drawing on the disciplines of anthropology, geography and material culture studies, Rose takes the reader on a journey that reveals not what photographs are but what photographs do. This 'doing' and the active nature of the image is significant because family photographs are embedded in specific practices, and it is the specificity of those practices, not simply their content, that define an image as a family photograph. In this way, their meaning is only part of their story, and Rose does not simply analyse these found materials, rather she moves them into a participatory framework that works with the creator of the images.

Arguably, these family photographs are 'found' in the sense that they were not produced by Rose, researcher initiated, or produced by participants for the purposes of the research, participatory productions; the images existed prior to and outside of the research, they are found images. Nevertheless, Rose's research framework moves them across these categorical boundaries as she did not simply try to interpret these images, rather she interviewed women in their own homes to gain a sense of the domestic space and the encounters between object and practice in family photography, namely subject positions and social relations. Rose presents her participants' photographs as indexical for they are dated, stored, displayed, looked at and circulated; and in this way they are involved in processes of 'doing' not simply being.

For all of the women in the study, photographs were about picturing happy moments but also about the ongoing process of revisiting and sharing the images, which would again generate pleasure and also enact familial integration. Discussing these found images with the women who created them, allowed for an insight into the enactment of family togetherness and the ways in which the integration of family photographs is both temporal and spatial. For Rose, photographs extend togetherness in time and space but this requires work. The labour of family photographs, can be seen as women's traditional responsibility for domestic order but it is also a way for women to negotiate a feminised subjectivity of acceptable motherhood. Photographs are presented as gifts for exchange, a commodity, but photographs also establish relationships between people and are not simply commodities. In the domestic sphere then, the global circulation of family photographs is complex, differentiated and cannot be seen as fully commodified; and it is the qualitative interviews with participants that engender an appreciation of the active nature of these 'found materials'.

The intersection between 'found materials' and more participatory frames can also be explored in relation to everyday objects or artefacts. The existential importance of things is most closely associated with the field of archeology. However, Olsen (2010) argues that although 'archaeology's long-held concern with things constitutes an intellectual skill', which should be acknowledged, much contemporary interest in material culture neglects the potential archeological contribution to the topics they address. This is a similar argument as the one presented here in relation to the accumulated knowledge of art historians, which can usefully inform current visual studies. Consequently, studies in the humanities, art, history and archeology, all offer a range of tools and techniques that can inform a social science engagement with 'found materials'.

What we do every day, in the fleeting moments when we discard a plastic bag, says something about consumer society and our transient and uncertain lives. The study of these artefacts can tell how a particular aspect of material culture is made use of, or even entangled in our everyday lives (Chapman 2000). The usefulness of the artefact in visual studies has been illustrated by the work of Hurdley (2006) who explored the display of material culture on domestic mantelpieces and many other focal points in participants' homes. For Hurdley, these were not just display spaces, but also sites where family and individual stories were constructed around individual objects and assemblages of photographs and collections of artefacts.

In line with Rose's (2010) work, introduced earlier in the chapter, Hurdley (2006) also moves between the boundaries that categorise artefacts as 'found materials' to engage with their participatory potential. For Hurdley (2006, p. 717), 'narratives and objects inhabit the intersection of the personal and the social'; and in her research she did not simply analyse these displays, rather the objects formed the basis for interviews with thirty people and their families. In discussing these artefacts with their possessors and exhibitors, Hurdley was able to explore how their materiality is not bound by temporal and spatial limits. Participants built stories of absent presences, where their artefacts acted as a horizon beyond past and future, and communicated their evolving biographies. In Chapter 6, I will return to the potentialities of introducing objects within an interview framework, with reference to my own work in the *Intergenerational Views and Experiences of Breastfeeding* project.

Found materials, which locate social scientists as image and narrative collectors, are a vast field of art works, family photographs, print press articles, online sources and everyday objects, some of which we have discussed here. Importantly, this section has emphasised that interest in found materials has a long history and a substantial body of valuable, cross-disciplinary work, which is useful to reflect on and incorporate in contemporary visual studies. It has also highlighted the permeable nature of Pauwels' (2010) categories and the ways in which access to conversations with image-creators and object owner can relocate 'found materials' from being the object of study to a tool of elicitation; a technique that will be explored further in relation to researcher-initiated productions.

## Researcher-initiated productions

Researcher-initiated productions position social scientists as image-creators (Pauwels 2011). In the category of researcher-initiated productions, researchers are the ones holding the paintbrush, sketching the outlines or behind the camera; and, in particular, it is the camera that has been employed to substantiate objective, scientific and reductive realism. Technological developments in the nineteenth century saw photographic methods centralised as an evidential base from which to analyse and represent 'other' cultures. The creation of these photographs, their dissemination and their analysis were firmly embedded in the power relations of Imperialism, where photography became part of the objectifying gaze of the colonial project.

The hierarchical ordering of race was presented as evidence of Western supremacy in which the reductive realism of the photograph was employed to maintain and enforce a prejudiced regulatory system. Photography provided this pseudo-science with a level of authenticity because of the 'truthfulness of the appearance of things' (Brown 2009, p. 14) and anthropologists and agencies of government were active in researcher-initiated work, which tended to present photography as a direct representation of reality. For example, Spencer (2011, p. 15) examines Landseer's 1890 plate drawing 'Negroes' and a 1935 photograph of a family of Aborigines in

Australia, to demonstrate the ways in which scientific disciplines used photography 'as part of their regimes of truth to catalogue and verify'.

As discussed in relation to the interpretation of found images and texts, researcher-initiated materials remain constructions of both individuals and specific cultures. Prosser (2006, p. 17) contends that a photograph does not simply show us how things look, 'it is an image produced by a mechanical device, at a very specific moment, in a particular context by a person working within a set of personal parameters'. Early photography in the social sciences was often filtered, censored and shaped through a propagandist manipulation of images and their accompanying text within an Imperialist tradition. However, by the twentieth century, there was a recognition that these highly constructed images could not act as authoritative evidence and that they contributed to 'the indignity of speaking for others' (Deleuze and Foucault 1990, p. 10).

A concern to move beyond 'the indignity of speaking for others' is often located in the documentary tradition's essentialist foundations, which aimed for verisimilitude, sympathy, relevance and the opportunity to illuminate social injustice. However, postmodern critiques contend that in such works causality is often vague, blame is not assigned and, therefore, the fate of those captured in the images cannot be overcome. Nonetheless, working between these contrasting positions it is possible to demonstrate the value of both more contemporary engagements and historical contributions, as well as acknowledging their dangers. Harper (2012, p. 18) contends that studying the documentary 'allows us to see how photographs create meaning in historical, sociological and political circumstances that are themselves in motion'; and he explores researcher-initiated production within the documentary tradition from the 1880s to the 1960s, documenting the work of key figures such as P. H. Emerson, Jacob Riis, Bill Brandt, Dorothea Lange and Bruce Davidson, and their impacts on contemporary visual sociology.

For Rose (2001, p. 130), 'reflexivity is an attempt to resist the universalising claims of academic knowledge and to insist that academic knowledge, like all other knowledge is partial'; and, as well as reflecting on the documentary tradition, Harper also sensitively returns to his early work. Revisiting a project that proposed a humanistic and artful ethnography of homelessness, Harper (2012) offers a form of autobiography in his writing where he reflects upon the emotional costs of ethnographic research, the shift from seeing photography as a means rather than an end, the lack of space to write in the first person and be reflexive before the 'cultural turn'; and why ethnography needs to include an account of its creation. Despite his critiques of researcher-initiated productions, Harper (2012, p. 55) retains an appreciation for the value of the visual image, arguing that 'trying to tell a complete story of a culture always fails, but adding a visual dimension makes the inevitable shortcomings much more interesting'.

The appreciation of reflexivity in researcher-initiated productions has generated a consideration of the position of the camera and the ways in which its gaze appears neutral, but is located and fixed in a particular position (Dicks et al. 2006). The recognition that photographs are inherently selective, reproducing the conscious and unconscious adoption of subjective perspectives, has helped to move researcher-initiated approaches beyond the reductive realism in earlier work. Harper's emphasis on ethnography also situates photographs within wider frameworks of social research, where they become one aspect of the fieldwork among other techniques within the researcher's tool box; an important point that I will return to in Chapter 6. However, both reflexivity and ethnography have their limits; therefore, it is useful to turn to what Pink (2007, p. 5) refers to as the 'hidden history' of applied visual anthropology, and reflect on the pioneering work of John Collier Junior, and the ways in which he advocated photo-elicitation, which was later developed into the participatory tool of photovoice.

While Goffman (1959) rejected posed photographs, Collier argued that all visual materials reveal something of the culture that produced them. A pioneer of visual anthropology, Collier argued that seeing and representing the visual is as important as speaking or writing words; and he applied visual anthropology to new forms of social intervention and produced a legacy of work that combined theoretical approaches with problem solving (Collier 2007). In terms of 'researcher-initiated productions' it is useful to revisit the controversial Vicos Project, which aimed to bring the indigenous population of Vicosinos into the twentieth century and integrate them into the market economy and Peruvian society. The project was sponsored by Cornell University and the University of San Marcos, and for Collier it provided an opportunity to apply his 'photography for social research', an approach that we would now term visual anthropology.

Between 1954 and 1955 Collier produced close to 9,000 still images as well as hours of film footage charting the visual ethnography of the community (Collier 2007); and this visual information was both for immediate use and part of a baseline record for later evaluation of the project. In providing an understanding of the material status of Vicosinos, this data was to be a comparative record, a before and after, of the applied development of schooling, healthcare and development of the physical and social infrastructure as well as the relationship of Vicosinos to the surrounding region and Peruvian society. However, Collier's images did not altogether present the view of a community that was demoralised and in need of a modernisation that desired outside information; and he was heavily criticised for recording happiness in the presence of extreme poverty (Collier 2007). Collier argued that his images, such as the Fiesta scene in front of Vicos church, belied outsiders' perceptions of a culturally deprived community, lacking in creativity and initiative. Furthermore, Collier felt that it was important to record the underlying cultural and personal vitality of the community – charting public events, private lives, ceremony, social relationships, and portraits that provided an insight into a community, which may not have been wealthy from a Westernised perspective but nevertheless had its own intrinsic value.

Researcher-initiated productions situate social scientists as image-creators and Collier's early photographic contributions were documentary in character; however, they became explicit tools for obtaining information and an understanding of the circumstances in which they were made. Collier was concerned with providing an insight into the cultural vitality of communities, which moved away from the desired baseline information of a community in need of regeneration. For Collier, the applied focus, in which the aesthetics of the images were centralised, while appreciated, became increasingly secondary, and in his later work, the photographs that Collier created moved from being simply documentary images to tools of elicitation. Collier is perhaps best known for his methodological contribution 'photo-elicitation' (Biella 2002), which is based on the simple idea of inserting a photograph into a research interview.

The term photo-elicitation originated from a paper published by Collier (1957), when it was initiated as a solution to the practical difficulties that research teams were having in relation to agreeing on categories for quality housing. Collier extended the method to examine how families adapted to residence among ethnically different people, and to new forms of work in urban factories, interviewing families and communities with photographs created by researchers. Reflecting on the use of photo-elicitation, Collier (1957, p. 858), argued that 'pictures elicited longer and more comprehensive interviews but at the same time helped subjects overcome the fatigue and repetition of conventional interviews' and noted the technique's 'compelling effect upon the informant, its ability to prod latent memory, to stimulate and release emotional statements about the informant's life'.

Photo-elicitation with researcher-initiated productions has been taken up by a range of researchers across the social sciences and related disciplines (see Harper 2002, 2012); and as we discussed earlier, photo-elicitation has also been utilised with 'found materials' or what could be positioned as 'participatory productions'; although importantly the family photographs and artefacts were not specifically 'produced' as part of the research process. For Harper (2002, p. 13), the potentiality of photo-elicitation has a physical basis because 'the parts of the brain that process visual information are evolutionarily older than the parts that process verbal information'. Consequently, images evoke deeper elements of consciousness than do words alone so that photo-elicitation interviews do not simply elicit more information, but rather evoke a different kind of information. Importantly, Harper does not argue for pictures without words but for the value of combining these two forms of symbolic representation; a position that resonates with the argument made in Chapter 1 that the visual needs to be embedded and understood in and with narrative forms.

This section has reflected on different forms of researcher-initiated productions and charted the move from the reductive nature of pseudo-science, which contributed to 'the indignity of speaking for others' (Deleuze and Foucault 1990, p. 10), to the documentary tradition, movements in ethnography, the reflexivity of the 'cultural turn', and the key impacts of photo-elicitation. There has also been a focus on the blurred lines between what is found, created by researchers or participatory; but this is not a criticism of the framework. Reflecting on his earlier work Pauwels (2011, p. 5) argues that 'few authors have ventured to provide an analytic and integrated approach to visual research as a whole'. Pauwels (2010, 2011), however, has ventured and his conceptual model is far more complex than this chapter can allow space to discuss; it considers the origin and nature of the visual, its research focus and design, and its format and purpose. It is difficult to relay this complexity by moving in so little space between the different approaches, naturally there will be overlaps and omissions. However, the basic outline framing applied here can still act as a useful starting point; and in the next section we will explore the move from photo-elicitation to photovoice where researchers 'hand over the camera' in methods embedded in collaboration and participatory research.

## Participatory productions

Chapter 4 focuses on participatory methodologies, exploring the relationship between the visual and the participatory. This later chapter explores how communities have used creative forms to 'speak out' visually, and with narratives, about political repression and human rights abuses; and it also challenges the ways in which this has led to an easy marriage between the visual and the participatory in contemporary research. In Chapter 4 there will be an emphasis on the dynamic and unequal relationships that continue to exist between researchers and participants but importantly also within wider networks, which are often not considered in accounts of participatory productions. Therefore, this section will not retrace the arguments and critiques that follow in Chapter 4; but instead consider some of the contemporary movements within social science research that have advanced the use of participatory frameworks; and spend some time offering an overview of the nature and forms of participatory visual data production.

Childhood requires us to think of law as a continually shifting cultural and social text (Monk 2009), and arguably the United Nations Convention on the Rights of the Child (1990) has acted as a precursor for the development of participatory research with children and young people. The Convention is the most widely ratified human rights instrument in history (Payne 2009) and it sets out a broad range of rights specifically for children including the right for children 'to express views in all decisions that affect them'. For Groundwater-Smith et al. (2015, p. 2), the Convention acted as a precursor for a move towards more participatory frames, in which children and young people have shifted from the positioning of data sources to one in which they have 'designed, enacted and interpreted inquiries and been honoured as an authentic critical voice'.

In the new sociology of childhood, and related fields, the Convention supported the argument that it is essential to conduct research 'with' rather than 'about' children (MacNaughton and Smith 2009). Participatory productions position the social scientist as the participatory facilitator and the approach is characterised by the guiding mantra of 'with' rather than 'about'; and this has contributed to the development of a range of visual and creative methods to engender understandings with children and young people in social research. This development was initially conceptualised within frames of child-centred or child-friendly methods, which highlighted children's competencies and experiences as different to those of adults, therefore, requiring different methods to match these competencies. However, this universalising approach to childhood has been rejected by arguments that such an approach can be both patronising and tokenistic. Instead, it is proposed that methods should be person centred, guided by what is appropriate for individual participants and be fit for purpose, in research with both children and adults (Punch 2002; Clarke 2011).

For MacNaughton and Smith (2009, p. 103) within these participatory frames there should not be a focus on what is 'child-friendly', rather there should be a consideration that knowledge is generated inter-subjectively through interactions and relationships; and that appropriate methods 'build trust and rapport between researchers and participants, show regard for the competencies of each and promote opportunities to demonstrate these'. This ethos can be seen across a range of visual and creative studies, for example, Holland *et al.*'s (2010) *(Extra)ordinary Lives* project involved ethnographic multi-media data generation methods with young people, which encouraged critical reflexive practices throughout. The study cautioned against the assumption that participatory research *per se* necessarily produces 'better' research data, equalises power relations or enhances ethical integrity; however, the study also demonstrated the potential contributions of participatory methodologies.

Much contemporary participatory research with children and young people has become saturated with visual and creative frames, which have generated new insights and contributed to a rigorous body of literature (see Fink 2012; Gallagher 2008; Hemming 2008; Ross *et al.* 2009). There has also been an increased interest in creative techniques with adults, particularly with vulnerable and marginalised communities (Mannay 2010; Richardson 2015); and again these studies make central the premise of giving voice and recognise the need to address the power relations that construct the research relationship. As Kara (2015, p. 3) contends, creative methods are increasingly positioned as 'effective ways to address increasingly complex questions in social science' and participatory productions are circulated in the forms of transformative frameworks, feminist research and de-colonising methodologies.

As will be discussed in the following chapters, the participatory nature of projects is variable. Some research studies take a more holistic approach, where participants are involved in all processes from design, to data production, analysis and dissemination – an approach often associated with the 'gold standard' of participatory research (see O'Neill 2012; Perez 2007). However, in a socio-economic climate where research evidence is tied to deadlines and budgets (Mills and Ratcliffe 2012), the availability of funding and temporal constraints mean that many projects can only be partial in their engagement with participatory approaches. Consequently, in relation to visual and creative methods, their participatory potential is often confined within the methods and techniques of data production.

These fieldwork techniques vary between projects but within them participants are positioned as active agents (Groundwater-Smith *et al.* 2015), who are involved in creating and producing data. For this reason, in participatory frames this fieldwork is positioned as 'data production' because data is produced 'with' participants, rather than 'data collection', which assumes a more passive role for participants and an active researcher who simply collects the data that already exists. Techniques of data production, then, are concerned with an active creative process where participants engage with drawing, collaging, mapping and taking photographs. In this way, researchers can be seen to hand back the camera so that rather than subjects being framed by the researcher, participants decide when, what and how to represent their subjective worlds.

This creative process is often followed by interviews where the data produced is shared and discussed with the researcher. Studies employing this approach in photograph-based research often use Collier's (1957) term photo-elicitation, introduced in the previous section, to describe this process; however, more recently some researchers have chosen to employ the term 'photovoice' (Harper 2012) to distinguish between photographs produced by the researcher and those produced by participants. The concept, 'photovoice' was introduced by Wang and Burris (1997) to emphasise the active role of participants, and they defined photovoice as a method through which knowledge would be generated by people who were normally passive objects in the research process.

In this way, photovoice offers a critique of photo-elicitation in that it argues that empowering participants necessitates putting them in control of processes of image creation. There is an argument against research-initiated productions in that the 'knowledge of outside researchers, no matter how involved they might have been with the community, could never approximate to the understandings reflected in the images made by the subject-collaborators' (Harper 2012, p. 191). Nevertheless, the elicitation interview remains important as researchers applying photovoice often contend that it is impossible to understand the meaning of an image in isolation from the context it emerged (Liebenberg 2009, p. 460). Interviews, then, allow for a more nuanced understanding of the meaning making of participants and engender an additional mode of communication, drawing on both visual and verbal narratives.

Despite the differences between traditional photo-elicitation, which comes from a researcher-initiated, documentary tradition, and photovoice, which allows creative control and freedom in a participatory framework, the terms are often used interchangeably by researchers as you will see in the following chapters. This is partly because much work with photovoice originated in health research; and the term is still filtering to other academic disciplines in the social sciences (Harper 2012). The attachment to photo-elicitation is also related to the way that 'elicitation' can exist separately in ways that 'voice' would not work so well. Photographs are only one creative technique and when using collages, narratives or drawings in my own work, I would tend to say that the data produced was discussed in elicitation interviews, 'voice' would not connote the same meaning. However, the framing of projects provides enough information for readers to establish who created the photographs and if a study has the ethos of photovoice, even when the term photo-elicitation is applied, the underlying philosophy remains visible; so the interchangeability of the terms is not too problematic. The diverse nature of participatory frameworks, their differential approaches and their similarities will be revisited and centralised within the following chapters.

## Conclusion

This chapter was concerned with outlining some of the main approaches to studying with visual and creative forms, in relation to found materials, researcher-initiated productions and participatory approaches, which will help to frame the following discussions across the book. As Margolis and Pauwels (2011) contend, 'the future of visual research will depend on the continued effort to cross disciplinary boundaries and engage in a constructive dialogue with different schools of thought'; and the chapter has highlighted the ways in which contemporary visual studies are situated within a body of historical and interdisciplinary work, which can help to guide and inform our practice. There is much to be learnt from the humanities, where art and artefacts have been thoughtfully considered by a range of scholars; and engaging with different fields and disciplines is fundamental in progressing visual studies. Importantly, the lenses of analysis employed to interpret and explore found materials can be usefully applied in interrogating images in documentary and collaborative approaches, and forms of analysis are fundamental within the social sciences; a point considered in more detail in Chapter 5.

Reflection on the documentary tradition is also useful, as its early relationship with the pseudo-science of classifying and marginalising communities, enables us to explore the ethical problems that we have attempted to move away from but that can still be evidenced, which will be revisited in Chapter 7. In moving researcher-initiated approaches beyond the reductive realism in earlier work, the chapter has also touched on the concepts of reflexivity, embedding the visual in wider methodological frames and the importance of elicitation; all these themes will be an area of focus throughout the book. Additionally, the section on participatory productions has set up some of the base ideas that are the focus of Chapter 4, where participatory methodologies are interrogated and evaluated in relation to their potential for 'giving voice' and the problematic nature of the easy marriage between the visual and the participatory, in relation to issues of power, positionality and research agendas.

Of all the frames discussed, arguably this book is primarily concerned with approaches that are participatory, or have some participatory potential. This emphasis is attached to my own research interests as my fieldwork has offered opportunities for participants to create data, producing photographs, narratives, collages, maps and a range of other materials, which have typically been discussed within elicitation interviews. However, as this chapter has documented, such categories are permeable and differentiating between what is found, researcher-initiated or participatory is never a straightforward task. This movement between frames, disciplines, visual and narrative modes, techniques and approaches is, for me, very much what makes working with creative methods an exciting undertaking. The following chapters journey through the evolving world of visual, narrative and creative research methods, considering and reflecting on their application, ethics potentialities and problematics. In the next chapter, Chapter 3, there will be an emphasis on the potentialities of creative data production in relation to the themes of familiarity, perspective and positionality.

# References

Bal, M. (2007) 'Lost in Space, Lost in the Library', in S. Durrant and C. M. Lord *Essays in Migratory Aesthetics: Cultural Practices between Migration and Art-making*, pp. 23–36. Amsterdam: Rodopi.

Banks, M. (2001) *Visual Methods in Social Research*. London: Sage.

Belton, R. (2002) *Art: The World of Art from Aboriginal to American Pop, Renaissance Masters to Postmodernism*. London: Flame Tree.

Bethlehem, L. and Harris, A. (2012) 'Unruly Pedagogies; Migratory Interventions: Unsettling Cultural Studies', *Critical Arts*, 26 (1): 3–13.

Biella, P. (2002) 'The Legacy of John Collier, Jr.', *Visual Anthropology Review*, 17 (2): 50–60.

Brown, R. (2009) 'Photography, Ongoing Moments and Strawberry Fields, the Active Presence of Absent Things', Conference Paper at the *International Visual Sociology Association, Annual Conference*, University of Cumbria, Carlisle.

Chadwick, W. (1990) *Women, Art and Society*. London: Thames and Hudson.

Chapman, J. (2000) *Fragmentation in Archaeology: People, Places and Broken Objects in the Prehistory of South-eastern Europe*. London: Routledge.

Clarke, J. (2011) 'Breaking Methodological Boundaries? Exploring Visual, Participatory Methods with Adults and Young Children', *European Early Childhood Education Research Journal*, 19 (3): 321–30.

Collier, J. (1957) 'Photography in Anthropology: A Report on Two Experiments', *American Anthropologist*, 59 (5): 843–59.

Collier, M. (2007) 'The Applied Visual Anthropology of John Collier: A Photo Essay', in S. Pink (ed.) *Visual Interventions: Applied Visual Anthropology*. London: Berghahn.

Deleuze, G. and Foucault, M. (1990) 'Intellectuals and Power', in R. Ferguson (ed.) *Discourses: Conversations in Postmodern Art and Culture*, pp. 9–16, Cambridge, MA: MIT Press.

Dicks, B., Soyinka, B. L. and Coffey, A. J. (2006) 'Multimodal Ethnography', *Qualitative Research*, 6 (1): 77–96.

Fink, J. (2012) 'Walking the Neighbourhood, Seeing the Small Details of Community Life: Reflections from a Photography Walking Tour', *Critical Social Policy*, 32 (1): 31–50.

Gallagher, M. (2008) 'Power is not an Evil: Rethinking Power in Participatory Methods', *Children's Geographies*, 6 (2): 137–51.

Goffman, E. (1959) *The Presentation of Self in Everyday Life*. Harmondsworth: Pelican.

Groundwater-Smith, S., Dockett, S. and Bottrell, D. (2015) *Participatory Research with Children and Young People*. London: Sage.

Harper, D. (2002) 'Talking About Pictures: A Case for Photo Elicitation', *Visual Studies*, 17 (1): 14–26.

Harper, D. (2012) *Visual Sociology*. London: Routledge.

Hemming, P. J. (2008) 'Mixing Qualitative Research Methods in Children's Geographies', *Area* 40 (2): 152–62.

Holland, S., Renold, E., Ross, N. J. and Hillman, A. (2010) 'Power, Agency and Participatory Agendas: A Critical Exploration of Young People's Engagement in Participative Qualitative Research', *Childhood*, 17 (3): 360–75.

Hurdley, R. (2006) 'Dismantling Mantelpieces: Narrating Identities and Materializing Culture in the Home', *Sociology*, 40 (4): 717–33.

Kara, H. (2015) *Creative Research Methods in the Social Sciences: A Practical Guide*. Bristol: Policy Press.

Lambert, T. (2014) 'Beauty Ideals', in M. D. Smith (ed.) *Cultural Encyclopedia of the Breast*. London: Rowman and Littlefield.

Liebenberg, L. (2009) 'The Visual Image as a Discussion Point: Increasing Validity in Boundary Crossing Research', *Qualitative Research*, 9 (4): 441–67.

MacNaughton, G. and Smith, K. (2009) 'Children's Rights in Early Childhood', in M. J. Kehily (ed.) *An Introduction to Childhood Studies* (2nd edn), pp. 161–76. Maidenhead: Open University Press.

Mannay, D. (2010) 'Making the Familiar Strange: Can Visual Research Methods Render the Familiar Setting more Perceptible?' *Qualitative Research*, 10 (1): 91–111.

Margolis, E. and Pauwels, L. (eds) (2011) *The Sage Handbook of Visual Research Methods*. London: Sage.

Mills, D. and Ratcliffe, R. (2012) 'After Method? Ethnography in the Knowledge Economy', *Qualitative Research*, 12 (2): 147–64.

Monk, D. (2009) 'Childhood and the Law', in M. J. Kehily (ed.) *An Introduction to Childhood Studies* (2nd edn), pp. 177–97. Maidenhead: Open University Press.

Olsen, B. (2010) *In Defense of Things: Archaeology and the Ontology of Objects*. Plymouth: AltaMira Press.

O'Neill, M. (2012) 'Ethno-mimesis and Participatory Arts', in S. Pink (ed.) *Advances in Visual Methodology*, pp. 153–72. London: Sage.

Pauwels, L. (2010) 'Visual Sociology Reframed: An Analytical Synthesis and Discussion of Visual Methods in Social and Cultural Research', *Sociological Methods and Research*, 38 (4): 545–81.

Pauwels, L. (2011) 'An Integrated Conceptual Framework for Visual Social Research', in E. Margolis and L. Pauwels (eds) *The Sage Handbook of Visual Research Methods*, pp. 3–23. London: Sage.

Payne, L. (2009) 'Twenty Years On: The Implementation of the UN Convention on the Rights of the Child in the United Kingdom', *Children and Society*, 23 (1): 16–28.

Perez, A. (2007) 'The Rhythm of our Dreams: A Proposal for an Applied Visual Anthropology', in S. Pink (ed.) *Visual Interventions: Applied Visual Anthropology*, pp. 227–46. Oxford: Berghahn.

Pink, S. (ed.) (2007) *Visual Interventions: Applied Visual Anthropology*. Oxford: Berghahn.

Prosser, J. (2006) 'Researching with Visual Images Some Guidance Notes and a Glossary for Beginners', *Working Paper: Real Life Methods*. University of Manchester and University of Leeds.

Punch, S. (2002) 'Research with Children: The Same or Different from Research with Adults?', *Childhood*, 9 (3): 321–41.

Richardson, M. (2015) 'Embodied Intergenerational: Family Position, Place and Masculinity', *Gender, Place and Culture*, 22 (2): 157–71.

Rose, G. (2001) *Visual Methodologies: An Introduction to Researching with Visual Materials*. London: Sage.

Rose, G. (2010) *Doing Family Photography: The Domestic, the Public and the Politics of Sentiment*. Farnham: Ashgate.

Ross, N. J., Renold, E., Holland, S. and Hillman, A. (2009) 'Moving Stories: Using Mobile Methods to Explore the Everyday Lives of Young People in Public Care', *Qualitative Research*, 9 (5): 605–23.

Spencer, S. (2011) *Visual Research Methods in the Social Sciences: Awakening Visions*. London: Routledge.

United Nations (1990) *Convention on the Rights of the Child* http://www.unicef.org.uk/Documents/Publication-pdfs/UNCRC_PRESS200910web.pdf (Accessed 23 March 2015).

Wang, C. and Burris, M. A. (1997) 'Photovoice: Concept, Methodology, and Use for Participatory Needs Assessment', *Health Education and Behaviour*, 24 (3): 185–92.

# 3

# MAKING THE FAMILIAR STRANGE

## Questions we would not think to ask

## Introduction

The previous chapter introduced different forms of visual materials; and the ways in which visual research methods and contemporary visual culture intersect in their use of visual images (Chamberlain *et al.* 2011; Rose 2013). Our 'ocularcentric culture' (Spencer 2011) was explored in relation to the useful framework of 'found materials as a data source', 'researcher-initiated production of visual data and meanings' and 'participatory-productions where the social scientist acts as the participatory facilitator' (Pauwels 2011). This chapter focuses on the later of these categories, 'participatory-productions where the social scientist acts as the participatory facilitator', examining how acts of participatory creation can work towards ameliorating some persistent difficulties in qualitative social science research. The potential of the visual is explored here in relation to the problematic nature of familiarity, perspective and positionality.

The centrality of the researcher and their position in relation to the research setting has been subject to controversy and long-standing debates threaded with the narratives of insider and outsider myths; and the response to Gillian Evans's (2006) book, *Educational Failure and Working Class White Children in Britain*, summed up in the UK press as 'how dare a middle-class person write about working-class people' (Butler 2006), illustrates the enduring and volatile nature of such insider and outsider divisions. Outsider myths assert that only researchers who possess the necessary objectivity and emotional distance from the field are able to conduct valid research on a given group. Conversely, according to insider myths, the attributes of objectivity and emotional distance render outsiders inherently incapable of appreciating the true character of a group's life. However, as Hammersley and Atkinson (2007) argue, these myths are not empirical generalisations; rather they are elements in a moral narrative, which seek to claim exclusive research legitimacy for a particular group.

Nevertheless, these moral narratives also highlight the practical problems of familiarity in empirical social science research. Insiders are frequently charged with the tendency to present their group in an unrealistically favourable light, and their work is often considered to be overshadowed by the enclosed, self-contained world of common understanding (Mannay 2010). Beyond the insider/outsider dichotomy, familiarity can act as a barrier in researching any field that we have previous experience of, as opportunities for discovery become clouded with the conventions of acquaintance (Geer 1964). This chapter explores the ways in which positionality and familiarity act to blunt traditional research tools, drawing on a body of empirical work to highlight the problem of familiarity; before revisiting some of my earlier work (Mannay 2010) to demonstrate how I, as an indigenous researcher, employed visual methods of data production in order to suspend my preconceptions of familiar territory, and facilitate an understanding of the unique viewpoints of my participants.

My article in *Qualitative Research* (Mannay 2010) drew upon visual data generated in a study of mothers and daughters residing in a Welsh, marginalised, urban housing area; and this chapter returns to that paper, revisiting and updating the key arguments. It was the difficulty of familiarity that first led me to pursue visual techniques of data production in my own work; and operationalising the visual engendered a recognition for its potential as a tool of defamiliarisation. The power of the visual to disrupt conventional ways of seeing for the researcher changed my patterns of empirical work and set me on the pathway to becoming a visualista.[1] Furthermore, the potential for defamiliarisation is always a dual process, for the creation of visual artefacts also works to make the familiar strange for research participants, who gain new perspectives on their own understandings of their subjective worlds. Following my initial engagement with fighting familiarity, visually there have been innovative and exciting projects in the social sciences that will be discussed in the following chapters, where researchers have engaged with the visual to move from simply seeing to engender a more active and productive gaze. In this chapter, there will be a specific focus on defamiliarisation techniques in the work of Richardson (2015) and Goff *et al.* (2013). In this way, the chapter focuses the usefulness of visual approach for making the familiar strange for both researchers and research participants.

## Epistemic privilege

Clear insider/outsider boundaries have traditionally been drawn for groups of respondents who are structurally marginalised in respect of class, ethnicity, sexuality and gender (Hodkinson 2005). For example, epistemic privilege can be found in the expression of feminist standpoint theory. The product of an age when women were claiming universal subjugation to establish their place on an academic agenda, feminist standpoint theory held that the experience of oppression engenders particular knowledges (Pilcher and Whelehan 2004). Accordingly, only those who have the appropriate experience of oppression are capable of researching and representing the experience. Paradoxically, this means that feminist standpoint theory aligns itself within the tradition of positivist science, which it sought to critique, as it 'grants an authority and hierarchy to certain groups and silences others' (Skeggs 1997, p. 26). Similarly, culturally sensitive research approaches have raised questions of who should conduct research in African-American communities and whose knowledge should be privileged (Tillman 2002).

Such discourses of epistemic privilege can be dangerous because they produce a false binary, which silences the multifaceted nature of identities, lifestyles and perspectives. Oakley (1981) illustrates a deceptively simple notion of identity with the claim that feminist interviewing of women was automatically a privileged knowledge because of the shared gender, which secured 'insider' definition. This assumption has since been criticised for discounting crucial differences between women such as class and ethnicity (Skeggs 2004); and much research is now concerned to recognise complexities and intricacies of the research relationship. For example, Song and Parker (1995) emphasise that their experiences of interviewing Chinese British young people as Korean American and Chinese British researchers were defined by a highly complex set of research relationships. The nuances and intricacies of their proximity in the research process led them to conclude that:

> *Dichotomised rubrics such as 'black/white' or 'insider/outsider' are inadequate to capture the complex and multi-faceted experiences of some researchers such as ourselves, who find themselves neither total 'insiders' nor 'outsiders' in relation to the individuals they interview.*
>
> *(Song and Parker 1995, p. 243)*

The notion of being an insider or an outsider, then, is inadequate in an absolute sense. However, to ignore questions of proximity is to assume that knowledge comes from nowhere, allowing researchers to become an abstract concept rather than a site of accountability. It may be misguided to privilege a particular type of knowledge but it is imperative to acknowledge that 'perspective is always premised upon access to knowledge' (Skeggs 2004, p. 14). Thus, inside/outsider discourses are important because they place the researcher at the centre of the production of knowledge. Therefore, despite the inadequacy of the insider/outsider binary in absolute terms the concept retains methodological usefulness. For example, Hodkinson's (2005) exploration of the Goth scene, a subculture centring around music and dress, discusses levels of group identity, commitment and distinctiveness, which reduce the level of ambiguity in respect to whether the researcher should regard themselves as an insider. This study resonates with my own location as a researcher where the proximity to my participants has often been characterised by a distinctive set of unifying characteristics.

For example, in a study of the everyday lives of mothers and daughters pairs in a marginalised housing area (Mannay 2010, 2013), as well as sharing the primary status of white woman with the participants, I also shared spatial containment. The mothers in the study were in my age group, we all had our children in our late teens and early twenties and we all had daughters. Beyond the pen and paper statistics, all of the mothers lived in areas that I had resided in or was familiar with; and in some cases our families had shared weddings, birthdays, football matches as well as fallouts, accidents and misfortunes, which impacted on the wider community. Our children had often shared playgroups, schools, extra curricula activities, and packets of crisps. The level of familiarity between the participants and me varied considerably in this study and carried feelings of 'belonging and not belonging (insider and outsider-ness) at once' (Hett 2014, p. 125); however, the relationship suggests a relatively clear position as researcher operating as an insider. Of course, it is true that outsiders and insiders may have immediate access to different kinds of information but they are also exposed to different kinds of methodological dangers. Positioning myself as an insider, therefore, made it important to explore and acknowledge both the benefits and drawbacks of being 'researcher near'.

## Researcher near

It is suggested that researchers working on familiar territory can elicit greater under-standing because cultural and linguistic barriers do not have to be negotiated and that participants may be more open and less likely to obscure aspects of their lives (Atkinson *et al.* 2003; Henry 2001; Aguilar 1981). Additionally, shared knowledge and shared understanding can counter the severe imbalance with regard to intimacy and distance between interviewer and interviewee, which is often common in research interviews (Rogan and de Kock 2005). The appeal of shared identity and shared experience, therefore, needs to be acknowledged. However, the status of indigenous observer has the ability to confer disadvantage as well as advantage. For instance, Vrasidas (2001) reports that by entering the research setting with pre-conceptions about the topic he may have been unable to notice that which is often taken for granted. The researcher, then, can never renounce their prior knowledge and the disadvantages of preconceived understandings were experienced in my earlier unpublished research, which formed part of an undergraduate dissertation as illustrated below.

> In the case of the third interview there was a small amount of vacillation because my own children attend the same school as those of the participant. Consequently, there was an element of my questions being unnecessary because I already knew the answers.
> (Mannay 2006, p. 21)

There was then, a two-way taken-for-granted cultural competence as I entered the interview with preconceived knowledge and the participant communicated an assumption that I already understood her experience. Thus, conducting research in a culture in which I was habituated had a deadening effect on the interview process in this case. However, although there was a small amount of vacillation in the inter-view, overall the elements of shared understanding and common ground contributed to a relaxed open atmosphere, which was reflected in the quantity and quality of the data. The experience of my undergraduate dissertation influenced the decision to select a sample from my own community. However, I felt that it was important to address the taken-for-granted cultural competence inherent to my insider status and to consider processes of 'making the familiar strange'.

## Making the familiar strange

Interpretive research aims to investigate the invisibility of everyday life but when a researcher is working in familiar territory there is a danger that their findings will be overshadowed by the enclosed, self-contained world of common understanding. As Sikes (2003) recalls when she was taught by outside 'experts' about working-class homes:

> Those people who, we were told, spoke in restricted codes, bought their children the wrong sort of toys, were not able to defer gratification, lacked cultural capital and didn't have dinner parties, were our friends, neighbours, families, our mums and dads, aunties and uncles, brothers and sisters.
>
> (Sikes 2003, p. 244)

Sikes acknowledged such outsider accounts as partial but was surprised to find that when she began her own research in working-class settings it was easy to assume commonalities. Sikes made a deliberate cognitive effort to question her taken-for-granted assumptions and learnt that much of what she had thought familiar was really very different. Of course, the problem of familiarity can be a challenge for all researchers as sites of investigation can throw up a range of knowledges based on firsthand experience. As Geer (1964) discloses 'I was bored by the thought of studying undergraduates … I had memories of my own college days in which I appeared as a child' (p. 337). Correspondingly, Becker (1971) laments educational researchers' inability to 'stop seeing only the things that are conventionally "there" to be seen', attributing the failure to the familiarity of the classroom setting and the researchers' lack of will and imagination (Becker 1971, p. 10).

The challenge of making the familiar strange in educational settings was taken up by Delamont and Atkinson (1995) who offer a range of strategies for fighting familiarity including adopting ethnomethodology, focusing on gender and studying unusual sites within the school setting. Similarly, Thorne (1993) attempts to make 'the child' strange by centring on the geography of gender and the culture of play in the classroom and the schoolyard. The success of such approaches can be seen in studies, which have contributed something new to the field, providing a deeper insight to educational settings by both focusing on gender and by researching within the somewhat neglected site of the school playground (Renold 2005; Mellor 2006).

Nevertheless, researchers still struggle with the practice of making the familiar strange and it remains fundamental to 'make strange social context that we assume to understand by virtue of taken for granted cultural competence' (Atkinson *et al.* 2003, p. 47). Thus, interpretive research needs to employ techniques which allow the researcher 'to make the familiar strange and interesting again' (Erikson 1986, p. 121). This desire to make the familiar strange has 'almost the status of a mantra among ethnographers' (Sikes 2006, p. 538) and the premise is evident across disciplines and paradigms; and the visual is one way to creatively fight familiarity.

## Fighting familiarity with creativity

For Deleuze (2000), making the strange familiar could be facilitated by abandoning the constraints inherent to language and adopting the stance of a nomadic thinker who is free to create new connections and open up experience. Creativity is also seen as a method of making the familiar strange in the field of engineering education, where Stouffer *et al.* (2004) suggest that stepping out of dominant paradigms may suspend taken-for-granted understandings and open up the possibility of a creative and critical research to understand the other. In order to expose that which is veiled by a web of taken-for-granted meanings, the researcher may then find it advantageous to employ techniques of 'defamiliarisation'. The concept of defamiliarisation was introduced by the Russian formalist Shklovsky who believed that over time our perceptions of familiar, everyday situations become stale; but that art can address this automisation by forcing us to slow down our perception, to linger and to notice (Gurevitch 1998).

Utilising children's drawings, Kaomea (2003) borrows defamiliarising analytical tools from literacy and critical theory to peel back familiar, dominant appearances and expose previously silenced accounts of the educational programme in postcolonial Hawaii. Kaomea uses the artwork of children to refresh her habitual responses to the educational system and to render the familiar setting more perceptible. Introducing a visual element to the process of data collection, then, can potentially provide different ways of knowing and understanding (Gauntlett 2007). Art, therefore, may be an element that can overcome the confines of language, open up experience and make the familiar strange.

Consequently, when I was conducting research within my own cultural milieu (Mannay 2010), in combination with earlier strategies for fighting familiarity, I selected visual methods of data production to specifically address the difficulties of insider research. Asking participants to independently record their own visual impressions and interpretations of their environment prior to interview, therefore, was seen as less problematic than a conventional interview design where the researcher is experience near. Participants in the study (Mannay 2010) were asked to create photographs, collages and maps of their everyday lives, in their own homes, without the presence of the researcher, which later formed the focus of elicitation interviews. The adoption of participant-directed visual methods of data production, then, aimed to act as an instrument for making the familiar strange and provide a gateway to destinations that lay beyond my repertoire of preconceived understandings of place and space.

## Windows to new worlds

Researchers are often apprehensive about entering a familiar research setting where their experience with the subject matter sets up a range of preconceptions about the

**FIGURE 3.1**   The night sky (Mannay 2010) (permission to reuse the image provided courtesy of SAGE Publications)

topic, and I was also concerned that the findings would be overshadowed by the enclosed, self-contained world of common understanding. If I had devised an interview schedule the questions would have been constrained by my prior knowledge and the answers in turn would be constrained by these questions. Therefore, I needed to find a method that promoted subject-led dialogue and, as discussed, employing self-directed visual data production techniques achieved this goal. The participants were not controlled by a predetermined interview schedule, they were simply asked to create a visual representation of their everyday lives; and they entered the interview setting with their own ideas. This gave me the opportunity to observe and learn about elements of our shared environment and aspects of the participants themselves that I would not necessarily have enquired about. The participants' visual data provided an opportunity to observe unseen or forgotten elements of the physical environment such as Tina's representation of the night.

Tina, a mother of two young children who resides in a marginalised housing estate, dedicates two hundred words to describing the importance that the night sky holds in her life. Tina describes the aesthetic pleasure of watching the stars, the contrast of the peace of the night compared with the pressure of the day, the space to think and the comfort that there is a window to the people that she loves in the heavens. Tina, then, places a high value on the night sky but, as Tina suggests, it was not a subject that I would have broached without the direction of the map.

TINA:   *You probably would have mentioned the college and the driving… and my Mum's house obviously but you wouldn't have known anything about the way I feel about the night.*

Thus, even though I was an indigenous researcher Tina offered me an insight into aspects of her world that I would not have considered salient and reveals a subjective relationship with the night sky that I have no prior knowledge of. This is important because although I would not have asked about the night sky in a traditional interview, for Tina the image is a central metaphor in the understanding of her everyday life. Tina is living in a marginalised area associated with folk devils and moral panics (Cohen 2011); and the criminal activities in her street leave her feeling trapped. At the time of the interview, Tina's transformation from 'stay at home mum' to college student also elicited a range of negative emotions in her family, such as inadequacy, anger and envy, which have been apparent in other studies of working-class upward social mobility (Lucey *et al.* 2003). Consequently, the night sky becomes a literal and metaphorical escape for Tina and her drawing allowed me an insight into this affective space, which may not have been accessible through a purely verbal interview encounter.

## Self-assessments and discoveries of the self

As Chamberlain *et al.* (2011) argue, visual methods of data production can locate researchers more firmly and more easily into the lifeworlds and spaces of the participants; this is achieved partially through processes of defamiliarisation that impact both on the researcher and the participants. In this study (Mannay 2010) participants also described the visual data production as a process in which their own lives were reconsidered, re-evaluated and made strange. The production of images required a lot of thought over an extended period of time and participants had to actively assess their sense of place, space and self. Suzie, a fifteen-year-old daughter in the study, commented on how the process of data production, using magazines, photographs and the internet, generated new ideas that she included in the finished collage such as the image representing her home as a jail.

Suzie cut a number of images from magazines and other visual resources and one of these featured the headless body of a person behind prison-like bars. When I asked Suzie about the inclusion of this image she told me, 'I feel like I'm in jail because I'm never allowed out'. Importantly, Suzie goes on to explain how the process of making the collage made her realise how much she felt like a prisoner; she was not searching for an image of incarceration but instead found the picture by chance and felt a resonance with her own situation.

It was important to consider the consequence of such discoveries of the self and of the other. In the same way that I embarked on analysing the data, the creators of the data would inevitably draw inferences about their own lives and find new meanings and connections. For example, improving narratives were related to many aspects of participants' lives as they were involved in improving their appearance; their bodies; their mind; their homes; their relationships; their future as illustrated in the extract from Juliet's (Suzie's mother) interview below where she discussed the process of making a collage of her everyday life:

JULIET: *Yeah it's made me think really what my life is all about and you know how I can sort of (.) get it better or what I think that I want to get better… and the things that I want to get rid of*

The daughters interviewed also spoke about their own anxieties. The desire for the perfect figure then was pitched against the love of forbidden foods such as chocolate and Suzie and sixteen-year-old Sophie both featured their favourite foods in their visual data. When I ask Sophie why she worries about her weight she answers:

SOPHIE: *I don't know why I just I don't know I just think it's probably natural for girls to just think ah like I look fat in this but that's because I hang round with my one friend she always says it*

Sophie then may be influenced by her peers and by the idea that image anxiety is a social norm for girls, but there is a wider influence in the form of media images as, drawing on the photographs she has taken in preparation for the interview, Sophie tells me that she loves magazines. This is followed by an account the world of celebrity and the 'stars' that Sophie likes and dislikes. Similarly, Suzie has an array of celebrities in her collage and her plans for cosmetic surgery, illustrated by advertising for liposuction, are seen as a necessary step if she wishes to achieve the same level of fame, wealth and success. Similar to the young women in Skeggs' (1997) study, Suzie and Sophie attempt to regulate their bodies. Then and now, 'Fat signifies immovability; social mobility, they maintain is less likely in a fat body' (Skeggs 1997, p. 83). Conceptions of self, then, are structured in all sorts of ways, both through the immediate locality and via broader social norms and power relations. The aspiration to stardom, then, documents place and space in a wider sense, where identity is inexorably linked to multi-media discourses of acceptable femininity.

This dual influence of the backyard and the wider world was important because my own research agenda was confined to the immediate locality. The freedom offered by the self-directed visual data production method acted as a vehicle for Sophie and Suzie to demonstrate not just the influence of friends, family, peers and local environment but to introduce an array of cultural artefacts such as television; magazines; advertising; food packaging; the internet and music. My proximity to the research site had blinded me to these wider images and their presentation acted as a salient reminder that it is impossible to compartmentalise life; for although we may be interested in the immediate locality this is just one factor to consider. In this way the visual helped me to move beyond my familiarity of the local and consider the global; and the ways in which the mediated forms and 'digital technologies add new dimensions' (Schevchenko 2014) to indigenous confinements.

## Deceptive assumptions of shared understanding

However, the danger that the study could be overshadowed by the enclosed, self-contained world of common understanding was not just restricted to the interpretation of the researcher. Chantelle (Tina's daughter), the youngest participant, who was ten years old at the beginning of the study, illustrates this point with a picture of her home.

**FIGURE 3.2** My house (Mannay 2010) (permission to reuse the image provided courtesy of SAGE Publications)

Chantelle provided a visual representation of the outside of her house. The picture is interesting because it is the archetypal representation of a house common to children's drawings but it is not an accurate image of Chantelle's home, which is terraced with two windows at the front, no smoke coming out of the chimney and no flowers in the front garden. Similar to the majority of visual tools, Chantelle's drawing is not an unambiguous record of reality (Ball and Smith 1992). When I take up the issue of the presence of the flowers in the picture with Chantelle she defends their inclusion.

I: *So have you got flowers like this by your house? Did you just put them on or are they there?*
CHANTELLE: *Um we've got trees there but there are flowers outside my house but they're just starting, just starting to grow*

The picture of the house then is a popular version of a house rather than an accurate representation that could be recognised as Chantelle's house. In this case then I am able to recognise discrepancies, nevertheless, the drawing illustrates that participants' visual images may not always be accurate, which must be kept in mind when utilising visual data; a point discussed in more detail in Chapter 6. When I have transcribed our conversation, I speak with Chantelle again about these discrepancies. The structural incongruity is explained as necessary as there are two windows at the rear of the house, which Chantelle has moved to the front in her picture to take account of these rooms. Painting and sketching, then, as Damon (2000) maintains are always dependent on the artistic ability of the author.

However, there is no attempt to elucidate the presence of the flowers in the garden. The inclusion of the flowers could be explained as an illustration of the gendered nature of children's drawing where young girls aspire to make their drawings pretty. Chantelle's drawing of her local environment was edged with gold stars and such elaboration is normative within the school setting. A correspondence between drawings and school-based activities is suggested with the use of the term 'work' in Chantelle's description of generating the pictorial data.

CHANTELLE: *I was happy when I did it (.) when I finished I was really happy because I was happy with my work, so happy*

Alternatively, the archetypal representation of home could be linked with Chantelle's desire to move away from her street.

I: *Do you like it on your street?*
CHANTELLE: *No I hate it*

As discussed in relation to Chantelle's mother's, Tina's account, the street that they live in is run down and plagues by crime; and Chantelle's aspiration to relocate is accompanied by descriptions of the preferred alternatives, which include large, detached houses whose gardens exhibit flowers and shrubbery. This could suggest that Chantelle's subjective representation of her home provides an insight to the intersection of the social and the psychic, a visual representation of fantasy, hope and longing. Perhaps, this is an analytical leap but in either case the drawing makes departures from actuality that Chantelle feels she does not need to justify or explain.

This departure is not problematic in itself for the research was interested in Chantelle's own subjective account of the lived specificities of classed location at a particular time and in a particular place. However, Chantelle's account becomes problematic when incredulous at my continued interest Chantelle informs me that it does not matter because I have been to her house and I know what it looks like. This is resonant of the two-way taken-for-granted cultural competence that I spoke of earlier in the chapter, a facet of my earlier research, which I hoped to suspend with a participatory methodology. Akin to the participant in my undergraduate research, Chantelle communicated an assumption that I already understood her experience. Thus, the relative disadvantage inherent to my insider status remains and Chantelle may have drawn her maps with the proviso that I already 'know' the landscape of her subjective world. This illustrates an underlying and potentially deceptive assumption of shared understanding, which persists despite the adoption of self-directed visual methods.

Nevertheless, overall the method of self-directed visual data provided an opportunity for the participants to share their own experience of space. Experiences of space, which reflect the simultaneous multiplicity of spaces that exist for the social relations of space are experienced differently and variously interpreted, by those holding different positions as part of it (Massey 1994). The technique provided an opportunity for mothers and daughters to create new connections and opened up experiences, which I had not envisaged, even though in many ways my own existence echoes that of my participants. In this way it enabled me to fight familiarity and travel beyond my vision of the local, to transcend my subjective experience and move from mere seeing to a more active gaze. Banks (2001) draws on Hindu philosophy to locate this more productive seeing in relation to '*darshan*'; the ability to see and understand multiple points of view and schools of thoughts. The visual was central in facilitating *darshan* in this study and the subsequent research I have undertaken. Fighting familiarity visually has also been a fundamental aspect in the work of other qualitative researchers and the following sections will explore the ways in which Michael Richardson (2015) and Sarah Goff *et al.* (2013) have successfully applied visual techniques of defamiliarisation.

## Masculinity, nationality and familiarity

As a man researching men and masculinities, Michael Richardson (2015) was aware of the power relations inherent in his position as researcher but also of the impact of his own background and embodied physical presence. Richardson worked with thirty-eight men from Tyneside, in the North East of England, across three generations within nineteen families of Irish descent to discuss masculinity, intergenerationality and place. The particular context of Tyneside Irish masculinities resonates with Richardson's individual genealogy; 'born of a family of Irish ancestry who had lived and worked on Tyneside since the nineteenth century, my Dad and his twin sister, former world champion Irish dancers, my Gran's maiden name, Monaghan, and I myself having performed as a 9-year-old Irish dancer' (Richardson 2015, p. 159). Consequently, he was interested in the ways in which visual methods can help overcome both perceived privilege and 'researcher nearness'.

As Edwards (2014, p. 180) contends, 'the body imprints its own emplaced past into its present experience' and the issue of researcher nearness was felt by Richardson; and resonated with his participants who engaged with strategies of recognition. For example, when interviewing Victor, a fourth generation Irishman, born on Tyneside in the 1940s, his wife joined the conversation and conveyed a familiarity based upon family resemblance; 'You know it's funny, Michael, you look just like my nephew . . . the spitting image in fact, only he's a little taller'. In order to disrupt this familiarity and move beyond his 'repertoire of preconceived understandings of place and space' (Mannay 2010, p. 96), like me, Richardson also drew on the potentialities of the visual; and produced a novel activity that both acted as a tool of defamiliarisation and facilitated an insight into the key study themes of masculinities.

Richardson provided participants with a visual outline of a man, which was an attempt to stimulate discussion about embodied masculinities by minimising the influence of his own masculinity. The cartoon-like outline became the frame of reference without privileging any particular masculinities; yet it remained recognisable as a 'symbolic man' from its appearance on 'toilet doors' and crime scene television

**FIGURE 3.3** Daniel
Source: Michael Richardson (2015)

programmes in the UK context. For Richardson, the participant interactions of his research needed to be conveyed by more than the written word; they needed to reflect the embodied identities of the men he was working with; and the visual provided a platform to engage at the level of affect. However, many men were reluctant to engage in the childlike activity of drawing, which was embraced by Chantelle as discussed in the previous section, a resistance seen in other visual studies (Mannay 2010; Johnson *et al.* 2012); and something that will be discussed in more detail in Chapter 6. Nevertheless, when participants did engage with the activity, Richardson found that the repeated processes of drawing and talking about, on and in the body helped participants to articulate their emotions.

For example, Daniel's drawing, illustrated in Figure 3.3, brought up a range of biographical reflections that encompassed family, sport, work and also religion; and the discussions around the soul and the transitions of belief throughout the life-course. The interview around the drawing elicited not only narratives but also laughter, song and reflexivity. Consequently, Richardson argues that the processes helped to articulate emotions; and he suggests that he gained insight to information that a pre-set semi-structured interview schedule would not have accessed. Even where participants did not engage in drawing within the initial meeting, there were instances where the activity still engendered time for reflection by participants and researchers alike.

Bill, a third generation Irishman, who was born in Scotland in the 1960s and moved to the North East of England as a young man, did not write or draw anything on the outline during his initial interaction with Richardson. However, Bill asked Richardson to leave the symbolic man with him to consider. Later Bill telephoned Richardson and asked him to take out three blank copies of the outlines; colouring the first in red, the second as a rainbow and the third in purple. In the same way that participants in my study created their images at home, away from me, the researcher, this temporal gap in Richardson's fieldwork allowed time for ideas and reflections to deepen and fill out.

In the following discussions Richardson learnt how the red image represented the 'hurt and anger' of Bill's early life where he was initially the victim of violence and later the perpetrator. The rainbow images represented the multiple influences that were significant in later stages in his life; while the present day, reflected in the purple image, symbolised Bill as a middle-aged man who had found a state of 'peace and calm'. In this way, the use of images allowed Richardson and his participants to move beyond the everyday commonalities of their connections. They acted to fight familiarity and engender a space of defamiliarisation, where issues of identity, masculinity and emotion could be articulated in a form that moved beyond the purely verbal communication of the mundane; and in this way Richardson was able 'to make the familiar strange and interesting again' (Erikson 1986, p. 121).

## Hospitals, waste and photo-elicitation

In contrast to Richardson's conceptual aims, the following empirical example emphasises the practical use of visual techniques for making the familiar strange in the mundane setting of the workplace. Sarah Goff, Reva Kleppel, Peter Lindenauer and Michael Rothberg were interested in contributing to efforts to reduce costs in the context of North American health services. Unnecessary costs within the service have been attributed to inefficiently delivered services, excess administrative costs, inflated prices, missed prevention opportunities and fraud (IOM 2012); but this study focused specifically on the category of 'waste'. The study was interested in eliciting the views of hospital workers around waste and wanted to avoid the closed categories of a clinical waste questionnaire and allow a process that would engender an element of reflexivity. Consequently, they chose to employ the technique of photo-voice: 'embedding the participant's perspective in the research' (Goff et al. 2013).

Twenty-one participants took 159 photographs and the main themes included types of waste and recommendations to reduce waste. In employing a visual element to the data production, Goff et al. (2013) found that healthcare workers' perceptions of what constitutes waste differed from the types of waste previously described in healthcare research. Sources of healthcare waste may be broadly categorised as operational or clinical in nature; however, participants tended to describe operational sources of waste, such as workflow inefficiencies, more than clinical sources of waste such as excess utilisation. Additionally, the visual approach introduced novel types of waste that have been less discussed in reference to healthcare waste such as energy and talent. The factor of time, illustrated with pictures of clocks by the participants, was related to multiple sites and contexts that are not common place in the previous academic literature. In this way, the familiarity of standardised categories was overcome by allowing health workers to reflect on their personal experiences and create their own images and interpretations of what constitutes waste.

Drawing on the visual as a resource provided a unique method for identifying healthcare waste; however, the authors also considered the limitations of the approach. Arguably it may have restricted examples of waste identified to those items that were easily photographed, represented waste that was most frequently encountered or that were most personally intrusive. Nevertheless, despite efforts to improve the value of healthcare, systemic waste remains a daunting challenge and visual methods can provide novel insights. The photographs in the study did not simply depict waste but led to discussions of interventions, particularly at the micro-level and meso-level, which may not have arisen in questionnaires or more formal interviews. The study also demonstrates the potential for using photo-elicitation to study other areas of healthcare and its value as a tool of action research.

## Conclusion

This chapter was concerned with exploring how visual techniques can act to 'fight familiarity'. The chapter illustrated the ways in which enabling a visual element in qualitative research can potentially open up new understandings for both the researcher and researched; presenting a range of concrete empirical examples, which demonstrate how photographs, maps, drawings and collages can render the familiar setting more perceptible. In each of the studies discussed, the use of participant-directed visual data production, and the subsequent elicitation discussions, tended to reveal far more than researchers would have expected using an entirely verbal approach for data production. The technique allowed time for the participants to reflect on their lives creatively without the direction of an intrusive research voice; which can be advantageous when the researcher is an insider who aspires to make the familiar strange.

Each of the studies discussed attempted to overcome some level of familiarity in relation to the research site, participants or area of study; and illustrated the pervasive nature of being researcher near in social science research. In the field, researchers are never complete insiders or absolute outsiders but there is always some level of familiarity and the potential for studies to be overshadowed by preconceptions and preconceived knowledge as opportunities for discovery become clouded with the conventions of acquaintance (Geer 1964). Consequently, the use of visual methods as a tool of defamiliarisation have multidisciplinary appeal and can be employed to fight familiarity in different contexts and academic fields; attending to conceptual enquiries and the practicalities of action research. Therefore, the appeal of the visual as a technique of data production is wide, as it lends itself to multiple sites and questions, although, as with all methods there remain practical problems with application and interpretation; issues that will be discussed in more detail in Chapters 5 and 6.

As Ball and Smith (2001, p. 131) suggest, 'the greater use of visual methods is not a panacea for all ethnography's ills nor is it the touchstone to startling ethnographic discoveries'. Nevertheless, the techniques discussed in this chapter acted to counter the tacit and normalising effect of knowledge, which operates by taking one's group experiences and assuming these to be paradigmatic of all. Employing these methods, then, can provide new insights into participants' worlds; thus, the application of self-directed visual data production provided a gateway to destinations that lay beyond researchers' repertoires of preconceived understandings of individuals, place and space; unravelling the diversity of experience and making the familiar strange and interesting again. The visual is a useful tool of defamiliarisation; however, when creatively applied, visual approaches can also act as a tool for participatory research across concrete, temporal and imaginative spaces, which will be the focus of Chapter 4.

## Note

1 Visualista was a term used by Eric Margolis to address an audience of visual researchers at the 2006 International Visual Sociological Association conference in Urbino.

## References

Aguilar, F. (1981) *Landlessness and Hired Labour in Philippine Rice Farms*. Norwich: Geo Books.

Atkinson, P., Coffey, A. and Delamont, S. (2003) *Key Themes in Qualitative Research*. Walnut Creek, CA: Alta Mira Press.

Ball, M. S. and Smith, G. W. H. (1992) *Analyzing Visual Data*. London: Sage.

Ball, M. S. and Smith, G. W. H. (2001) 'Technologies of Realism? Ethnographic Use of Photography and Film', in P. Atkinson, A. Coffey, S. Delamont, J. Lofland and L. Lofland (eds) *Handbook of Ethnography*, pp. 302–20. London: Sage.

Banks, M. (2001) *Visual Methods in Social Research*. London: Sage.

Becker, H. (1971) 'Footnote', in M. Wax, S. Diamond and F. Gearing (eds) *Anthropological Perspectives on Education*, pp. 3–27. New York: Basic Books.

Butler, P. (2006) 'Down and Out in Bermondsey? Not at All', *Society Guardian*, 11 October.

Chamberlain, K. Cain, T., Sheridan, J. and Dupuis, A. (2011) 'Pluralisms in Qualitative Research: From Multiple Methods to Integrated Methods', *Qualitative Research in Psychology* 8(2): 151–169.

Cohen, S. (2011) *Folk Devils and Moral Panics*. London: Routledge.

Damon, F. H. (2000) 'To Restore the Events? On the Ethnography of Malinowski's Photography', *Visual Anthropology Review* 16(1): 71–7.

Delamont, S. and Atkinson, P. (1995) *Fighting Familiarity: Essays on Education and Ethnography*. Cresskill, NJ: Hampton Press.

Deleuze, G. (2000) *Proust and Signs* (R. Howard, trans.). London: Athlone.

Edwards, E. (2014) 'Out and About: Photography, Topography, and Historical Imagination', in O. Shevchenko (ed.) *Double Exposure: Memory and Photography*, pp. 177–210. London: Transactional.

Erikson, F. (1986) 'Qualitative Methods in Research on Teaching', in M. C. Wittrock (ed.) *Handbook of Research on Teaching*, pp. 119–58. New York: Macmillan.

Evans, G. (2006) *Educational Failure and Working Class White Children in Britain*. London: Palgrave Macmillan.

Gauntlett, D. (2007) *Creative Explorations: New Approaches to Identities and Audiences*. London: Routledge.

Geer, B. (1964) 'First Days in the Field', in P.E. Hammond (ed.) *Sociologists at Work*, pp. 372–98. New York: Basic Books.

Goff, S., Kleppel, R., Lindenauer, P. and Rothberg, M. (2013) 'Hospital Workers' Perceptions of Waste: a Qualitative Study Involving Photo-elicitation', *BMJ Quality & Safety* 22: 826–835.

Gurevitch, Z. D. (1998) 'The Other Side of Dialogue: On Making the Other Strange and the Experience of Otherness', *American Journal of Sociology* 93(5): 1179–99.

Hammersley, M. and Atkinson, P. (2007) *Ethnography: Principles in Practice* (3rd edn). London: Routledge.

Henry, A. (2001) 'Looking Two Ways: Identity, Research, and Praxis in the Caribbean Community', in B. Mercher and A. Ingram-Willis (eds) *Multiple and Intersecting Identities in Qualitative Research*, pp. 61–8. Mahwah, NJ: Lawrence Erlbaum.

Hett, G. (2014) 'She is an English Speaker, but that is not her Identity! Exploring Teachers' Language Practices in a Syrian English-as-a-Foreign-Language Institute'. Unpublished Doctoral thesis, University of East Anglia

Hodkinson, P. (2005) 'Insider Research in the Study of Youth Cultures', *Journal of Youth Studies* 8(2): 131–49.

IOM (Institute of Medicine). (2012) *Best care at lower cost: The path to continuously learning health care in America*. Washington, DC: The National Academies Press.

Johnson, G. A., Pfister, E. A. and Vindrola-Padros, C. (2012) 'Drawings, Photos, and Performances: Using Visual Methods with Children', *Visual Anthropology Review* 28 (2): 164–177.

Kaomea, J. (2003) 'Reading Erasures and Making the Familiar Strange: Defamiliarising Methods for Research in Formerly Colonized and Historically Oppressed Communities', *Educational Researcher* 32(2): 14–25.

Lucey, H., Melody, J. and Walkerdine, V. (2003) 'Uneasy Hybrids: Psychological Aspects of Becoming Educationally Successful for Working-class Young Women', *Gender and Education* 15(3): 285–99.

Mannay, D. (2006) 'Structural Constraints and School Choice: The Theory of Reasoned Action and the Theory of Planned Behaviour', Unpublished BA thesis. Cardiff: Cardiff University.

Mannay, D. (2010) 'Making the Familiar Strange: Can Visual Research Methods Render the Familiar Setting more Perceptible?', *Qualitative Research* 10(1): 91–111.

Mannay, D. (2013) '"Keeping close and spoiling" revisited: exploring the significance of "home" for family relationships and educational trajectories in a marginalised estate in urban south Wales', *Gender and Education* 25(1): 91–107.

Massey, D. (1994) *Space, Place and Gender*. Cambridge: Polity.

Mellor, D.J. (2006) 'Playground Romance: An Ethnographic Study of Friendship and Romance in Children's Relationship Cultures', Unpublished PhD thesis, Cardiff University.

Oakley, A. (1981) *Subject Woman*. London: Martin Robertson.

Pauwels, L. (2011) 'An Integrated Conceptual Framework for Visual Social Research', in E. Margolis and L. Pauwels (eds) *The Sage Handbook of Visual Research Methods*, pp. 3–23. London: Sage.

Pilcher, J. (1995) *Age and Generation in Modern Britain*. Oxford: Oxford University Press.

Pilcher, J. and Whelehan, I. (2004) *Fifty Key Concepts in Gender Studies*. London: Sage.

Pink, S. (2004) 'Applied Visual Anthropology Social Intervention, Visual Methodologies and Anthropology Theory', *Visual Anthropology Review* 20(1): 3–16.

Radnofsky, M. L. (1996) 'Qualitative Models: Visually Representing Complex Data in an Image/Text Balance', *Qualitative Inquiry* 2(4): 385–410.

Renold, E. (2005) *Girls, Boys and Junior Sexualities*. London: Routledge Falmer.

Richardson, M. (2015) 'Embodied Intergenerational: Family Position, Place and Masculinity', *Gender, Place and Culture* 22 (2): 157–171.

Rogan A. I. and de Kock, D. M. (2005) 'Chronicles from the Classroom: Making Sense of the Methodology and Methods of Narrative Analysis', *Qualitative Inquiry* 11(4): 628–49.

Rose, G. (2013) 'On the Relation between "Visual Research Methods" and Contemporary Visual Culture', *Sociological Review*, 62 (1): 24–46.

Schevchenko, O. (ed.) (2014) *Double Exposure: Memory and Photography*. London: Transaction Publishers.

Sikes, P. (2003) 'Making the Familiar Strange: A New Look at Inequality in Education', *British Journal of Sociology of Education* 24(2): 243–8.

Sikes, P. (2006) 'Travel Broadens the Mind or Making the Strange Familiar: The Story of a Visiting Academic', *Qualitative Inquiry* 12(3): 523–40.

Skeggs, B. (1997) *Formations of Class and Gender*. London: Sage.

Skeggs, B. (2004) *Class, Self and Culture*. London: Routledge.

Song, M. and Parker, D. (1995) 'Commonality, Difference and the Dynamics of Discourse in In-depth Interviewing', *Sociology* 29(2): 241–56.

Spencer, S. (2011) *Visual Research Methods in the Social Sciences: Awakening Visions*. London: Routledge.

Stouffer, W. B., Jeffrey, S. and Oliva, M. G. (2004) 'Making the Strange Familiar: Creativity and the Future of Engineering Education', in *Proceedings of the 2004 American Society for Engineering Education Annual Conference and Exposition*, Washington, DC: American Society for Engineering Education, Session 1615.

Thorne, B. (1993) *Gendered Play: Boys and Girls in School*. Brunswick, NJ: Rutgers University Press.

Tillman, L. C. (2002) 'Culturally Sensitive Research Approaches: An African-American Perspective', *Education Researcher* 31(9): 3–12.

Toynbee, P. (2003) *HardWork – Life in Low-Pay Britain*. London: Bloomsbury.

Vrasidas, C. (2001) 'Interpretivism and Symbolic Interactionism: "Making the Familiar Strange and Interesting Again" in Educational Technology Research', in W. Heinecke and J. Willis (eds) *Research Methods in Educational Technology*, pp. 81–99. Charlotte, NC: Information Age Publishing.

# 4

# PARTICIPATORY METHODOLOGIES

## Questions of power and positionality in creative research

## Introduction

The previous chapter focused on the potential of creative methods to 'fight familiarity' and engender a space where both researchers and participants can move beyond the enclosed world of familiarity. In this way, where familiarity can act as a barrier in researching any field that we have previous experience of, and opportunities for discovery become clouded with the conventions of acquaintance (Geer 1964), creative methods of data production were presented as a possible solution. It was recognised that this solution was partial; however, in terms of the positions of research nearness and participants' familiarity with their own lifeworlds, these techniques were seen to disrupt positionality and provide different ways of knowing and understanding (Gauntlett and Holzwarth 2006). Positionality has also been widely debated in terms of power relations, where an easy marriage between visual data production and participatory practice is well versed and in vogue within the field of social science; however, although participatory techniques offer an opportunity to disrupt power relations they are unable to transcend these hierarchies. This chapter argues that we need to reconsider relationships between participants and researchers, and acknowledge that even when the 'intrusive presence' of the researcher steps out of the site of visual data production this leaves a space that is often filled by the 'intrusive presence' of significant others.

Visual images are widely recognised as having the potential to evoke emphatic understanding of the ways in which other people experience their worlds (Belin 2005; Mizen 2005; Pink 2004; Rose 2010). Furthermore, the case for limiting the intrusive presence of the researcher, extending the restrictions set by the linearity of verbal narrative and gaining a more nuanced understanding of the lives of others through visual techniques has been upheld by a large body of academic work (Dodman 2003; Harper 2002; Mason 2005; Packard 2008; Twine 2006; Woodward 2008).

As I have discussed in the previous chapter and elsewhere (Mannay 2010), methods of visual data production also have the potential both to 'fight familiarity' (Delamont and Atkinson 1995), and engender participatory practice. However, the idea of an easy marriage between the visual and the participatory has been challenged by a number of researchers. For example, Luttrell and Chalfen (2010) comment that the explosion of participatory media projects has not resolved the goal of 'giving voice', and that a recurring and unresolved issue for researchers is that of whose voice is being spoken and, simultaneously, whose voice is being heard – particularly when research participants are children.

Large comparative research often involves cultural assumptions that are symptomatic of 'what children are and what children should be'; and participatory visual methods have become an important theme in a sociology of childhood where the voice of the child is prioritised. Consequently, it has become common place within academia, particularly the social sciences, to discuss the importance of 'allowing' the voices of marginalised communities to speak for themselves. Yet as Barrera (2011, p. 5) contends, this statement 'masks the awkward question of how it was those voices were silenced in the first place' and it also engenders a consideration for the continuance of silences in marginalised communities and the limits of social sciences to effectively address such silence. As Lomax *et al.* (2011) argue, there is a danger with linking the visual and the creative with the participatory, which becomes problematic practice; not least because visual and narrative outputs cannot speak for themselves. For even where children are involved in planning, filming and editing, as they were in Lomax *et al.*'s study, films and photographs were still produced through dynamic relationships – children's (unequal) relationships with each other, the researchers and the residents on their estate.

Therefore, participatory visual approaches that make central the premise of giving voice need to address the power relations that construct not only the research relationship but also, importantly, the wider social context. Artefacts do not exist in a vacuum; they are based on the background experiences and feelings of the person that created them and, importantly, on the power relations that surround them. The relationship between researcher and researched is key to the collection of reliable data (Pole 2007), but researchers are not the only intrusive presence. Consequently, it is important to explore what we mean by 'the participatory' and the interplay between researchers, participants and the wider community. As Joanou (2009) suggests, researchers should continually reassess their research practices and this chapter engages with the call for reassessment; first, by exploring why creativity itself is centralised as a vehicle of empowerment and the potentialities for transferring this conceptualisation into research methodologies. The chapter then examines multiple conceptions of participatory practice, how these interpretations are actualised by researchers in the field and the need to explore issues of power and positionality beyond the boundaries of the researcher/participant relationship. The chapter also explores the difference between 'speaking' and being 'heard', which is not always fully considered in the participatory ideology of 'giving voice'.

## Creativity and voice

Visual and creative methods are often presented as a panacea for resolving issues of power and positionality (Lomax *et al.* 2011); and it is important to understand how this relationship has been established. The appeal of visual artefacts can be traced, in part, to the ways in which images have been employed as a tool by marginalised and silenced communities. For example, the term 'story cloth' is used in craft art literature to refer to a form of narrative, pictorial textile craft art, presenting single scenes and narrative sequences in either embroidery or appliqué; and this format has been utilised by groups who are silenced through illiteracy, patriarchy and coercive political control. Exploring collective memory in post-Apartheid South Africa, a needle worker explains her engagement with story cloth, commenting, 'I quilt because I don't want my history, my story to die. Quilting gives me a voice when I can't write or speak' (Goggin 2003). Similarly, Roberta Bacic (2013) has curated politically significant stories that document the lived experience of Pinochet's Chile. As illustrated in Figure 4.1, arpilleras, tapestries or quilts sewn by women, 'speak out' visually about political repression and human rights abuses. Through their stitches and their materials, often consisting of the clothing of the regime's missing and dead, they convey processes of resistance, memory and the search for truth and justice in a context of repression.

**FIGURE 4.1**  ¡Adiós Pinochet! Goodbye Pinochet! Chilean arpillera, anon., c1980. Photograph Colin Peck – courtesy of Roberta Bacic (2013)

The visual has also been a tool to 'speak out' in the unsettled political geography of the United Kingdom, where Welsh, Scottish and Irish nationalists have challenged their enrolment into political union as a form of forcible integration (Clarke 2009). The War of Independence saw the partition of Ireland in 1921, and Northern Ireland was left with pervasive divisions between Catholic nationalists who wanted single Irish rule and a Protestant population who opposed home rule in favour of union with Britain. In an artificial state, devoid of geographical, historical or political logic, mural painting became a way of claiming space visually. The Protestant domination of politics engendered a discrimination in housing, education and employment for the Catholic population and when civil protest was met with a harsh police response on 30 January 1972, Bloody Sunday, resulting in the death of fourteen civilians killed by British soldiers, this spiral violence led to the beginning of the 'Troubles' (Blakeley and Saward 2009).

The 'Troubles' saw an explosion of mural painting that featured both Unionist and Republican art; and these wall paintings were often a means of communication that represented messages suppressed in the media. The iconic print media image of the 'Boy Petrol Bomber', at the Battle of Bogside, Londonderry 1969, presented contradictory metaphors of the innocent child with gas mask and petrol bomb in his hand. This visual representation was canonised through its appearance in a series of murals in Northern Ireland, where each artist casts the boy differently according to their political loyalties (Wright 2011). These images become signs of their times but can be reformatted to act as signs beyond their times; reinvented and mediating new messages, acting as affective practices that can be experienced as both empowering and disempowering for different communities.

Wahl (2014) explored processes of negotiating representation in Israel and Palestine and the notion of visual representation in this heavily documented region. Wahl was interested in understanding how local visual practitioners negotiated the work of photography and worked within issues such as victimhood, representation and the ambiguous nature of photography. Wahl focused on protected images that are often invisible in press coverage such as hunger strikes, protests, and the destruction of homes. The problematic nature of media coverage was taken up by a photographer Tania Nasir who commented:

> sometimes I'm bored with the way we're portrayed, in a sense, as you say these stereotype images. And at the same time I feel, photographs are really a very very powerful tool about showing what's happening . . . I don't know if there's an instance in the world where the general media can take up a mission to show something different, it's individuals I think who will do that.
>
> (Wahl 2014, p. 6)

Similar to the case in Northern Ireland, individuals do engage with offering new perspectives that may be silenced in the media and wall murals employ both images and words to communicate representations and experiences across Israel and Palestine.

As well as offering representations of ongoing political unrest, creativity has also been used to 'give voice' in relation to one-off events where people feel their views have been overlooked. In 1965 the Welsh village, Tryweryn, near Bala, was flooded to provide water for Liverpool. Local people had campaigned against the proposal but in the end they had to leave their village in Wales so that their land could be exploited to provide water for the neighbouring city over the border in England. 'Cofiwch Dryweryn', 'Remember Tryweryn' was first daubed in red paint on a derelict wall at the side of the A487, overlooking Llanrhystud, in the early 1960s and the message has faded and been repainted several times over the decades. In 2005, the city of Liverpool officially apologised for the flooding of the community forty years earlier. The graffiti has since become an unofficial national landmark and an example of the ways in which the visual message can become a symbol for communities whose voice was silenced in the wider national politics, which forced seventy residents to leave their homes while their village disappeared under the waters of the new lake.

These examples all demonstrate the power of creativity and its connection to the idea of 'giving voice' through cloth work, photography and painting. However, these examples can be positioned as grass-roots movements and forms of individualised political activism, which demonstrate flexible and decentralised network forms. In this way, they can be conceptualised as 'knotworking' collaborations between partners that take place without rigid predetermined rules or fixed central authority (Engeström 2007). Negotiation is the central coordinating mechanism of the distributed agency required in knotworking within social production; and 'wild fire activities' (Engeström 2007) of activism do not necessarily translate successfully into hierarchical and institutionally constrained projects of social research. Therefore, the potential of the visual as a tool to 'speak out' and the ideology of participatory practice in social research needs to be carefully considered.

## Participatory practices

Chalfen (2011) notes that the term 'participant visual methods' covers a diverse range of approaches, and projects have different end points. Participatory approaches are often conceptualised in line with the underlying assumptions and common principles of inclusive practice (Walmsley and Johnson 2003), which attempt to centralise the views and experiences of participants and engender an approach resonant with the aims of 'giving voice'. One principal objective of such research, then, is to eliminate the conceptual and practical filters applied both literally and metaphorically by researchers; and to engender access to more authentic views. As Thompson (2008) contends, children and young people are capable of providing expert testimony about their experiences, associations and lifestyles; and in 'giving voice' there is a recognition that all participants are competent 'beings' and 'political selves' (Kallio 2008) whose views, actions and choices are of value.

For Pauwels (2011) participatory productions situate the social scientist as the participatory facilitator, conducting research 'with' and not 'on' participants so that research becomes a joint enterprise or one that is participant led. However, participatory practices are not all or nothing, rather they exist on a continuum in which studies illustrate differential participatory potentials and practices. A gestalt approach to the participatory would engender a relationship between researcher and participants at all stages in the research process, from design to data production, analysis and dissemination; and some researchers have managed to follow this holistic endeavour in their creative work with communities.

For example, Maggie O'Neill (2012, p. 158) argues that both the narrative and the visual 'can be defined as critical theory in practice and an example of public scholarship'. In her research practice, O'Neill (2012) works within a framework of 'ethno-mimesis', which captures the combination of ethnographic participatory research and the visual or poetic representation of research. O'Neill has designed projects in the UK and Canada that draw on the framework of ethno-mimesis and can be conceptualised as Participatory Action Research, which involves a commitment to facilitating both the development and outcomes of research. Importantly, her work positions participants as co-researchers and community members as experts through a democratic decision-making process at all stages of the research project.

A clear example of ethno-mimesis can be seen in a project undertaken by Maggie O'Neill and Rosie Campbell, which explored prostitution in South Walsall, UK. Importantly, the project began by involving a range of local agencies and groups; and the recruited and trained local community researchers who were residents of South Walsall. The project worked in conjunction with local art agencies and employed the theme of safety as the research topic so that the fieldwork was careful to shift the focus from prostitution as the causal factor of the problems in the area. The project engaged sex workers and other local residents to work collaboratively on a number of outputs including displays in art galleries, information leaflets and a website. In this way, participants were involved at all stages of the research and working collaboratively across communities acted to transgress barriers, with the visual and narrative productions acting as a vehicle for participants and researchers to view the difficulties in the local area from multiple perspectives. Additionally, the findings of the project contributed to the wider policy discourse as they were central in the 2006 Home Office strategy on prostitution; consequently, it is evident that combining community arts, social research and genuinely participatory practices is a powerful tool for facilitating social change.

Another best practice example of Participatory Action Research is offered by the community film-making and empowerment project 'The Rhythm of our Dreams' ('*Al Compás de Los Sueños*'), facilitated by Anne Matinez Perez (2007). The project aimed to produce a documentary film that would generate awareness of social inclusion, its causes and how it should be tackled. Perez was working in a marginalised area in Córdoba, Spain and, arguing that the poverty that is closest to us remains invisible, Perez aimed to raise visibility of the local problems. Importantly, Perez was careful to situate the difficulties as an effect of wider social structures rather than local residents and she employs the analogy below to communicate this distinction;

> *The water reaches all the orange trees equally. If we translate water into social justice it becomes housing, employment, education. When the water is spread out equally no orange tree rots; no person would break down causing social conflict. When the water does not reach the tree the problem is not with the tree itself, which smells, but with the water that never got there.*
>
> *(Perez 2007, p. 229)*

The methodological focus combined applied anthropology and visual ethnography in a participatory film-making project concerned with 'giving voice' and working side-by-side with participants; and centralising the salience of dreams. Dreams offer a simple and graphic way of illustrating the distance that both separates and unites us, as while some of us dare to imagine a better future and struggle to achieve it, others dare not even mention desires that are unattainable. This contrast between the dreams of those who have access to basic resources, and those who do not, was foregrounded in the creative data production, which centralised the voices and interpretations of the participants. Participants worked alongside researchers to create a book, CD-ROM and film, which were disseminated to local residents and policy makers.

The film making was careful to avoid the media tendency to sensationalise and the journalistic reductionism, which often acts to 'voice over' the perspectives of marginalised communities and curtail the opportunities for forms of 'direct witness'. The project examined dreams through a music therapy approach because dreams project our fantasies and desires; and are part of the creative and imaginative practice of being an individual, which forms part of our agency to instigate processes of change. In this way, the work of Perez and O'Neill can be seen as the gold standard in participatory practice, where there is considerable work throughout the project to creatively disrupt the traditional binaries and power relations between researcher and participant.

However, many research projects are unable to attain this level of participant involvement across the journey from design to dissemination. Consequently, even where creative techniques of data production are employed, questions remain about who is seen, how they are seen and who is viewing, which are all part of the social power relations that produce specific versions of social hierarchies (Haraway 1991). The opportunity to involve participants in a meaningful way is often curtailed by the wider socio-economic climate where research evidence is rapidly becoming subservient to political expediency (Haggerty 2004, p. 219). For Mills and Ratcliffe (2012), this reflects the requirements of national and international polities and economies to train knowledge workers within an intense circulation of concepts and commodities. This push for efficiency potentially narrows the opportunities to engender 'the unpredictable, the tangential and the creative': so that all that remains is 'methodological instrumentalism' (Mills and Ratcliffe 2012, p. 152).

These external market contingencies continue to stress the business case for research output and often prevent researchers from indulging in 'slow science', which engenders flexibility and serendipity – as a combination of both chance and intuitive reasoning (Rivoal and Salazar 2013). The qualitative researcher is expected to condense their time in the field, be reflective without time for reflexivity; and write and publish at speed to keep their ethnographic account relevant before it becomes obsolete and void of economic value (Mannay and Morgan 2014). These discussions will be taken up in more detail in Chapter 6; however, it is important to acknowledge the consequences for creative participatory research. In time-bounded research projects that are tied to the requirements of funders and an ideology of methodological instrumentalism, the gold standard of participatory practice set by researchers like Perez and O'Neill are difficult to attain.

Consequently, the aims of 'giving voice' can be compromised and many projects can only be seen as partial in their commitment to participatory practice. This partial participatory practice is often concentrated in methods of data production where the techniques of community film making, photo-elicitation, drawing and poetry workshops offer an opportunity to disrupt power relations; however, they are unable to transcend the hierarchies between researcher and participants. In this way, projects that employ creative techniques of data production cannot be necessarily seen as participatory. They may have elements of participatory practice but the balance of power will be graduated towards the researcher and impact on the design, implementation and dissemination of research. It is important then to acknowledge the impact of the researcher but also of 'intrusive others' who influence the process and outcomes of social inquiry; and explore the power relations between participants and significant individuals in participants' lives.

## Power relations and participants

Conducting research in the classroom, Gallagher (2008) notes how the existing power relations between the pupils impacted on the data production process in situations where he attempted to step back and displace the intrusive voice of the researcher. The visual data produced with building blocks was often a reflection of the views of the more dominant children to the neglect of the views of children who were lower down in the classroom hierarchy. Children did not necessarily engage in an equitable form and Gallagher (2008) acknowledges that the participatory ideal of the design did not manifest in the actuality of the fieldwork. Therefore, although creative methods of data production are popular in participatory projects, these techniques are not participatory in themselves; and although they may displace the intrusive voice of the researcher, they are ill equipped to eradicate existing power relations in the field.

Gallagher (2008) illustrates how his attempts to introduce participatory methods to children were circumscribed by the pre-existing landscape of power within the school, charting the ways in which the more dominant children in the classroom thwarted his attempts to intervene in these power relations. Similarly, although

I attempted to introduce participatory techniques and remove myself from the physical site of data production in my research, I was unable to circumvent processes of power and control inherent in the complex sets of relations that constitute the field of that data production, namely mothers and daughters' homes.

The *Mothers and Daughters on the Margins* project, introduced in the earlier chapters, was interested in participants' perspectives; nevertheless, as Chalfen (2011) comments, there is always some form of assignment in participatory work; and although participants were primarily concerned with constructing their own visual and narrative production, in terms of ownership, there was, of course, an element of guidance. The research design aspired to minimal instruction but even asking participants to create data to reflect their everyday lives affected some form of assignment at the point of data production; and this assignment necessarily guided data analysis.

The research design carefully considered the researcher/researched relationship as I have documented in detail in Chapter 3 and elsewhere (Mannay 2010, 2011); however, beyond this relationship, 'the importance of voice, whose story is being told and for whose benefit, looms large' (Walmsley and Johnson 2003, p. 41). For this reason, the following sections are concerned with presenting data around wider research relationships with participants' siblings, parents and partners that were not fully appreciated or adequately contemplated at the outset of the study. As the research was interested in intergenerational perspectives, on the one hand, including other individuals who are of importance to the participant could be viewed as beneficial. On the other hand, the presence of these knowledgeable others at the site of data production could be viewed as an implicit silencer of the participant's voice. The following sections revisit my earlier publication (Mannay 2013a) to explore this tension; and the associated methodological outcomes, concerns and relationship with the ideology of participatory practice.

## Parental involvement

In my attempt to empower participants by stepping back from the site of data production, rather than radically reconfiguring adult/child power relations, I have, in some cases, provoked a reconfiguring of those power relations where the mother or another family member steps in as the powerful adult. This was evident when I interviewed eight-year-old Bryony about her visual data, which demonstrated clear familial influence. Initially Bryony completed 'space and place' maps, using pencil crayons, to tell me about her everyday life as illustrated in Figure 4.2. These maps seemed to have been created by Bryony without overt interference and in the following interviews Bryony had a clear foundation on which to communicate her experience of home and the immediate locality.

However, at the second stage of data collection – possible future selves – Bryony's step-father became enthusiastic about the project and wanted to take part. I explained that I was only producing data with mothers and daughters but this did not dampen his enthusiasm to 'help'. While Bryony's maps were handmade, the

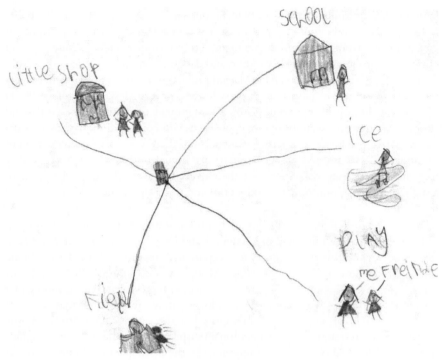

FIGURE 4.2  Bryony – place and space map

collage was produced collaboratively utilising computer graphic software; and rather than being a representation of Bryony's ideas of her future self it was a contemporary representation of favourable pastimes with the label 'I like ...' as demonstrated in the extract from her collage in Figure 4.3.

The technical standard of the collage implies adult assistance but it could be argued that the selection of images was based upon Bryony's preferences; suggesting collaboration rather than control. However, the quote below, and the related image illustrated in Figure 4.4, suggests that Bryony was not in agreement or even

FIGURE 4.3  Bryony – I like ...

# I like nice cars

**FIGURE 4.4**  I like nice cars

perhaps completely aware of all of the image-based and textual additions to her data production activity.

BRYONY:  (reading from the collage) *I like nice cars, who put that on there, I know I like nice cars but, I don't really really really like them (pause) I don't watch Top Gear, I don't watch anything about cars*

The elicitation interviews around this collage were not as embedded in Bryony's data; Bryony did not direct our conversation around the collection of images in the way that I would have expected from our previous interview with her map. In this way, the collage was unable to provide such an emotive basis for discussion as the initial hand-drawn map, where Bryony was eager to talk through the images that she had created. There seemed to be a lack of ownership and engagement with the collage and, as a researcher, I felt that the production was not so much a reflection of Bryony, but rather the images presented here and in other pictures of idyllic holidays and consumer lifestyles, were an idealised form: a presentation of what a young girl in a caring, successful and secure family should both 'like' and 'have'.

The 'intrusive other' in Bryony's collage, her step-father, does not consider the activity instructions; and I am presented with a collage that neither meets the requirements of the research, nor interests Bryony as a self that can be shared. The visual data production activity seems to have travelled beyond assistance and interaction, to some extent expected with younger participants (Clark-Ibanez 2004), to one of adult control. Again, arguably the collage offers some insight into a central adult's performance of family but in a study interested in the views of mothers and daughters, where voices of participants themselves are placed centre stage in research as the 'knowers' and 'tellers' of their own stories and experiences, Bryony's opportunity to narrate her ideas about her possible future self was diminished.

## Sibling suggestions

This is not to suggest that power is solely wielded by adults, as children and young people with their actions and in some cases their mere presence can restrict, dictate or influence the content of their mother's and siblings' visual and narrative data production. For example, this extract from Roxanne's positive possible self-narrative was a line that her younger brother added in while she was away from the computer.

*I have a lovely brother which comes round the house now and then and chills with (boyfriend) and kids.*

The added line is left intact by Roxanne and it leads to conversations around the sibling relationship and also the relationship between her boyfriend and her brother. Arguably, without the additional line our conversation may have taken the same direction; Roxanne did not write about her brother specifically, although she mentions family, but neither does she omit his inclusion or contradict its meaning in her/their future selves. For this reason we can see the individual account set out by Roxanne as different but not necessarily truer or fuller; and perhaps the collaborated account is in fact more naturalistic.

Yates (2010) conducted photo-elicitation research with young people whose lives had been disrupted by chronic illness; and she raises similar concerns about the complete exclusion of family members. Initially, both our thinking relegated familial interference as a constraint on participants to speak freely and a contamination of participants' data. However, for Yates (2010, p. 285) the 'banishing the parents' perspective and involvement' was not viewed as a natural or appropriate way to proceed by either the parent or the young person. Perhaps, then, in some cases, discussion with other family members can be advantageous, allowing participants to more fully explore their sense of self, checking their own ideas and understandings with others, who know them well; but from a different, subjective perspective, which could arguably build a fuller picture.

This idea of assistance and collaboration may be particularly useful in research exploring 'possible selves' of the future. Adulthood does not occupy a 'grown up' static state and neither does childhood; rather there is a constant and continual state of fluidity in an ever changing landscape of who we might have been and who we might still become. A continuous fluidity that Renold and Ringrose (2011) argue is intensified in the lives of girls and women. Thus, inevitably some possible selves will come to be, permanently and temporarily, while others will be lost along the way but sometimes recover (King and Hicks 2007). It is important to explore the idea of 'lost' and 'recovered' possible selves, and here the family and their ability to remind, refocus and reboot our sense of selfhood raises some concerns about 'banishing the parents' (Yates 2010 p. 285) to engender access to a true, clear and singular self.

Similarly, Clendon (2006) discusses the benefits of intergenerational perspectives in exploration of mothers' and daughters' thoughts around why they have kept their baby health books. Clendon employed joint elicitation interviews around these books and argued that the dyad format was more naturalistic as it acknowledges that women traditionally communicate with one another within the referents of family; and that this format elicited a greater depth of interview material. For Clendon (2006), then, interaction between mothers and daughters in her study enabled a richer perspective on intergenerational differences to be uncovered. However, she concedes that in some dyads the dialogue was more restrained and in these cases she moved to a more participatory style of interviewing where her input as a woman and as a mother were obvious and the interview became a construction between the researcher and the participants.

I also adopted this approach in the interviews where I would share my own similar experiences in the manner of a conversation about mutual topics of interest rather than rely on traditional question and answer technique. In this way, rather than trying to engender a 'true' account and employing participatory methods to elicit a singular perspective or 'give voice' to an individual participant, the 'intrusive presence' of significant others, both family members and the researcher, could potentially offer more nuanced and differentiated accounts.

## Imagined audiences

In his seminal chapter on the history of social psychology, Allport (1954, p. 5) provided a definition for the sub-discipline stating that 'Social psychology is the attempt to understand and explain how the thoughts, feelings, and behaviours of individuals are influenced by the actual, imagined, or implied presence of other human beings'. The definition retains centrality in contemporary social psychology but the concept of imagined audiences can be viewed as relevant across the discipline of social sciences. For example, in the present study it is worth noting that where adult participants, mothers, created data single-handedly, with no overt manipulation, in some cases there were still images and words that were not included because of the risk that data could be viewed by family members.

As Luttrell and Chalfen (2010, p. 199) contend, 'imagined audiences can change and play important roles in what is said or left unsaid'; a reminder that visual research should always be interested in not just that which can be seen but with what is hidden, erased (Kaomea 2003) and absent. In mothers' accounts this was specifically salient in terms of data that presents the darker side of family life and explores the 'affective landscapes of trust, confidentiality, silence, and the unintended consequences that encroach upon, and beyond, research relationships in indigenous qualitative inquiry'; as I discuss in more detail elsewhere (Mannay 2011, p. 962).

In many of the interviews I conducted with mothers their visual data was not simply a collection of images but rather, resonating with the 'turn to practice' in social theory, a set of social practices (Reckwitz 2002). Focusing on social practices, Rose (2010) drew on the disciplines of anthropology, geography and material culture studies to explore not what photographs are but what photographs do. Rose (2010) interviewed women in their own homes to gain a sense of the domestic space and the encounters between object and practice in family photography; and she argues that family photographs can be seen as part of women's traditional responsibility for domestic order and a way for women to negotiate a feminised subjectivity of acceptable motherhood and enact family togetherness.

This enactment of family togetherness was a process touched upon earlier in the chapter when I discussed the idealised form of Bryony's life presented by Bryony's step-father. In this way, the meaning of images is only part of their story because their presentation can be employed to engender a particular kind of intimate viewing public. Arguably, there is always some form of presentation of self (Goffman 1959); however, in the accounts of mothers it was often omissions rather than additions that were active in the practice of the maintenance of a happy family life. When stories are troubling, in the form of domestic and familial abuse, especially when the participant has remained with an abusive partner or is worried about her children accessing and interpreting symbolic meaning of visual data, omissions serve a protective and necessary purpose; but also act to silence subjective truths.

The focus of the study was not domestic abuse; however, the prime ethnographic maxim is that one cannot know what one is exploring until it has been explored (Rock 2007, p. 33) and the academic work and consultations on violence against women supports the ongoing and pervasive nature of abuse in the UK (Mannay 2013b, 2013c; Barter et al. 2009; Jarvinen et al. 2008; Rights of Women 2010; Women's National Coalition 2010). This suggests that researchers need always to be aware of and sensitive to these related silences; even, and perhaps especially, when the focus of the research is removed from discourses of abuse and data is unexpected.

Having been made aware of such interference and omission, in the interview situation, where appropriate, I asked about the process of production and if there were any other images or themes that participants thought of but did not include in their data. As Gabb (2008) argues in empirical qualitative studies of family life, the researcher inevitably becomes embedded in the personal worlds of those being researched; and the willingness of participants to share these accounts within the interview setting is testimony both to the centrality of violence in mothers' and daughters' lives, and the strength of the research design, which engendered a high level of trust between researched and researcher. The interview then does provide an opportunity to intervene in the complex sets of power relations that constitute the field of data production and elicit silenced accounts; but such an intervention is never a complete solution. Removing the researcher from the site of data production may be advantageous but as Gallagher (2008) maintains, 'participatory techniques may provide interesting ways to intervene in games of power... but they do not provide a way to transcend such games' (2008, p. 147).

## Conclusion

This chapter has illustrated the ways in which creative practices form a valuable and powerful source of expression in grass-roots movements and forms of individualised political activism. The link between creativity and voice is apparent in these individual constructions and 'knotworking' collaborations (Engeström 2007). In research, the 'visual might contribute to extending understanding of the ways social inequalities are imagined, constituted and reinforced' (Fink and Lomax 2012, p. 1); however, social science studies are always embedded in a differential and complex set of power relations. As Luttrell and Chalfen (2010, p. 200) contend, 'in the service of equality and social justice, we will continue to be pressed to ask how some voices continue to be unrepresented, muted, unheard, "voiced over" and silenced'; and this chapter makes visible the act of image and narrative production, in order to explore the ways in which data gains its meaning from the process through which it is produced.

The chapter has explored processes at the macro level through a consideration of the invisibility of marginalised groups including those living under the conditions of oppressive governance, poverty, gendered power relations and ideas of what 'children are and should be'. At the meso level the chapter has reflected on the unequal power relations in communities, schools and families; and how the projects conducted by O'Neill (2012) and Perez (2007) act to address inequalities and enable creative spaces where individuals can both 'speak' and be 'heard'. At the micro level, the dynamics between researchers and participants and others were introduced because, although the intrusive presence of the researcher is routinely considered in contemporary social research, the influence of intrusive presence of others – friends, parents, adults – is less likely to be the focus of debate.

In this chapter such interaction has been seen to influence, restrict and control data that participants produce. However, arguably, interaction can also be positioned as a more naturalistic form of inquiry and a tool to promote the production of more reflective, nuanced and considered visual and narrative data. Parents, friends and family, the researcher and research aims, and wider social norms and values are a continuing and constant influence. Unless our participants are Harlow's monkeys[1] (Miller 2011), cruelly separated from company and society, then perhaps we need to expect, embrace and evaluate such influence; and appreciate the ways in which family involvement can enable a richer perspective on intergenerational differences to be uncovered (Clendon 2006; Mannay 2013a; Yates 2010). More than looking at data, then, we need to look beyond data and consider how much assistance, guidance and interaction participants are party to in the creative process; and whether the 'intrusive presence' of significant others is a threat, a benefit or simply an inescapable facet of social science research, where meanings are always negotiated, revised and co-constructed.

Returning to Allport (1954, p. 5), this chapter has demonstrated how the 'thoughts, feelings, and behaviours of individuals are influenced by the actual, imagined, or implied presence of other human beings'. However, if social science is interested in a multiplicity of understanding of the complexities of lived experience, which are continuously configured, then relationships undoubtedly mediate individual identities and experiences; and rather than trying to exclude 'intrusive voices', perhaps it would be more useful to examine the ways in which they can act to further our understandings. This raises important questions about how we interpret visual and narrative creations and the salience of the elicitation process in gaining a sense of the message the image-creator intended to convey, a discussion that will be centralised in the following chapter.

## Note

1 The reference to Harlow's monkeys is used as a metaphor and it relates to the controversial experimental psychology of Harry Harlow. Harlow was interested in the basis of attachment and set up a number of different conditions to study this with primates. Harlow studied the impacts of maternal deprivation with rhesus monkeys by isolating them for study in a cage without their mother or other primates.

## References

Allport, G. W. (1954) *The Nature of Prejudice*. New York, NJ: Perseus Books.

Barrera, P. (ed.) (2011) *Seeking Sanctuary: Journeys of Despair and Hope*. Cardiff: Communities First Ethnic Minorities Programme.

Bacic, R. (2013) 'Arpilleras: Evolution and Revolution' Keynote Paper and Exhibition, *3rd International Visual Methods Conference*, Victoria University of Wellington, Wellington, New Zealand, 2–6 September 2013. http://www.cain.ulst.ac.uk/quilts/exhibit/followup.html#wellington03091 (Accessed 19 August 2015).

Barter, C., McCarry, M., Berridge, D. and Evans, K. (2009) *Partner Exploitation and Violence in Teenage Intimate Relationships*. London: NSPCC.

Belin, R. (2005) 'Photo-elicitation and the Agricultural Landscape: "Seeing" and "Telling" about Farming, Community and Place', *Visual Studies*, 20 (1): 56–68.

Blakeley, G. and Saward, M. (2009) 'Political Ordering', in S. Bromley, J. Clarke, S. Hinchcliffe and S. Taylor (eds) *Exploring Social Lives*, pp. 347–90. Milton Keynes: The Open University.

Chalfen, R. (2011) 'Differentiating Practices of Participatory Media Production', in E. Margolis and L. Pauwels (eds) *The Sage Handbook of Visual Research Methods*, pp. 186–200. London: Sage.

Clarke, J. (2009) 'Making National Identities: Britishness in Question', in S. Bromley, J. Clarke, S. Hinchcliffe and S. Taylor (eds) *Exploring Social Lives*, pp. 203–46. Milton Keynes: The Open University.

Clark-Ibanez, M. (2004) 'Framing the Social World with Photo-elicitation Interviews', *American Behavioral Scientist*, 47 (12): 1507–27.

Clendon, J. (2006) 'Mother/daughter Intergenerational Interviews: Insights into Qualitative Interviewing', *Contemporary Nurse*, 23 (2): 243–51.

Delamont, S. and Atkinson, P. (1995) *Fighting Familiarity: Essays on Education and Ethnography*. Cresskill, N.J.: Hampton Press.

Dodman, D. R. (2003) 'Shooting in the City: An Autobiographical Exploration of the Urban Environment in Kingston, Jamaica', *Area*, 35 (3): 293–304.

Engeström, Y. (2007) 'From Communities of Practice to Mycorrhizae', in J. Hughes, N. Jewson and L. Unwin (eds) *Communities of Practice: Critical Perspectives*. London: Routledge.

Fink, J. and Lomax, H. (2012) 'Introduction: Inequalities, Images and Insights for Policy and Research', *Critical Social Policy*, 32 (1): 1–8.

Gabb, J. (2008) *Researching Intimacy in Families*. Basingstoke: Palgrave Macmillan.

Gallagher, M. (2008) 'Power is not an Evil: Rethinking Power in Participatory Methods', *Children's Geographies*, 6 (2): 137–51.

Gauntlett, D. and Holzwarth, P. (2006) 'Creative and Visual Methods for Exploring Identities', *Visual Studies*, 21 (1): 82–91.

Geer, B. (1964) 'First Days in the Field', in P. E. Hammond (ed.) *Sociologists at Work*, pp. 372–98. New York: Basic Books.

Goffman, E. (1959) *The Presentation of Self in Everyday Life*. Harmondsworth: Pelican.

Goggin, D. (2003) 'Introduction', in C. McEwan, 'Building a Postcolonial Archive? Gender, Collective Memory and Citizenship in Post-Apartheid South Africa', *Journal of Southern African Studies*, 29 (3): 748.

Haggerty, K. D. (2004) 'Displaced Expertise: Three Constraints on the Policy Relevance of Criminological Thought', *Theoretical Criminology*, 8 (2): 211–311.

Harper, D. (2002) 'Talking About Pictures: A Case for Photo Elicitation', *Visual Studies*, 17 (1): 14–26.

Haraway, D. J. (1991) *Simians, Cyborgs and Women: The Reinvention of Nature*. London: Routledge.

Jarvinen, J., Kail, A. and Miller, I. (2008) *Violence Against Women: Hard Knock Life*. London: New Philanthropy Capital.

Joanou, J. P. (2009) 'The Bad and the Ugly: Ethical Concerns in Participatory Photographic Methods with Children Living and Working on the Streets of Lima, Peru', *Visual Studies*, 24 (3): 214–33.

Kallio, K. P. (2008) 'The Body as a Battlefield: Approaching Children's Politics', *Geografiska Annaler/Human Geography*, 90 (3): 285–97.

Kaomea, J. (2003) 'Reading Erasures and Making the Familiar Strange: Defamiliarising Methods for Research in Formerly Colonized and Historically Oppressed Communities', *Educational Researcher*, 32 (2): 14–25.

King, L. A. and Hicks, J. A. (2007) 'Lost and Found Possible Selves: Goals, Development and Well-being', *New Directions for Adult and Continuing Education*, 114: 27–37.

Lomax, H., Fink, J., Singh, N and High, C. (2011) 'The Politics of Performance: Methodological Challenges of Researching Children's Experiences of Childhood through the Lens of Participatory Video', *International Journal of Social Research Methodology*, 14 (3): 231–43.

Luttrell, W. and Chalfen, R. (2010) 'Lifting up the Voices of Participatory Research', *Visual Studies*, 25 (3): 197–200.

Mannay, D. (2010) 'Making the Familiar Strange: Can Visual Research Methods Render the Familiar Setting more Perceptible?', *Qualitative Research*, 10 (1): 91–111.

Mannay, D. (2011) 'Taking Refuge in the Branches of a Guava Tree: The Difficulty of Retaining Consenting and Non-consenting Participants' Confidentiality as an Indigenous Researcher', *Qualitative Inquiry*, 17 (10): 962–4.

Mannay, D. (2013a) '"Who put that on there … why why why?" Power Games and Participatory Techniques of Visual Data Production', *Visual Studies*, 28 (2): 136–46.

Mannay, D. (2013b) '"I Like Rough Pubs": Exploring Places of Safety and Danger in Violent and Abusive Relationships', *Families, Relationships and Societies*, 2 (1): 131–7.

Mannay, D. (2013c) 'The Permeating Presence of Past Domestic and Familial Violence: So Like I'd Never Let Anyone Hit me but I've Hit them, and I Shouldn't have Done', in J. Ribbens McCarthy, C. Hooper and V. Gillies (eds) *Family Troubles? Exploring Changes and Challenges in the Family Lives of Children and Young People*, pp. 151–62. Bristol: Policy Press.

Mannay, D. and Morgan, M. (2015) 'Doing Ethnography or Applying a Qualitative Technique?: Reflections from the "Waiting Field"', *Qualitative Research*, 15 (2): 166–82.

Mason, P. (2005) 'Visual Data in Applied Qualitative Research: Lessons from Experience', *Qualitative Research*, 5 (3): 325–46.

Miller, P. H. (2011) *Theories of Developmental Psychology* (5th edn). Worth: New York.

Mills, D. and Ratcliffe, R. (2012) 'After Method? Ethnography in the Knowledge Economy', *Qualitative Research*, 12 (2): 147–64.

Mizen, P. (2005) 'A Little "Light Work"? Children's Images of their Labour', *Visual Studies*, 20 (2): 124–39.

O'Neill, M. (2012) 'Ethno-mimesis and Participatory Arts' in S. Pink (ed.) *Advances in Visual Methodology*, pp. 153–72. London: Sage.

Packard, J. (2008) '"I'm Gonna Show you What it's Really Like Out Here": The Power and Limitation of Participatory Visual Methods', *Visual Studies*, 23 (1): 63–76.

Pauwels, L. (2011) 'An Integrated Conceptual Framework for Visual Social Research', in E. Margolis and L. Pauwels (eds) *The Sage Handbook of Visual Research Methods*, pp. 3–23. London: Sage.

Perez, A. (2007) 'The Rhythm of our Dreams: A Proposal for an Applied Visual Anthropology', in S. Pink (ed.) *Visual Interventions: Applied Visual Anthropology*, pp. 227–46. Oxford: Berghahn.

Pink, S. (2004) 'Applied Visual Anthropology Social Intervention, Visual Methodologies and Anthropology Theory', *Visual Anthropology Review*, 20 (1): 3–16.

Pole, C. (2007) 'Researching Children and Fashion: an Embodied Ethnography', *Childhood*, 14 (1): 67–84.

Reckwitz, A. (2002) 'Toward a Theory of Social Practices', *European Journal Social Theory*, 5 (2): 243–63.

Renold, E. and Ringrose, J. (2011) 'Schizoid Subjectivities: Re-theorising Teen-girls' Sexual Cultures in an Era of Sexualisation', *Journal of Sociology*, 47 (4): 389–409.

Rights of Women (2010) *Measuring Up? UK Compliance with International Commitments on Violence Against Women in England and Wales*. London: Rights of Women.

Rivoal, I. and Salazar, N. B. (2013) 'Contemporary Ethnographic Practice and the Value of Serendipity', *Social Anthropology*, 21 (2): 178–85.

Rock, P. (2007) 'Symbolic Interactionism and Ethnography', in P. Atkinson, A. Coffey, S. Delamont, J. Lofland and L. Lofland (eds) *Handbook of Ethnography*, pp. 26–39. London: Sage.

Rose, G. (2010) *Doing Family Photography: The Domestic, the Public and the Politics of Sentiment*. Farnham: Ashgate.

Thompson, P. (2008) *Doing Visual Research with Children and Young People*. Abingdon: Routledge.

Twine, F. W. (2006) 'Visual Ethnography and Racial Theory: Family Photographs as Archives of Interracial Intimacies', *Ethnic and Racial Studies*, 29 (3): 487–511.

Wahl, H. (2014) 'Negotiating Representation in Israel and Palestine', *Visual Studies*, 29 (1): 1–14.

Walmsley, J. and Johnson, K. (2003) *Inclusive Research with People with Learning Disabilities: Past, Present and Futures*. London: Jessica Kingsley Publishers.

Women's National Coalition (2010) *A Bitter Pill to Swallow: Report from WNC Focus Group to Inform the Department of Health Task Force on the Health Aspects of Violence Against Women and Girls*. London: WNC.

Woodward, S. (2008) 'Digital Photography and Research Relationships: Capturing the Fashion Moment', *Sociology*, 42 (5): 857–72.

Wright, T. (2011) 'Press Photography and Visual Rhetoric', in E. Margolis and L. Pauwels (eds) *The Sage Handbook of Visual Research Methods*, pp. 317–36. London: Sage.

Yates, L. (2010) 'The Story they want to Tell, and the Visual Story as Evidence: Young People, Research Authority and Research Purposes in the Education and Health Domains', *Visual Studies*, 25 (3): 280–91.

# 5

# PROBLEMATISING INTERPRETATION

## Applying auteur theory, disrupting the surface and breaking the frame

### Introduction

The preceding discussions have focused very much on fieldwork and the ways in which visual and narrative data production allow the opportunity to fight familiarity but also the inherent hierarchies and power relations that exist in sites of research. This chapter shifts the focus from processes of visual and narrative data production to questions of interpretation; particularly the seeing and reading of images. Our visually saturated culture reflects the power of the 'media sphere' in which the proliferation of digital images through social networking sites (Mitchell 2011) contributes to an ocularcentric climate (Spencer 2011, p. 1), where digital photographic images become seductive because of their seeming realism and their capacity for dissemblance and deception. However, seeing or vision simply refers to the physiological capabilities of the human eye, while visuality accounts for the far more complex ways in which vision is constructed.

Beyond vision, visuality, and the overlapping term scopic regime, refer to the ways in which audiences bring their own ways of seeing and other knowledges to bear on an image (Rose 2001). Images and narratives may belong to a world of things that we feel we know about – immensely and conventionally – but the connections between them can be clouded by our subjectivities and often remain unrevealed by our reading. Imagery evokes memories, reflections and feelings but interpretation depends on our accumulated cultural knowledge, and experience imposes a set of available frames for reference. There is a need to frame and fix our understandings as tropes, metaphors or analogies as 'no sooner is an image seen than it must resemble something: humanity seems doomed to analogy' (Barthes cited in Spencer 2011, p. 19).

As Steedman (1986, p. 137) contends, it is generally recognised in literary accounts of metaphor that

> *the connective device on which metaphor turns, that is, on the perception of real similarities between entities in the real world, is often actually no more than the recognition*

*of culturally highly specific contingent relations: we are used to comparing certain things with particular other things and metaphor often works through this connection, rather than perceived similarity.*

Reading literature and artwork from other cultures often serves to reveal the connections of our own metaphoric system, accordingly images have no inherent or structural association, other than that which 'the audience is educated to expect by convention' (Banks 2001, p. 10). Where there is not the vision that permits an understanding of these new connections, then 'a story cannot be told' (Steedman 1986, p. 138); or where a story is constructed it may be one that has no relationship with the meaning making of the original creator.

There is often a juxtaposition between the audience's reading and interpretation and the internal narrative of images, as intended by their creator. In this way, the reading of visual images and texts is predicated on the interpretation of the viewing self, an 'I' that is not an objective entity but a position of accumulated subjectivities. As Berger (1972, p. 370) contends, 'the present tense of the verb to be refers only to the present: but nevertheless with the first person singular in front of it, it absorbs the past, which is inseparable from it. "I am" includes all that has made me so. It is more than a statement of immediate fact: it is already biographical'. The audience, then, actively make their own meanings from an image. Thus, the reading of visual images suggests that the message lies within the visual image and analysis provides the opportunity for the image to speak but cultural assumptions, personal knowledge and the context guide our reading and interpretations.

Consequently, if the research is interested in the ways in which people assign meanings to pictures, the study of images alone, as data whose meaning is intrinsic, is a mistaken method (Banks 2001). To gain an understanding of the internal narrative of the image it is imperative to acknowledge the role of the image-maker; and the notion that the most salient aspect in understanding a visual image is what the maker intended to show is often referred to auteur theory (Rose 2001). Auteur theory is often required on a practical level because the interpretation of the audience is not necessarily the same as the narrative the image-maker wanted to communicate; indeed it can often be markedly different (Kearney and Hyle 2004). Consequently, the practice of asking participants to explain the visual images and narrative texts that they create has become a common feature of social science research (Belin 2005; Darbyshire *et al.* 2005; Lomax *et al.* 2011; Morrow 2001; Richardson 2015); in this way participants are provided with the opportunity to both 'show' and 'narrate' their experiences and lives.

This chapter returns to the study, *Mothers and Daughters on the Margins: Gender, Generation and Education* (Mannay 2010, 2012), and introduces data from the project, *University Challenge: How can we foster successful learning journeys for non-traditional students in a School of Social Science?* (Mannay and Edwards 2013, 2014), to demonstrate the salience of auteur theory in gaining an understanding of participants' creative productions. However, the chapter also considers the argument that 'the notion that meaningful interpretation is contingent on knowing its creator's intentions is nonetheless problematic, not least because these are not always available to viewers' Lomax (2012, p. 228). Returning to Pauwels' (2011) classifications of visual approaches set out in Chapter 2 (found materials, researcher-initiated productions and participatory productions), the chapter will consider cases where the creator's intentions are not accessible; and the implications of these absences for the analyses of visual images. Consequently, the chapter explores four different approaches to knowing the image, when it is not possible to apply auteur theory and ask participants to share their subjective interpretations of their creations.

## Applying auteur theory

As discussed in the previous chapters, in the *Mothers and Daughters on the Margins* project I was interested in participants' subjective interpretations of their everyday lives and participants were asked to create narratives, maps and collages to represent their experiences. These activities can be framed as participatory productions, situating the social scientist as the participatory facilitator (Pauwels 2011); and participants created materials in their own homes with minimal direction. This data production was followed by elicitation interviews to acknowledge the polysemic nature of the participants' creations. All of the data was polysemic because of the ambiguous and multiple meanings that could be generated. As Reavey (2011, p. 5) contends, 'the interpretation of an image cannot always be fixed' and it was important that my own interpretations did not act to frame and fix the data in a way that silenced the meaning making of the participants. Accordingly, the interviews were not so much about an understanding *of* the data produced, as an understanding *with* the data produced about the lives of the participants (Radley 2011).

In an elicitation interview, drawing on the image from her map, illustrated in Figure 5.1, one of the mothers in the study, Tina, described how drawing her two daughters acted to clarify aspects of the maternal relationship. When I looked at the picture I assumed that Chantelle had been presented as bigger than Louise simply because she is older and taller. However, Tina made clear that this was not the case and I could only understand the intended meaning of the image with Tina's interpretation:

TINA: *Louise she's small and if you look at that she ain't even in line with Chantelle because she's in the background and in my drawing I did that because sometimes I feel like Chantelle takes all the attention away from Louise*

In order to gain an understanding of the internal narrative of the image, then, it was imperative to acknowledge the role of Tina as a mother and the image-maker. My own interpretation of the visual data would have been inadequate for, both literally and metaphorically, it is human beings who speak to one another and the lone image is an inadequate tool for understanding other people's worlds (Banks 2001); in this way it is our conversation around the image that acts as the vehicle for communicating meaning. The practice of creating visual data, then, presented an opportunity for Tina to transcend the visible and actual physical difference by

**FIGURE 5.1**　Tina's daughters – Chantelle and Louise (Mannay 2010) (permission to reuse the image provided courtesy of SAGE Publications)

distorting generalities of alignment, she has placed one child at the forefront and the other in the background. My singular interpretation was still veiled by a web of taken-for-granted meanings, a one-dimensional focus on the two sisters, which was informed by assumptions about age difference. However, the combination of Tina's creativity and explanation contributed to a more nuanced understanding of the maternal relationship for both the researcher and the researched (Mannay 2010), allowing an opportunity to visualize the more multi-dimensional dynamic of the daughters' relationship with each other and their mother.

This example illustrates the salience of the distinction between readings of images that 'look at' and those that 'look behind' (Wright 1999); and the conversation allowed an opportunity to move beyond the two children that can be seen, to the participant's use of the visual image to mediate their understandings of their world and the subjectivities of their familial relationships within that world. Importantly, it is the act of drawing that also clarifies the maternal relationship for the participant, as in the interview discussions Tina tells me that she did not realise the extent to which Chantelle had pushed Louise in to the background until she created her map (Mannay 2010). This realisation would have remained inaccessible to the reader without Tina's interpretation as the visual image itself represents an ambiguous, polysemic and multimodal form of data, which offers alternative surface interpretations.

The polysemic, ambiguous and multimodal nature of visual data is often contrasted with the positioning of the written word as a source of data that is fundamentally mono-modal (Reavey 2011); however, in the *Mothers and Daughters on the Margins* project the narratives produced by participants also afforded opportunities for mis-reading or missing the depth of meaning attached to the use of language. In the same way as my own interpretations of the visual data of place and space would have been inadequate, the representations of narratives, although generally in written rather than visual form, must be theorised in terms of the relationship between reader and text/image. The reader needs to understand text by situating it within an extra-textual interpreting field of reference, which consists of the reader's individual experiences of the world (Duncan and Ley 1993).

Therefore, just as images are open to misinterpretation, the reader will often produce a different interpretation of the text from that which the author intends; in this manner the need for clarification is extended to all modes of data. For example, the following extract taken from ten-year-old Nicole's written narrative account of a positive future possible self (Mannay 2012) engenders a misreading:

*When I'm grown up I would like to be a teacher. I want to get married but not too early. I want to learn how to drive. I will have children when I'm 26 years old. I am going to take off my Mum and Dad.*

The expression 'take off my Mum and Dad' could be interpreted as expectation of continued parental support, particularly in a socio-economic climate where young people demonstrate an extended financial dependency on their parents (Da Vanzo and Goldscheider 2010). However, when we discuss the narrative and I ask Nicole about this turn of phrase a different meaning is presented.

NICOLE: *Yeah it sort of means like um yeah it sort of means take things off their hands like*
INTERVIEWER: *Ah yeah*
NICOLE: *The responsibilities that they shouldn't be doing 'cause they're too sick or old to do it and it might hurt their back or something*
INTERVIEWER: *Ah right*
NICOLE: *For them to break their spine or something*
INTERVIEWER: *So taking all the stress off them all the bad things like*
NICOLE: *Yeah*

In this example the misreading is semantic but the interviews also allowed an exploration beyond the surface of participants' texts. The following extract comes from a narrative written by Zoe, a mother in the study who is trying to reconstruct her ideas about her positive future self from the retrospective perspective of being the same age as her daughter. This example also demonstrates the salience of the elicitation interview:

*The difference in career prospects though are I wanted to be a nurse when I was younger. I've always had a very caring side that wanted to help other people and feel that my daughters are the same.*

Zoe's narrative fits with wider discourses of appropriate work for women and the naturalisation of women's capacity to care. However, when we examine the accompanying interview we see how the career aspiration is related to the prevalence of domestic violence within the childhood home.

INTERVIEWER: *You wanted to be a nurse when you were little*

ZOE: *Mmm*

INTERVIEWER: *Why d'you think you didn't do it at the time*

ZOE: *I didn't think I would be able to, I didn't think I was intelligent enough to become a nurse, so I never bothered, but I think I only wanted to be a nurse because of what my Mother went through and everything, 'cause I wanted to stop people getting hurt*

INTERVIEWER: *Yeah*

ZOE: *Well to help people that got hurt*

INTERVIEWER: *Yeah*

ZOE: *I think that's what it was basically*

Zoe also created a negative possible future self-narrative, which did discuss the violence in the familial setting of her childhood home (Mannay 2013a); however, the interview around the positive possible future self allowed an exploration of this abuse in relation to the career aspirations for nursing and Zoe's later employment as a carer. In this way, the narratives did not serve as stand-alone data sources. Rather, as in the case of the visual data, these written narratives were explored in individual interviews, which both incorporated and went beyond this data. As Galman (2009, p. 204) maintains, artefacts of research are created to be objects of a conversation for alone they can be interpreted only as a 'snapshot of the ever evolving performance of self, encapsulated for a brief moment on the page'. Thus, to move beyond a surface meaning of the narrative and visual data showcased to the researcher, it is imperative to build auteur theory into the design of the interview process, a commitment that I have built into my later qualitative research studies; as illustrated in the following section which discusses a project that draws upon 'the world technique' (Lowenfeld 1939).

## The world technique

Non-traditional, mature students face a number of complex psychological and structural barriers to higher education and their journeys are often characterised by initial aspirations and later disappointments, when classed, gendered and relational positionings conflict with students' identities and contribute to their withdrawal from academia (Mannay 2013b; Mannay and Morgan 2013; Mannay and O'Connell 2013; Reay *et al.* 2010; Rose-Adams 2013). The project *University Challenge: How can we foster successful learning journeys for non-traditional students in a School of Social Science?* (Mannay and Edwards 2013, 2014) was interested in building on this previous research and exploring initiatives to meet the needs of non-traditional students in higher education.

The project was designed in relation to the premise of action research as a 'process of reflective problem solving at the school level', which allows practitioners to identify an issue of study to determine if and how changes can be implemented to improve processes, procedures and programs (Howard and Eckhardt 2005, p. 32). The study was interested in eliciting participants' experiences of being a non-traditional student drawing on visual techniques and participatory approaches. The data production techniques drew on sandplay therapy in which clients create three-dimensional scenes, pictures or abstract designs in a tray filled with sand and a range of miniature, realistic and fantasy, figures and everyday objects (Weinrib 2004). However, rather than adopting a Jungian-informed approach that is popular in therapeutic work we worked with 'the world technique' (Lowenfeld 1939) as this best aligned with the authors' approach to visual inquiry, which centralises the meaning making of participants.

Having explored the centrality of applying auteur theory to gain an insight into participants' subjective experience in previous work (Mannay 2010, 2013b), it was important to consider how the sandbox technique could retain this participant-focused understanding of visual data production. For Lowenfeld (1939), it is important to centralise the subjective perspective of the participants, rather than applying the researchers' own interpretations and assumptions to the scenes. As Hutton (2004) maintains, Lowenfeld's work has often been overlooked, anonymously integrated and misrepresented in later applications. Lowenfeld was aware of this misrepresentation and in relation to its application to tests of traits, temperament and personality, she was anxious that 'the world technique' should not be 'misunderstood or distorted when part of the equipment is borrowed and adapted for a different purpose' (Lowenfeld 1950, p. 325).

In applying 'the world technique' as a method of visual data production not as a therapeutic intervention, distortion is unavoidable; however, what is central in both applications is auteur theory, or the salience of participants' interpretations of their visual creations; and in this way, I would hope that Lowenfeld would approve of the current incorporation of her innovative work.

For Lowenfeld, the worlds created by children with figures in the sand tray are a projective tool allowing the expression of thoughts and feelings on a symbolic level. Lowenfeld respected the work of Jung and was influenced by Freudian theory; however, for Lowenfeld the therapist should not attempt to interpret the symbolism of the world but rather wait for the meanings to be identified by the child, 'in recognition of the multiplicity of meanings the world may contain' (Hutton 2004, p. 607).

In this way, the figures in the sand tray become a primary vehicle for intra-personal and inter-personal communication, where 'each figure holds unique and personal meaning for individuals' (Sangganjanavanich and Magnuson 2011, p. 266). The emphasis of the importance of the individual's discovery of their own meaning both resonates with the tenets of auteur theory and takes up a democratising and dialogical stance, which other psychoanalytically informed approaches have been accused of precluding. Lowenfeld (1939, p. 329) discusses the way that the child gradually comes to 'find himself' in the medium of 'the world technique'; and in the

**FIGURE 5.2** You feel quite isolated

data production there was a high level of reflection where participants also expressed the way in which they were party to 'defamiliarisation' (Gurevitch, 1998); in relation to their re-thinking of their educational experiences and interpersonal relationships.

As in Lowenfeld's (1939) work, metaphors created in the sand scene also enhanced participants' understandings of the self so that as in previous visual work there were new discoveries of the self (Mannay 2010; Thomson and Holland 2005). Importantly, rather than eliciting the rational responses to successive questions inherent to traditional interviewing (Hollway and Jefferson 2013), 'the world technique' engendered a thoughtful engagement at the level of affect and a reflexive engagement with the realm of emotion, in which isolation was a central theme as illustrated in Figure 5.2.

In this section of their sand tray scene the participant employed replica figures to represent the subjective sameness of traditional students, in contrast to her position as different. The significance of this visual metaphor is clearly articulated in the following quote:

> and there'd be like two hundred of, two hundred of these very similar people sat there, and me …the dinosaur because I was much older and then all these very similar people, just that in a way, they probably didn't, I was probably just invisible, I don't think

*they were all like glaring at me thinking what's she doing here the odd one out, it was more about, they all were the same and were friends and I was just, just this sort of strange entity in the lecture theatre*

Accordingly, the figures act as clear metaphors for participants to communicate memories of their first year at university; however, again it is the elicitation interview that engenders an understanding of these metaphors. Importantly, the student uses the dinosaur, both as a visual metaphor and a metaphorical figure of speech, to illustrate how she imagines her status as a student and her experiences of the lecture theatre. 'The world technique' also has the benefits of scenes being made-and-remade. Many visual methods lack this level of fluidity as they become fixed once collage pieces are glued, the camera is clicked or ink comes into contact with paper.

In mainstream visual research, arguably, LEGO® SERIOUS PLAY®[1] offers opportunities to encourage experiential forms of expression and analysis that can help participants see and experience familiar situations in a new way (see Gauntlett and Holzwarth 2006; Hinthorne and Schneider 2012); however, although Lego bricks have the potential to be built and rebuilt, they do not necessarily have the flexibility of 'the world technique'. Applying elicitation interviews allowed an opportunity for participants to talk through these constructions and re-constructions and share their thinking. In this way, adapting the psychoanalytical base of 'the world technique' afforded a space in which participants could both 'show' and 'narrate' their experiences and lives; again centralising the importance of auteur theory in gaining an understanding of participants' meaning making in relation to their visual productions.

## Readings without writers

Reflecting on the limitations of auteur theory, this section considers Helen Lomax's (2012, p. 228) important point that 'the notion that meaningful interpretation is contingent on knowing its creator's intentions is nonetheless problematic, not least because these are not always available to viewers'. Drawing on Pauwels' (2011) framework, researcher-initiated productions, where the social scientist acts as image-creator, producing images themselves; and participatory productions, where the social scientist as the participatory facilitator works with participants who produce images themselves, best lend themselves to auteur theory. These approaches are centralised throughout this book; however, when we consider found materials and locate social scientists as image collectors, the problem of positioning the intentions of the image-creator as central in the understanding of the image raises significant challenges. However, even in the case of found images there are sometimes opportunities to connect with the intentions of the image-creator, which will be discussed in the following iconic images of the *Boy Petrol Bomber, Londonderry 1969* and *Migrant Mother 1936*.

As Brown (2009) contends, we are seduced by the truthfulness of the appearance of things in the photograph as we want to believe in the image. Historically, this seduction has been central in the photograph's role in a regulatory system that has stigmatised marginalised groups: patients, the poor and colonised races (Fink and Lomax 2014; Spencer 2011; Tagg 2003). In relation to contemporary images, Wright (2011, p. 317) argues that although print media can be disparagingly viewed as tomorrow's fish-and-chip wrapping, the presence or absence of visual images has 'the power to make or break the worthiness of any news story'. Wright supports this observation by charting the ways in which articles that do not have readily available images for publication do not make the headlines; because they lack the impact of the visual metaphor.

Wright (2011) revisits the iconic print media image *Boy Petrol Bomber, Londonderry 1969*, photographed by Clive Limpkin, which contains contradictory metaphors as a young boy – the innocent child – stands wearing a gas mask and holding a petrol bomb in his hand. Wright analyses this image, and demonstrates the power of the image by charting the way that it has been canonised through its appearance in a series of murals in Northern Ireland; where each artist casts the boy differently according to their political loyalties. As Fink and Lomax (2014, p. 82) argue, all images are 'products of the historical contexts in which they are produced as well as the dominant discourses that are at play in those contexts'. In this way, images become signs of their times but can be reformatted to act as signs beyond their times; reinvented and mediating new messages.

It is this reinvention and the mediating of new messages that can become problematic when applied to exploring visual productions in ethnographic research; particularly now that digital technologies to retouch and manipulate images are so readily available and photographs, themselves, are online commodities (Fink and Lomax 2014). However, importantly Wright does not simply read the found image but in researching the image he makes connections with the image-creator, by reading his online profile and book (Limpkin 1972). This move beyond the photographic representation means that Wright was able to offer the interpretations and insights of the original photographer at the Battle of Bogside, allowing the image-creator to have a voice in the analysis of a found image.

However, Limpkin (1972) interprets the image in relation to his own political stance, suggesting a young delinquent on the road to ruin, an interpretation that is juxtaposed to the heroic Republican representation of a boy that is speaking out against the oppression of his community. Wright's (2011) analysis speaks to this multiplicity of meaning making, however, the *Boy Petrol Bomber* remains voiceless; his very presence creates the impact of the image but his personal narrative remains silenced beneath the layers of interpretation assigned by the photographer, researcher, discourses of children and childhood, and the subjects of its 'audiencing' in the multimodal forms of the print press, books, mural paintings and its online presence.

The legacy of early anthropological work, which essentialised indigenous peoples with an authoritative voice, was critiqued in postmodernism with a recognition of the 'indignity of speaking for others' (Spencer 2011, p. 15). However, it is easy to forget the propagandist manipulation of imagery and the 'management of visibility' (Thompson 2005). Therefore, in contemporary visual ethnography it remains important that the original meaning of an image does not become silenced; and that in interpreting visual images, ethnographers are giving voice rather than simply voicing over. *Migrant Mother* is arguably the most famous documentary photograph representing the North American depression of the 1930s and it is also an example of how the photograph can take on 'a life of its own', presenting a series of different messages rather than its makers or that of the photographed subjects (Curtis 1986).

Dorothea Lange was travelling around California in March 1936 documenting the plight of the sharecroppers, displaced farm families, and migrant workers for the Farm Security Administration, part of Roosevelt's New Deal programme, when she photographed Florence Thompson and her children. The photograph become an icon of American suffering and stoicism and was printed, distributed and consumed in the global media market. The global audience actively made their own meanings from the image and there was a classical distinction between the mimesis (showing) and diegesis (telling); fraught with interpretation and (mis)interpretation (Spencer 2011). As Curtis (1986, p. 1) argues, 'lost in the appreciation of *Migrant Mother* as a timeless work of art is its personal and cultural genesis'; and to explore what has become lost it is important to consider the views of the photographer and the photographed.

In her notes of the encounter with Thompson, Lange wrote: 'I did not ask her name or her history. She told me her age, that she was 32. She said that they had been living on frozen vegetables from the surrounding fields and birds that the children killed. She had just sold the tires from her car to buy food' (Meltzer 2000, p. 133). Lange's images are often singled out because her photos appear to offer compassion to those in the middle of the economic crisis; however, some argue that in creating ragged heroes and heroines Lange actually deflects the true cause of their plight; the structural failure of capitalism (Harper 2012). There was an element of romanticism in Lange's work and her belief that photography should be restrained and uplifting, even when its subject matter was not. Her subjective take on the purpose of photography and her ability to represent the stoicism of the dispossessed embedded a particular frame on the American consciousness through the art of photography.

The subjects of the photograph remained captured in this trope and Thompson was displeased with her incarceration and the commodification of her image; and in a later interview she says of Lange, 'I wish she hadn't of taken my picture' (Hariman and Lucaites 2007, p. 65). Despite the popular interpretation of the image, Thompson was not a white American but a Cherokee who had lived on the margins of American society, while Lange's portrait of her was reproduced around the globe, becoming an icon of American suffering and stoicism. Gordon (2009) argues that the reputation of the image grew because it symbolised white motherhood and white dustbowl refugees. The photograph may not have garnered such popularity if viewers had known its subject was a Cherokee woman. These ironies echo the contradictions that attend America's collective notion of nationhood and also highlight the ways in which the simple reading of a photograph can misrepresent both visual creator and the subject of the image.

## Images in isolation

The photographs of the *Boy Petrol Bomber, Londonderry 1969* and *Migrant Mother 1936* have an iconic status, immediately identifiable historical contexts and elements of controversy, which allow a reading beyond the surface interpretation of the photograph. Therefore, there is a need to obtain wider contextual information and an understanding of the circumstances in which visual images were made. Where there is an absence of these contextual factors, reading can be guided by theoretical frameworks, for without theory, arguably our seeing is blind or tends to rest on unexplained views and expectations, as well as emotional responses and socio-cultural interpretations. This section will explore strategies and frameworks that have been successfully applied to explore the visual image, drawing on the idea of 'breaking the frame', cultural studies, social representations theory and semiotics.

These are only a selection of the possible applications to visual inquiry but they are strategies that I found useful in my research and teaching. For example, in a current research project *Negotiating Young Parenthood: A study exploring the ways in which mediated stereotypes of teenage parents impact on their perceptions of their parenting practices; and their engagement with service providers*, funded by the Wales Institute of Social & Economic Research, Data & Methods, I have been working with colleagues, Dr Amy Grant and Ruby Marzella, to explore social representations of motherhood. The project, discussed in more detail in Chapter 6, has involved exploring visual images of motherhood on an online search engine, comparing the search terms mother and baby to the alternative young/teenage mother and baby. In addition to drawing on a social representations framework to analyse these images, we have also employed the same images as a tool of elicitation in interviews with young parents to explore their perceptions of these mediated forms. In relation to teaching, my third year undergraduate students are assessed on their ability to select and analyse a found image, drawing on multiple lenses of analysis; and in my workshops with postgraduates and researchers, consideration is always given to how we can come to know an image without the account of its creator.

The accounts presented here represent a selection of the approaches that I draw from, they are not exhaustive; but there are many textbooks and research guides that work with each approach separately and in depth, for example Scholes' (1982) *Semiotics and Interpretation*; Sturken's and Cartwright's (2009) *Practices of Looking: An Introduction to Visual Culture* or Wells' (2003) *Photography Reader*. However, the section offers the reader a flavour of the ways in which these perspectives can be usefully applied; to interrogate images, moving beyond their surface, considering the circumstances of their production, examining their temporal and geographical placement; and exploring the philosophy, politics, religion and power relations that impact on the viewer's interpretations of creative forms.

## Semiotics – the theory of signs

All human communication has the dual feature of denotation and connotation as it both denotes something specific and connotes further meanings. Visual images, without a supporting narrative, operate at the level of connotation and where there is a high level of complexity this results in what Roland Barthes called 'myths'. This presents difficulties for any simple reading of an image because as Banks (2001, p. 7) argues, 'our initial understandings or readings of images are always pre-scripted'. The interpretation of sight is culturally and historically specific as meaning is created in the situated act of viewing. Beyond the cultural lens used to interpret an image the immediate context of the image, art gallery, magazine, book, also contributes to its connotation. Semiotics, the study of signs, which stems from the early work of Saussure, invites us to study hidden meanings and critique the power relations inherent to visual representations, for this reason applying semiotics is particularly useful when exploring advertising and promotional media.

Hetherington and Havard (2014, p. 135) argue that sometimes 'messages are encoded into commodities through design and logo', which 'might be more important than the thing itself' and in the same way the images surrounding the product connote meanings, which act to seduce the viewer. For example, in advertising the purchase of the beautiful and powerful car is not simply about the car itself, the projected image suggests that in the act of consumption the consumer will become the person portrayed in the car advertisement: powerful, sexy, attractive and wealthy. It is not the car itself but the second level of meaning that takes the buyer to the purchase; however, once seduced the car itself becomes inadequate. As Harper (2012, p. 119) argues, 'because it is a phony promise the consumption will be empty and meaningless'.

For Richards (1998), advertisements carry implicit meanings, presenting consumers with the lure of buying a material object that is associated with a desired identity. Analysing a series of Wallis fashion label advertisements, Richards argues that there is a shared syntagm that applies to each advert: attractive woman dressed in Wallis clothes attracts the undivided attention of a man at work, who becomes so engrossed by her appearance, he becomes oblivious to his actions thus endangering either his life or the lives of others. The signifier is the woman, as the focal point of the advert, Wallis is aimed at a female market; and the model wears the products the company wants to sell, with the simultaneously metaphorical and literal caption *Dress to Kill*. Richards argues that the images connote that women can have sexual control over men, and all of these connotations can be associated with modern-day views on femininity; however, this is only one reading. At its most deterministic, semiotics suggest that academics can read a truer meaning of what is signified by the visual than audience members can; however, academics can also be seduced by their own commitment to a symbolic way of seeing.

Advertisements have more than one meaning, depending on how it operates, how signs and their ideological effects are organised within the text, and in relation to its production and circulation (Dyer 1982, p. 115). This complexity was highlighted in Harper's and Faccioli's (2000) study of twenty public billboard advertisements featuring interaction or reaction between men and women. The project was interested in revisiting Goffman's (1979) seminal work around the gender politics of advertising, and the physical grammar of the ritualised subordination of women, and the Italian billboard images were discussed in interviews with American and Italian women. There were significant differences in the interpretations of the images between the two groups. The American women saw the gendered interactions as threatening, violent, demeaning and upsetting. Conversely, the Italian women interpreted the advertisements as mutually seductive and amusing; and found the illustrations of male physical power as a signifier of sexual pleasure. The study illustrates the complexity and multiplicity of connotation in the situated act of viewing; and also arguably the power and savvy of the Italian marketing industries who achieved the requisite product placement to seduce their target home audience.

## Cultural studies

The field of cultural studies has been criticised as an approach to exploring the visual and narrative, with accusations of little empirical work and weak application of theory (Harper 2012). However, this appears to be unnecessarily dismissive in light of the body of work produced from the 1970s by the University of Birmingham's Centre for Contemporary Cultural Studies and more recent applications in the field. The Centre for Contemporary Cultural Studies aimed to understand how the mass arts, for example, cinema, print press and pop music, achieve their effects by breaking up the ordered surfaces of popular culture and reinterpreting, politicising and reconstructing meanings (BBC 2014). Early studies were characterised by a focus on highly visible, spectacular subcultures that were lived out at the level of the street, which identified the product of collective subcultural styles; however, later studies moved beyond this purely descriptive endeavour to focus on the underlying issues of power and control that contribute the mediation and circulation of ideas.

For example, in *Policing the Crisis* (Hall *et al.* 1978) the mediation of disorderly behaviour was linked explicitly to wider diverse forms of social and political dissent and the State's agenda to regain power and control. Hall *et al.* (1978) analysed British print press media and documented the ways in which a 'moral panic' (Cohen 1973) was constructed around the 'black mugger'. The reporting of street crimes committed by young, black men was exaggerated in the media representation creating urban 'folk devils' (Cohen 1973). For Hall *et al.* (1978), this mediation was a deliberate attempt to distract the viewing public from the wider, deep-seated origins of social conflict, chiefly inequality. In this way, the construction of folk devils acted to obscure these issues and devalue the work of social movements that aimed to provoke social change. Importantly, in creating a moral panic the government was able to secure public support to 'crack down on crime', which included the introduction of new measures that were used to police not only street crime but civil protests. For Hall *et al.*, the statistical analysis of the prevalence of crime, in relation to its mediation, was able to demonstrate the ways in which both visual and textual forms can be used to distort public perception and create a moral panic.

More recently, Tyler (2008) tracked the repetition of specific figures across different media and found that classed figures accrue affective value in ways that have significant social and political impact; in particular negative emotions and associated moral judgements become harnessed to the figure of the 'chav'. Tyler (2008) demonstrates how the figure of 'chav mum' circulates within a wide range of celebrity media, reality television, comedy programming on British television, consumer culture, print media, literature, news media, films and websites. Figures such as the BBC caricature Vicky Pollard are brought to life and endowed with affect through mediation. These visual images engender emotion and class disgust is re-invoked and deployed in instrumental ways, marking difference and reframing the same classed and gendered folk devils of previous generations; 'in camouflaged versions of traditional well-known evils' (Cohen 2011, p. viii).

Visual images can engender emotions, which can be expressed as a sickening feeling of revulsion, loathing, or nausea but also through laughter and as Tyler (2008) argues laughter is often at the expense of another; and when we laugh we effectively fix the other, as the object of comedy. Laughter may seem less harmful than overt forms of demonisation; however, as Sennett (2003, p. 3) contends, 'lack of respect, though less aggressive than outright insult, can take an equally wounding form'. The figure of 'chav mum' engenders a publicly sanctioned wave of middle-class contempt, which not only ridicules already marginalised mothers but also impacts on public perceptions and social policy as television caricatures are discussed as real entities within political discourse. These examples demonstrate the important role that cultural studies plays in disrupting the ordered surfaces of popular media to explore discourses of power, class and politics.

Cultural studies have also contributed to an understanding of the development of masculinities and femininities within consumer society. McRobbie's and Garber's classic study, *Girls and Subcultures*, explored the salience of the teenage bedroom space for young girls and its connections to the wider adolescent culture (McRobbie 1991). McRobbie and Garber analysed publications such as *Jackie* magazine and argued that the issues were saturated with ideological messages within the codes of domesticity, romance and make-up. The original work was groundbreaking in its focus on the everyday worlds of young girls but it received some criticism for the positioning of young people as passive in their consumption of popular culture. In more recent work, Lincoln (2012) conceptualises identity as always under-construction and a work in progress and situates the bedroom as a key site within which the media can be appropriated and transformed; helping people to make sense of their own lives.

Lincoln documents how young people who have grown up as digital natives are immersed in media cultures as a normalised part of their everyday lives. Applying the theoretical framework of zoning, Lincoln also examines young people's engagement with both old and new forms of media and the way that media zones can be opened and closed through a young person's media practices, in the continuous interplay of sociality and solitude. Lincoln draws on Goffman's (1959) presentation of self to explore the use of social networking sites and the oscillation between authentic and deceptive selves, and strategies of both self-exposure and self-preservation.

Photographs are seen as a form of identity currency and symbolic exchange; and there is a pressure to display and update these images of self (Ringrose 2013).

However, the young people in Lincoln's study distinguish between the 'truer' more authentic self that they can be within their bedrooms, as compared with the production of an acceptable online self. Accordingly, Lincoln (2012, p. 219) suggests that in a postmodern, mediated world of flux, change and uncertainty, 'young people seek out, perhaps more than ever before, those spaces that can offer some form of stability... and the bedroom is one of those spaces'.

Again, this work highlights the disjuncture between young people's self-presentation in online images and the stories behind these images, where they feel their 'truer' self can be understood. Importantly, Lincoln studied both the visual culture of young peoples' bedroom and online spaces, and asked them to discuss their visual artefacts in elicitation interviews. It is in these discussions that the young people draw distinctions between the mediated self and the self behind this perfor-mance; highlighting both the usefulness of auteur theory and the constructed and distorting capacity of visual images themselves.

## Social representations

Moscovici's (1998) theory of social representations has also been central in the study of culture and the analysis of 'common sense' shared meanings and understandings. Social, political and historical forces shape and are shaped by individuals' meaning making and sharing common social representations among a group makes them into a cohesive assemblage. In contemporary society, the media plays a crucial role in the circulation of ideas and the development of new social representations, where social representations are both produced by and reflected by the media. Consequently, analysing the linguistic aspects and visual images circulated in the media is one way of detecting the social representations that circulate in a particular society.

The theory of social representations proposes that individuals, social groups and the media enact two processes in the development of social representations, anchoring and objectification. Anchoring is a naming process, which involves cat-egorisation and serves to make sense of one thing by linking it to another familiar sphere of knowledge. Objectification involves the transformation of an abstract concept into a tangible image or object; in this way visual images become objecti-fications of social representations and these objectifications conjure up associations as anchors to other spheres.

Morant (1998, p. 251) explored representations of motherhood in media adver-tisements and noted that 'motherhood is objectified as a young, feminine woman. She seems to have the stereotypical rosy glow of motherhood and looks calm and contemplative ... the nurturant and caring mother ... being a good mother involves staying close to your baby'. Importantly, these dominant objectifications of motherhood set up the boundaries of acceptable femininity and parenting; closing down any space to consider the practices, troubles and tensions of contem-porary motherhood (Lomax 2013). These social representations are also exclusion-ary, 'images of young, white, heterosexual, able bodied women, which are the norm on women's magazines, work to define what forms of femininity are socially acceptable and desirable. But at the same time they also render invisible women of different race, age, or physical ability' (Morant 1998, p. 253).

Advertisements also illustrate objectifications of masculinity and, while women have traditionally been constructed as the focus of the male gaze (Mulvey 1975), the related scopophilia, or pleasure of looking, has more recently been associated with the female audience. In contemporary media images there is a growing representation of men as objects of the gaze, rather than merely bearers of the look. For example, David Beckham is positioned as the centrepiece of what Ramchadani (2007) reports as 'art-cum-porn' in a series of advertisements for Armani underwear. Gill (2011) explores the position of David Beckham as both sportsman and father, in this way the objectification of masculinity conjures up associations as anchors to other spheres of hegemonic manliness. However, the objectification of sexuality is different from similar representations of women, as rather than demonstrating 'ritualised subordination' (Goffman 1979) men's positioning is often more active so that even the reclined body looks back at the viewer, asserting a certain dominance.

There is an argument, then, that in relation to sexual objectification, idealised-eroticised images of men are constructed in a way that allows them to symbolically hold on to power. The category of men is not homogenous and in the same way that some mothers are made invisible within mediated forms (Morant 1998) so too are particular men and masculinities disregarded (Gill 2011). Social representations theory may not privilege the tenets of auteur theory but, arguably, its concepts of anchoring and objectification offer one approach to understanding the ways in which mediated images act to both reflect and actively construct the dominant ideologies that circulate in particular societies.

## Breaking the frame

A further approach to exposing the mechanisms of power that enable the production of images and the cultural mediation of images can be engendered with Butler's (2009) notion of 'breaking the frame'. For Butler (2009, p. 12), when a frame is broken 'a taken for granted reality is called into question exposing the orchestrating designs of the authority who sought to control the frame'. In this way, the viewer can move beyond the image itself and their own emotional response to its content, conceptualised by Barthes' (1981) 'punctum' as a piercing or bruising action. In breaking the frame the audience has an opportunity to explore both the internal organisation of the image itself and the salience of the multiple contexts in which the image is seen, felt and interpreted.

Drawing on Butler, Zarzycka (2012) examines a work by Yuri Kozyr, which took First Prize in the Portrait category at the annual 2009 World Press Photo competition. In the competition, Kozyr's image is presented with a short text overview that informs the viewer about the subjects of the composition, Rajiha Jihad Jassim and her son. The caption explains that the photograph was taken in Baghdad, Iraq and that Rajiha's husband has been kidnapped, leaving her with five children and no family income. In analysing Kozyr's work, Zarzycka (2012) discusses how Rajiha and her son are positioned in a black background with their faces, looking in different directions, illuminated with the use of light; the composition of the image creates a form of 'beautiful suffering' (Reinhart *et al.* 2006). Zarzycka interprets the dramatic composition of the scene as inviting a sense of timelessness and the shift from light to shade as a momentary pause from movement; a stagnation within the emotional circuit of grief. The dark background, broken by the light on the subjects' faces, can also be read as representative of overwhelming loneliness, imposed silence and the disjuncture within the community.

Importantly, in seeking to account for how meanings are constructed in connection to gendered identities, Zarzycka situates this single image within the iconographical tradition of gendered representations of loss. As Ahmed (2004) contends, in the visual sphere images of women often form the symbolic embodiment of the nation and its lost lives; and the beautiful suffering of their mourning acts to imply some form of closure through the process of mourning. Breaking the frame of this image, Zarzycka argues that these representations shield us from the realities of death, rather than presenting a valid testimony of the structural violence that engendered the loss. 'Women as emblematic figures of genocide and dispossession' (Zarzycka 2012, p. 77) act to sanitise and make palatable the unpalatable for audiences who are dulled by the aesthetics and repetition. There is no mention of any perpetrators in such images and the photographs are divorced from the wider socio-political framework that could have acted to legitimise and give voice to their subjects' lived reality.

Furthermore, the presentation of this particular image within the World Press creates an additional layer of shielding. The photograph is decontextualised from the original collection, *Victims of the Iraq War*, where men, women and a child, all against a deep black background with a single ray of light upon their faces, testified to the acts of violence committed against them and their families. In moving from being part of a series to a singular representation, the image becomes reframed and limited in its ability to connect with the viewer. This reframing also deleted the textual support that was available with the *Victims of the Iraq War* collection as sentences were omitted that had supported the original exhibition, their meanings cut out in the editing process. For Zarzycka (2012, p. 81) the iconographic construction of images and their decontextualisation 'inscribe on the image tropes that have been eternally presented in societal discourse, dismissing the ruptures that might occur in their readings'. Breaking the frame offers an opportunity to move beyond forms of essentialism that represent the simple reading of an image. The representation of beautiful suffering offers eternal, easily consumable and familiar tropes but a space is needed to recognise the mechanics of production and consumption, systematic power relations, and the silencing and distancing of the *other*, which is evoked in photogenic misery.

## Conclusion

As Rose (2010, p. 26) contends, 'visual imagery is never innocent; it is always constructed through various practices, technologies and knowledges'. Consequently, there is a need to adopt a critical approach to reading visual images, one that thinks about the agency of the image, considers the social practices and effects of its viewing, and reflects on the specificity of that viewing by different audiences. As academics we need to question our own readings of images and narratives and in doing so recognise our own ideological commitments and specific ways of knowing. This chapter has acknowledged the role of the image-maker in visual and narrative productions, and drawn on auteur theory (Rose 2001), which argues that the most salient aspect in understanding a visual image is what the maker intended to show.

Auteur theory was presented in the chapter as a technique of working with researcher-initiated productions and participatory productions, approaches that are centralised throughout this book. However, the chapter also explored the ways in which auteur theory can be successfully applied to the reading of found images to some extent. While supporting the premise of auteur theory as a useful approach to analysing with visual and narrative artefacts, the chapter was also careful to acknowledge the limitations of auteur theory (Lomax 2012), presenting strategies to explore images without the interpretations of their creator. The chapter provided a brief overview of four approaches that I have found useful in my research and my work with students, namely semiotics, cultural studies, social representations theory and the concept of breaking the frame. These accounts were in no way exhaustive but my aim was to convey a sense of the importance of the wider socio-cultural context and offer the reader a starting point from which to engage with these approaches in more depth.

The chapter has stressed the need to move beyond vision and consider visuality, and the inherent power relations, misinterpretations, silences and subjectivities, which come to bear on both visual and narrative culture. The chapter has also focused on the importance of context and decontextualisation in the interpretation in visual and narrative representations. In Chapter 6, the theme of context will be revisited in relation to the situated nature of the production of visual images and narratives within the research process. In understanding the visual it is important always to have a sense of the mechanisms of production and the following chapter engages with the everyday issues of creative research with a series of practical, reflexive and reflective tales from the field. In Chapter 7, again some of these issues will be revisited in relation to discourses of ethics, affect and reflexivity.

## Note

1  The LEGO® SERIOUS PLAY® methodology was developed by the Lego Group between 1998 and 2010. LEGO® SERIOUS PLAY® consists of a progressive sequence of model building exercises that encourage participants to think abstractly about complex problems using the iconic plastic Lego bricks. Participants then share their models with others sitting around the table, creating opportunities for both self-expression and shared learning. LEGO® SERIOUS PLAY® methodology aims to deepen the reflection process and support an effective dialogue. In this model communication is purposefully designed to allow time for individual reflection and provide opportunities for all participants to express their thoughts on an equal footing.

# References

Ahmed, S. (2004) *The Cultural Politics of Emotion*. Edinburgh: Edinburgh University Press.

Banks, M. (2001) *Visual Methods in Social Research*. London: Sage.

Barthes, R. (1981) *Camera Lucida: Reflections on Photography*. New York: Hill and Wang.

Belin, R. (2005) 'Photo-elicitation and the Agricultural Landscape: "Seeing" and "Telling" about Farming, Community and Place', *Visual Studies*, 20 (1): 56–68.

Berger, J. (1972) *About Looking: Writers and Readers*. London: Penguin.

British Broadcasting Corporation (2014) *Bingo, Barbie and Barthes: 50 Years of Cultural Studies*. London: BBC Radio 4 http://www.bbc.co.uk/programmes/b03c2zw4

Brown, R. (2009) 'Photography, Ongoing Moments and Strawberry Fields, the Active Presence of Absent Things'. Conference Paper at the *International Visual Sociology, Annual Conference*, University of Cumbria, Carlisle.

Butler, J. (2009) *Frames of War: When is Life Grievable?* London: Verso.

Cohen, S. (1973) *Folk Devils and Moral Panics*. London: Paladin.

Cohen, S. (2011) *Folk Devils and Moral Panics*: London: Routledge.

Curtis, J. C. (1986) 'Dorothea Lange, Migrant Mother, and the Culture of the Great Depression', *Winterthur Portfolio*, 21 (1): 1–20.

Da Vanzo, J. and Goldscheider, F. K. (2010) 'Coming Home Again: Returns to the Parental Home of Young Adults', *Population Studies: A Journal of Demography*, 44 (2): 241–55.

Darbyshire, P., MacDougall, C. and Schiller, W. (2005) 'Multiple Methods in Qualitative Research with Children: More Insight or Just More?', *Qualitative Research*, 5 (4): 417–36.

Duncan, J. and Ley, D. (eds) (1993) *Place/Culture/Representation*. London: Routledge.

Dyer, G. (1982) *Advertising as Communication*. London: Routledge.

Fink, J. and Lomax, H. (2014) 'Challenging Images? Dominant, Residual and Emergent Meanings in On-line Media Representations of Child Poverty', *Journal for the Study of British Cultures*, 1 (21): 79–95.

Galman, S. (2009) 'The Truthful Messenger: Visual Methods and Representation in Qualitative Research in Education', *Qualitative Research*, 9 (2): 197–217.

Gauntlett, D. and Holzwarth, P. (2006) 'Creative and Visual Methods for Exploring Identities', *Visual Studies*, 21 (1): 82–91.

Gill, R. (2011) 'Bend it Like Beckham? The Challenges of Reading Gender and Visual Culture', in P. Reavey (ed.) *Visual Methods in Psychology: Using and Interpreting Images in Qualitative Research*, pp. 29–42. London: Routledge.

Goffman, I. (1959) *The Presentation of Self in Everyday Life*. New York: Doubleday.

Goffman, I. (1979) *Gender Advertisements*. New York: Macmillan.

Gordon, L. (2009) *Dorothea Lange: A Life Beyond Limits*. New York: W. W. Norton & Company.

Gurevitch, Z. D. (1998) 'The Other Side of Dialogue: On Making the Other Strange and the Experience of Otherness', *American Journal of Sociology*, 93 (5): 1179–99.

Hall, S., Critcher, C., Jefferson, T., Clarke, J. and Roberts, B. (1978) *Policing the Crisis: Mugging, the State, and Law and Order*. London and Basingstoke: Macmillan.

Hariman, R. and Lucaites, J. L. (2007) *No Caption Needed: Iconic Photographs, Public Culture, and Liberal Democracy*. Chicago: University of Chicago Press.

Harper, D. (2012) *Visual Sociology*. London: Routledge.

Harper, D. and Faccioli, P. (2000) 'Small, Silly Insults, Mutual Seduction and Misogyny: the Interpretation of Italian Advertising Signs', *Visual Sociology*, 15 (1): 23–50.

Hetherington, K. and Havard, C. (2014) 'Consumer Society? Identity and Lifestyle', in G. Blakeley and J. Allen (eds) *Making Social Lives*, pp. 115–46. Milton Keynes: Open University Press.

Hinthorne, L. L. and Schneider, K. (2012) 'Playing with Purpose: Using Serious Play to Enhance Participatory Development Communication in Research', *International Journal of Communication*, 6: 2801–24.

Hollway, W. and Jefferson, T. (2013) *Doing Qualitative Research Differently: Free Association, Narrative and the Interview Method* (2nd edn) London: Sage.

Howard, J. K. and Eckhardt, S. A. (2005) 'Why Action Research? The Leadership Role of the Library Media Specialist', *Library Media Connection*, 24 (2): 32–4.

Hutton, D. (2004) 'Margret Lowenfeld's World Technique', *Clinical Child Psychology and Psychiatry*, 9 (4): 605–12.

Kearney, K. S. and Hyle, A. E. (2004) 'Drawing Out Emotions: The Use of Participant produced Drawings in Qualitative Inquiry', *Qualitative Research*, 4 (3): 361–82.

Limpkin, C. (1972) *The Battle of Bogside*. London: Penguin.

Lincoln, S. (2012) *Youth Culture and Private Space*. Basingstoke: Palgrave Macmillan.

Lomax, H. (2012) 'Shifting the Focus: Children's Image-Making Practices and their Implications for Analysis', *International Journal of Research and Method in Education, Special Issue – Problematising Visual Methods*, 35 (3): 227–34.

Lomax, H. (2013) 'Troubled Talk and Talk about Troubles: Moral Cultures of Infant Feeding in Professional, Policy and Parenting Discourses', in V. Gillies, C. A. Hooper and J. Ribbens McCarthy, J. (eds) *Family Troubles? Exploring Changes and Challenges in the Family Lives of Children and Young People*, pp. 97–106 Bristol: Policy Press.

Lomax, H., Fink, J., Singh, N and High, C. (2011) 'The Politics of Performance: Methodological Challenges of Researching Children's Experiences of Childhood through the Lens of Participatory Video', *International Journal of Social Research Methodology*, 14 (3): 231–43.

Lowenfeld, M. (1939) 'The World Pictures of Children', *British Journal of Medical Psychology*, 18: 65–101.

Lowenfeld, M. (1950) 'The Nature and Use of the Lowenfeld World Technique in Work with Children and Adults', *The Journal of Psychology*, 30 (2): 325–31.

Lowenfeld, M. (1979) *The World Technique*. London: Allen and Unwin Press.

Mannay, D. (2010) 'Making the Familiar Strange: Can Visual Research Methods Render the Familiar Setting more Perceptible?' *Qualitative Research*, 10 (1): 91–111.

Mannay, D. (2012) *Mothers and Daughters on the Margins: Gender, Generation and Education*. PhD Thesis, Cardiff University.

Mannay, D. (2013a) 'The Permeating Presence of Past Domestic and Familial Violence: So Like I'd Never Let Anyone Hit Me but I've Hit Them, and I Shouldn't have Done', in V. Gillies, C. A. Hooper and J. Ribbens McCarthy, J. (eds) *Family Troubles? Exploring Changes and Challenges in the Family Lives of Children and Young People*, pp. 151–62. Bristol: Policy Press.

Mannay, D. (2013b) 'Keeping Close and Spoiling: Exploring Discourses of Social Reproduction and the Impossibility of Negotiating Change and Maintaining Continuity in Urban South Wales', *Gender and Education*, 25 (1): 91–107.

Mannay, D. and Edwards, V. (2013) 'It's Written in the Sand: Employing Sandboxing to Explore the Experiences of Non-traditional, Mature Students in Higher Education. Presented at: *Society for Research into Higher Education (SRHE) Annual Research Conference 2013*, Celtic Manor, Newport, Wales, UK, 11–13 December 2013.

Mannay, D. and Edwards, V. (2014) 'Coffee, Milk and a Sprinkling of Sand: An Initiative to Assist Non-traditional, Mature students Form Supportive Networks in Higher Education'. Presented at: *2014 FACE Annual Conference*, Salford University, Salford, UK, 2–4 July 2014.

Mannay, D. and Morgan, M. (2013) 'Anatomies of Inequality: Considering the Emotional Cost of Aiming Higher for Marginalised, Mature Mothers Re-entering Education', *Journal of Adult and Continuing Education*, 19 (1): 57–75.

Mannay, D. and O'Connell, C. (2013) 'Accessing the Academy: Developing Strategies to Engage and Retain Marginalised Young People on Successful Educational Pathways', *Socialinė Teorija, Empirija, Politika ir Praktika – Social Theory, Empirics, Policy and Practice*, 7:133–40.

McRobbie, A. (1991) *Feminism and Youth Culture: From Jackie to Just Seventeen*. Basingstoke: Macmillan.

Meltzer, M. (2000) *Dorothea Lange: A Photographer's Life*. New York: Syracuse University Press.

Mitchell, C. (2011) *Doing Visual Research*. London: Sage.

Morant, N. (1998) 'Social Representations of Gender in the Media', in D. Miell and M. Wetherell (eds) *Doing Social Psychology*, pp. 234–83. London: Sage.

Morrow, V. (2001) 'Using Qualitative Methods to Elicit Young People's Perspectives on their Environments: Some Ideas for Community Health Initiatives', *Health Education Research*, 16 (3): 255–68.

Moscovici, S. (1998) 'Social Consciousness and its History', *Culture & Psychology*, 4 (3): 411–29.

Mulvey, L. (1975) 'Visual Pleasure and Narrative Cinema', *Screen*, 16 (3): 6–18.

Pauwels, L. (2011) 'An Integrated Conceptual Framework for Visual Social Research', in E. Margolis and L. Pauwels (eds) *The Sage Handbook of Visual Research Methods*, pp. 3–23. London: Sage.

Radley, A. (2011) 'Image and Imagination', in P. Reavey (ed.) *Visual Methods in Psychology: Using and Interpreting Images in Qualitative Research*, pp. 17–28. London: Routledge.

Ramchadani, N. (2007) 'Golden Balls Strikes Again'. *The Guardian*, 17 December 2007.

Reavey, P. (2011) 'The Return to Experience: Psychology and the Visual', in P. Reavey (ed.) *Visual Methods in Psychology: Using and Interpreting Images in Qualitative Research*, pp. 1–16. London: Routledge.

Reay, D., Crozier, G. and Clayton, J. (2010) 'Fitting in or Standing Out: Working-class Students in UK Higher Education', *British Educational Research Journal*, 32 (1): 1–19.

Reinhart, M., Edwards, H. and Duganne, E. (eds) (2006) *Beautiful Suffering: Photography and the Traffic in Pain*. Chicago: University of Chicago Press.

Richards, S. (1998) *A Semiotic Analysis of Wallis Adverts*. Available at: http://www.aber.ac.uk/media/Students/sar9502.html (Accessed 13 Apirl 2015).

Richardson, M. (2015) 'Embodied Intergenerational: Family Position, Place and Masculinity', *Gender, Place and Culture*, 22 (2): 157–71.

Ringrose, J. (2013) *Postfeminist Education: Girls and the Sexual Politics of Schooling*. Abingdon: Routledge.

Rose, G. (2001) *Visual Methodologies: An Introduction to Researching with Visual Materials*. London: Sage.

Rose, G. (2010) *Doing Family Photography: The Domestic, the Public and the Politics of Sentiment*. Farnham: Ashgate.

Rose-Adams, J. (2013) 'Leaving University Early: Exploring Relationships between Institution Type and Student Withdrawal and Implications for Social Mobility', *Widening Participation and Lifelong Learning*, 15 (2): 96–112.

Sangganjanavanich, V. F. and Magnuson, S. (2011) 'Using Sand Trays and Miniature Figures to Facilitate Career Decision Making', *The Career Development Quarterly*, 59: 264–73.

Scholes, R. (1982) *Semiotics and Interpretation*. New Haven, CT: Yale University Press.

Sennett, R. 2003. *Respect: The Formation of Character in an Age of Inequality*. London, New York: Penguin Books.

Spencer, S. (2011) *Visual Research Methods in the Social Science: Awakening Visions*. London: Routledge.

Steedman, C. (1986) *Landscape for a Good Woman: A Story of Two Women*. London: Virago.

Sturken, M. and Cartwright, L. (2009) *Practices of Looking: An Introduction to Visual Culture* (2nd edn). Oxford: Oxford University Press.

Tagg, J. (2003) 'Evidence, Truth and Order: Photographic Records and the Growth of the State', in L. Wells (ed.) *The Photographic Reader*. Abingdon: Routledge.

Thompson, J. B. (2005) 'The New Visibility', *Theory, Culture and Society*, 22 (6): 31–51.

Thomson, R. and Holland, J. (2005) 'Thanks for the Memory: Memory Books as a Methodological Resource in Biographical Research', *Qualitative Research*, 5 (2): 201–19.

Tyler, I. (2008) 'Chav Mum Chav Scum', *Feminist Media Studies*, 8 (1): 17–34.

Weinrib, E. L. (2004) *Images of the Self: The Sandplay Therapy Process*. Cloverdale, CA: Temenos.

Wells, L. (ed.) (2003) *The Photography Reader*. Abingdon: Routledge.

Wright, T. (1999) *The Photographer's Handbook* (2nd edn). London: Routledge.

Wright, T. (2011) 'Press Photography and Visual Rhetoric' in E. Margolis and L. Pauwels (eds) *The Sage Handbook of Visual Research Methods*, pp. 317–36. London: Sage.

Zarzycka, M. (2012) 'Madonnas of Warfare, Angels of Poverty: Cutting through Press Photographs', *Photographies*, 5 (1): 71–85.

# 6

# VISUAL AND NARRATIVE DATA PRODUCTION

## Time, artistic ability and incongruence

## Introduction

The last chapter was concerned with the reading of visual images, focusing on the salience of auteur theory and the ways in which the researcher can work with found images, where there is no access to the image-creator. This chapter returns to the creation and use of images in social research fieldwork and explores the practicalities of applying different modes of visual data production. Fieldwork was discussed in Chapter 3, in relation to the potential of visual and creative data as a tool to fight familiarity, and in Chapter 4, where there was a focus on positionality and participatory approaches. In this chapter, there is a move away from these areas of interest to a concrete engagement with the everyday processes, practicalities, experiences and challenges of visual and narrative fieldwork.

Drawing on my own 'tales from the field' and the reflexive accounts of a range of qualitative researchers, this chapter sets out the difficulties of applying creative techniques in terms of encroaching on the time of participants. The chapter explores the idea of artistic ability and how this can impact on the quality of images and, more importantly, on the items that are included and excluded in participants' drawings (Mannay 2010, 2013a). The chapter also examines the ways in which visual and narrative data production can be incongruent with the everyday lives of participants; and the need for researchers to be aware that engaging with drawing, and other creative methods, can be a site of embarrassment and discomfort (Abrahams and Ingram 2013; Johnson et al. 2012). Consequently, it is argued here that researchers need to be flexible in their use of research methods and that some approaches will not necessarily be appropriate to use with some participants, accordingly techniques need to be tailored to fit the needs of each participant.

Importantly, the chapter also restates the significance of more traditional ethnographic methods such as participant observation and unstructured interviews and the ways in which visual and narrative techniques need to be seen as embedded in ethnographic fieldwork; rather than as separate and isolated research tools. There is often an over-investment in visual and narrative techniques that fails to recognise the holistic process of fieldwork and the chapter attempts to redress this balance by situating modes of data production within wider frameworks of qualitative inquiry. The chapter is also concerned with looking beyond the immediate relationships between researcher and participants to consider how wider institutional regulations and funding priorities can both enable and constrain creative approaches to fieldwork.

In this way, the chapter moves from the micro, to the meso and then to the macro to explore key processes in visual and narrative data production. At the micro level there is a consideration of the issues of time, artistic ability and incongruence, which surface in everyday interactions between researchers and participants. The meso perspective begins to consider creative techniques within wider research designs and frameworks; and explores the need to engage with the 'spaces previous to' and 'spaces of reflection' in the 'waiting field' (Mannay and Morgan 2015). Taking a macro perspective, the chapter also draws on Mills and Ratcliffe's (2012, p. 152) sobering account of the impact of the knowledge economy on qualitative research where the push for efficiency potentially narrows the opportunities to engender 'the unpredictable, the tangential and the creative' so that all that remains is 'methodological instrumentalism'. The requirements of national and international polities, economies and external market contingencies have a profound impact on the ways in which visual and narrative approaches can be actualised. In particular, they make demands on the researcher's time that precludes 'slow research'; we will return to this point later in the chapter, for now we will explore time in relation to micro interactions in the process of fieldwork.

## Time, artistic ability and incongruence

A fundamental problem of employing participatory visual methods is the enormous amount of time that such activities take to complete. In traditional interview methods the researcher sets a date, arranges a convenient time and that part of the fieldwork is complete. However, when participants have been asked to produce visual data prior to interview, a meeting cannot take place until this has been completed. For example, in the *Mothers and Daughters on the Margins: Gender, Generation and Education* project (Mannay 2010, 2012), participants created their data in their own homes and follow-up interviews were carried out when the visuals or narratives were completed. The response to the visual and narrative data production was met within very different time frames. In advantageous circumstances, participants completed their visual and/or narrative data production within a week. Overall, children were quicker to engage with the tasks and able to share them in the elicitation interviews. However, for the adult participants, the framework was considerably longer and in some cases the data production activities were not completed for a few months.

This can be frustrating for researchers when there is a deadline to meet so it is something that needs to be considered carefully at the research design stage of a project. This brings up issues of when and how often to remind participants about the project when aspiring to a participatory research relationship. Participants may not want research to impinge on their time, as time, after all, is a precious resource. Therefore, it is important to recognise that participants have their own lives, where participating in research is often an additional burden on their commitments. In response to this problem of time, in later studies I have tried to adopt approaches that build data production into the fieldwork itself so that participants make their visual artefacts when the researcher is physically present. The move away from participants creating visuals and narratives away from the intrusive voice of the researcher needs to be considered; but as discussed in Chapter 4, it is important to acknowledge that even when the 'intrusive presence' of the researcher steps out of the site of visual data production this leaves a space that is often filled by the 'intrusive presence' of significant others (Mannay 2013a).

Producing narrative and visual data in situ, then, can attend to some of the difficulties associated with participants' time and the time of the researcher in suspending interviews until the artefacts are produced, as well as the issues around the presence of intrusive others beyond the research relationship. In the project *University Challenge: How can we foster successful learning journeys for non-traditional students in a School of Social Science?* (Mannay and Edwards 2013, 2014), participants took part in data production within the scheduled interview framework. As discussed in more detail in Chapter 5, drawing on 'the world technique' (Lowenfeld 1939), participants created three-dimensional scenes, pictures or abstract designs in a tray filled with sand and a range of miniature, realistic and fantasy, figures and everyday objects. In contrast to the techniques of photo-elicitation, collaging and mapping, participants working with 'the world technique' did not have to source any materials or have any drawing skills. They could create sand scenes by simply selecting from the items provided and placing them in the sand tray. Therefore, while the activity required some thought and reflection, it was less demanding in terms of time.

For some participants, then, the delay in response may be because the project has to fit in with their busy work schedule and social life and an *in situ* task can partially address this difficulty. However, for other participants it can also be due to an initial aversion to the method of data production. As has been illustrated in a range of studies, visual methods of data production may not be suitable for everyone or may need adjusting to suit particular age groups or communities. For example, Johnson *et al.* (2012) asked participants to draw their experiences of oncology treatment. The participants' drawing introduced topics that had not emerged in previous interview-based research; and the study demonstrated the benefits of combining drawings with interviews, particularly the ways in which the approach shed light on unexpected issues. However, although the drawing activity worked well with younger children, older children tended to associate the technique with school exercises and there were questions around its suitability in relation to 'childishness'.

Drawing also brings up issues in relation to artistic ability and how well ideas and themes can be represented. For example, in the *Mothers and Daughters on the Margins: Gender, Generation and Education* project (Mannay 2010), Tina, one of the mothers in the study, lacked confidence in her artistic abilities and found the request to draw unconventional and alien to her everyday life (Kearney and Hyle 2004). As a result, Tina delayed the interview because she did not want to draw the maps or show me her drawings:

TINA:   *Before I drew um I was just worried about what to do and what you'd think of them and that you know because I'm so crap*

Reflecting on the process, Tina did talk about enjoying the activity after her initial aversion; however, the lack of confidence in her drawing led to omissions. One of these omissions came to light in the interview but there may have been other items that Tina did not feel able to represent visually. In response to my question about her pets she replied:

TINA:   *Ah no I was going to draw them I can't draw (laughs) (both laugh) I should have put them in the corner*

As Luttrell and Chalfen (2010, p. 199) contend, 'imagined audiences can change and play important roles in what is said or left unsaid'; a reminder that visual research should always be interested in not just that which can be seen but with what is hidden, erased (Kaomea 2003) and absent (Mannay 2013a). Tina's lack of confidence in her drawing ability meant that an important aspect of her everyday life was made invisible. One way to counter such omissions might be simply to ask questions towards the end of elicitation interviews about things that were not included. In the *Mothers and Daughters on the Margins: Gender, Generation and Education* project (Mannay 2010, 2012) participants also worked with photographs and collaging and, in these frames, there was less concern about accuracy and a tendency to apply metaphors. Where images were not readily available that exactly reflected the point that participants wanted to discuss, metaphors were employed such as a picture of a kitchen bin to symbolise a problem with littering in the local area or a snowflake to centralise the importance of Christmas for connecting with extended family.

A further example of a symbolic image is illustrated in Figure 6.1, where a mother in the study, Caroline, summarised the problems her family and neighbours have encountered in their street with a photograph of graffiti. The photograph is not in her street and does not represent the type of anti-social behaviour that she wants to discuss; however, when she is out shopping she takes a photograph of this graffiti as a reminder to herself of an aspect that she wants to discuss in our elicitation interview. In our meeting we discuss a wide range of incidents, such as tipping over wheelie bins, arson, car crime, and burglary, which are transient activities, not amenable to being captured with a camera. In this way, the photograph removed the anxiety of the technical ability to reproduce an accurate representation of a thing or event in a drawing, and allowed for the symbolic use of a subjectively representative image.

Drawing is commonly related to artistic ability and its proficiency is associated with discourses of the proficient schooled subject (Damon 2000; Barker and Weller 2003).

**FIGURE 6.1** Vandalism

In contrast, when George Eastman introduced the Kodak camera in 1888, he coined the advertising slogan 'you press the button we do the rest'; a marketing mantra that allowed amateur photographers a sense of mastery over the previously professionalised area of photography (van Dijck 2014). Consequently, taking photographs has become a naturalised and relatively straightforward visual data production technique for adults and young people. The instant nature of the photograph can arguably limit the opportunity to address the issue of automisation, where the act of drawing acts to force participants to slow down their perception, to linger and to notice (Gurevitch 1998). However, being behind the lens in itself engenders a decision-making process about the choice of images and moments, from an infinite number, which the camera will capture (Goldstein 2007). Furthermore, as illustrated in Figure 6.1, participants employed the camera to create symbolic representations of the stories that they want to share with the researcher.

Photo-elicitation, then, can overcome some of the practical issues associated with mapping and drawing in social science research; however, as with other visual techniques, creating photographs can intrude on participants' time. There can also be technological problems, for example, photographic images may not always be effectively developed or represent what the participant intended to create, particularly when disposal cameras are used. However, as I have discussed elsewhere (see Mannay 2014a), the quality of the photograph itself is not always important, as elicitation interviews are not so much about an understanding of the data produced, as an understanding with the data produced about the lives of the participants.

For example, the photograph in Figure 6.2 has 'gone wrong' as it is not aesthetically pleasing and its subject matter escapes from the lens; consequently, the image does not clearly represent the content that Adele was attempting to communicate. However, the photograph retains its usefulness as an elicitation tool. Adele, a daughter in the *Mothers and Daughters on the Margins: Gender, Generation and Education* project (Mannay 2010, 2012) had attempted to take a photograph of her car from her living room window but the separating glass pane acted to reframe the subject so that the viewer is presented with Adele's hands and the camera inside her home. The camera was disposable so Adele did not see the image until I delivered the unopened package of photographs to her, so there was no opportunity to retake the shot.

Adele was a university student, commuting to a local university from home, and she had purchased a car with her university grant. This material item was symbolic of the journey to the different and conflicting world of higher education (Mannay 2013b); however, the reflective image places Adele firmly back 'home'. The conflict between wanting a better life and achieving social mobility but remaining in her locality, and not distancing herself from her family, characterised Adele's interview

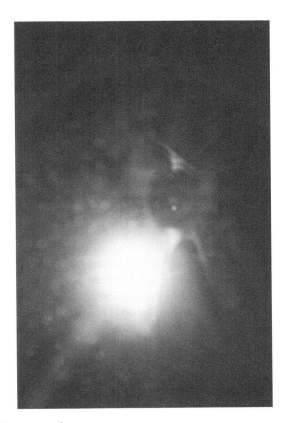

FIGURE 6.2 'Gone wrong'

talk; and the image itself contributed to these discussions. In this way, despite the poor quality of the image, the photograph enabled an exploration of the positioning of inbetweenness, where the nexus of biographical, social and local factors conjoin possibilities with the contexts and conditions of lived practices and future expectations.

Issues of quality in photography, then, are not necessarily problematic and participants can discuss the content and meanings of an image even when it has not retained the essence of its chosen subject. However, photography can act to complicate the widespread notion that ethical social enquiry necessarily requires preserving the anonymity of the research participants. Visual researchers have been concerned with questions of how and when to anonymise images that contain people, places and other identifying characteristics (Wiles *et al.* 2011) and there are debates around the 'ethics of recognition' (Sweetman 2009). In a climate of Open Access publishing and dissemination these concerns around the ethics of photographic data are particularly pertinent (Mannay 2014b); and these concerns will be explored in detail in Chapter 7. However, one way to avoid the issue of identification is for researchers to move from the role of 'social scientist as the participatory facilitator' to the role of the 'social scientist as image creator' (Pauwels 2011).

In researcher-initiated productions the camera can pass to the hands of the researcher so that they frame the content of the photographic images produced. This allows an element of control over what is recorded, which can be useful in circumventing ethical issues around recognition. As Wagner (2007, p. 29) contends, 'a photographer's selectivity in one dimension makes it wholly suspect in all others' and this movement to a documentary approach can preclude the participatory potential of visual research. However, there are still opportunities to involve participants in the staging of the photograph so that the researcher-initiated production is directed by the research participants. This approach was adopted in the Children and Young People's Research Network (CYPRN) funded project, *Inter-generational Views and Experiences of Breastfeeding* (Mannay *et al.* 2014), which will now be discussed.

The benefits of breastfeeding have been widely publicised and breastfeeding is positioned as having the potential to reduce harm and minimise avoidable harm in relation to the health and well-being of infants and children. However, according to the Health and Social Care Information Centre (2010) Infant Feeding Survey, breastfeeding rates in Wales are very low, with only one per cent of Welsh women breastfeeding their babies exclusively for six months, in line with World Health Organisation (2014) guidance. The *Inter-generational Views and Experiences of Breastfeeding* project was interested in the experiences of new mothers and grandmothers in relation to infant feeding practices. However, this is a sensitive area in which policy agendas and contemporary notions of the 'good mother frame infant feeding practices, rendering them a site of moral and interactional trouble' (Lomax 2013, p. 97).

Consequently, we wanted the method of data production to allow participants some control about the topics for discussion and decided to employ artefacts as the impetus for the interview discussions. Participants were asked to collect items that represented their experiences of new motherhood in preparation for the accompanying

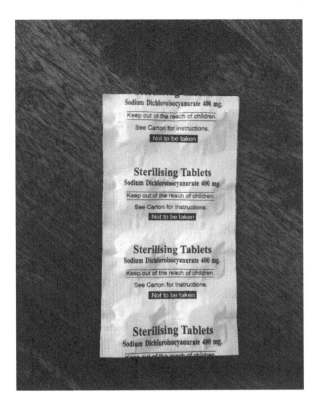

**FIGURE 6.3**   Sterilising bottles

interviews; and these artefacts then acted as tools of elicitation, leading the conversations. The artefacts were then photographed by researchers who were careful to position items so that the photographs did not include participants, their children or other identifying information, as illustrated in Figure 6.3. The inclusion of artefacts offered many of the benefits of other visual approaches. Additionally, if artefacts are close to hand, as they were in this study, their collection does not significantly impose on participants' time. Furthermore, participants' photographs can be created with the ethics of recognition in mind as they can be employed in disseminating the project, without raising ethical issues about visibility and confidentiality.

In the *Inter-generational Views and Experiences of Breastfeeding* project the majority of participants put together a set of useful artefacts that provided a more nuanced insight into their everyday experiences of infant feeding; and opened up new areas of interest that were not envisaged at the outset of the project. However, some participants did not engage with the process and said that they had forgotten or not had time before the interview, in some cases artefacts were then brought together *in situ* and in others the interviews were conducted without any objects of elicitation. Overall, the elicitation interviews around artefacts generated more in-depth conversations than those without this visual element; but participants cannot always be expected to engage with these pre-tasks. Accordingly, it can be useful to explore the potentialities of introducing found materials that situate the researcher as an image collector (Pauwels 2011).

Arguably, limitations can be imposed by employing researcher-, rather than participant-, generated images because the researcher's framing of visual elicitation tools may not have relevance in the context of the participant's lived life. However, they do mean that participants' time does not have to be encroached on outside of the scheduled interviews. Indeed, the use of found images has proved successful in previous research. For example, in their 'Men-as-fathers' project Henwood *et al.* (2008) presented a sequence of images depicting sociocultural change in ideas of fatherhood and masculinity over time to participants. In interviews participants were invited to comment on each individual image before being presented with the next. The technique proved valuable as it enabled men to reconfigure their thoughts about fatherhood. Participants were able to re-represent themselves in relation to the flow of the images and 'articulate their shifting and coexisting identifications with ideas of masculinity encoded in more traditional and modern representations of fatherhood' (Henwood and Shirani 2012, p. 113).

Similarly, in a project conducted with Amy Grant and Ruby Marzella, *Negotiating Young Parenthood: A study exploring the ways in which mediated stereotypes of teenage parents impact on their perceptions of their parenting practices; and their engagement with service providers* (2014), we introduced found images as a photo-elicitation tool. As Tyler (2008) argues in her paper 'Chav Mum Chav Scum', the figure of 'chav mum' circulates within a wide range of celebrity media, reality television, comedy programming on British television, consumer culture, print media, literature, news media, and 'chav hate' websites. Importantly, these caricatures impact on public perceptions and social policy: and young parents' perceptions of their own parenting practices and capabilities. In this way, mediated figures accrete form and accrue affective value in ways that have significant social and political impact (Lomax and Fink 2014). This negative portrayal can have a number of problematic outcomes as young parents may feel isolated and be wary of engaging with support services because of the way that they feel they are perceived. Furthermore, any reluctance to engage with services for parents and children can further disadvantage young parents so that they are unable to develop their skills to their full potential and engage with community activities and events.

For this reason, it is important to direct research to examine mediated forms of young parenthood and the experiences of young parents. In this study we were interested in young parents' subjective understandings of their depiction in the mediascape and the ways in which this impacts on their everyday negotiation of parenthood. We ran small focus groups with three to four parents who all knew each other to ensure that participants felt that they were in a comfortable and safe environment to discuss their experiences. We began the interviews with a more general conversation around being a parent and the pressures more specific to young parents. Following this we introduced a number of images sourced from the search engine Google in response to the terms 'parent and child' and 'young/teenage parent and child'. The images illustrated a disjuncture between idealised and demonised representations and allowed further discussion about how these images permeated the lived experience of parenthood beyond the print press, internet and television programming that forms the mediascape. Arguably, this approach precludes the reflexive engagement afforded by a pre-task centred on participants' visual creations; however, it does address some of the practicalities of time, artistic ability, technological issues and the ethics of representation.

These discussions have explored 'tales from the field' focusing on the practicalities of visual data production and the advantages and disadvantages associated with different techniques. Importantly, when drawing on the visual, whether the social scientist is acting as the participatory facilitator, image-creator or employing found images (Pauwels 2011), ongoing reflective practice is crucial. The relative success of visual data production techniques with the majority of participants in a project can have a negative impact in that they act to blind the researcher to other techniques, which may be more suitable for some of the research sample. It is often useful to have a range of options, rather than dictating particular data production techniques, if research is going to be truly participatory.

Therefore, if participants are not engaging with the visual data production process it is important to offer alternatives, visual, narrative and oral. Providing only visual techniques can be prescriptive as the research then carries the subliminal message 'You will use my participatory visual method'. Consequently, it is important to offer flexibility in the research approach, and as well as offering a range of visual production options, also providing the opportunity for participants to take part in a more traditional interview, or to offer their own suggestions that could be incorporated into the study. The visual then should not become centralised as a necessity or be enforced where it is seen as unsuitable, unwelcome or undesirable by research participants. Importantly, researchers also need to be mindful that research is wider than a set of visual techniques and think of the process as embedded within a considerably wider set of practices. This will be the focus of the following section.

## The 'waiting field'

As I have argued previously (Mannay and Morgan 2015), contemporary social science research is often concerned to engage with and promote particular forms of innovative data production, such as photo-elicitation, autoethnography or participatory film making. This fascination with the latest techniques has been accompanied by an ever more fragmented range of research methods training for students where the week-by-week shift between approaches engenders a disjointed view of becoming the researcher. This individualisation of techniques has set up rival camps and critiques where the common ground of being embedded in qualitative inquiry is often forgotten. For researchers, who began their academic careers in the ethnographic tradition, there is an appreciation of the holistic base of enquiry from which a family of methods can be effectively employed. However, more recently qualitative researchers have been distracted by 'the technique'; a distraction that can blind them to the occupation of ethnography.

The emphasis on 'the technique', rather than a holistic approach to qualitative inquiry, has arguably been fostered by the critiques of, and inevitably defences of, the ethnographer's tools. The scrutiny of individual tools, although necessary, can also work as a distraction, in that there is so much emphasis on the tools that the tool box of ethnography becomes invisible. For example, interviewing is a tool widely used by social researchers and in contemporary research, and many qualitative studies rely entirely, or primarily, on interview data (Hammersley 2008). The charge of over reliance has attracted criticism alongside a more radical appraisal of interviews in which the potential for the interview to engender access to information about the social worlds in which informants live is challenged (Atkinson and Coffey 2002).

More recently, autoethnography has been critiqued as a narcissistic preoccupation (Roth 2009), lazy (Delamont, 2007, 2009) and antithetical to career progression (Poulos 2010). Of particular interest here, is the point that even the recent attractiveness of the visual has moved to a more critical juncture where the researchers are discussing the limitations of participatory visual methods (Packard 2008). There has been a more critical approach to visual studies and its related philosophies, ethics and methodologies in special issues such as the *International Journal of Research and Method in Education* recent edition '*Problematising Visual Methods*' (Lomax 2012; Wall *et al.* 2012).

The problems attributed to one technique of data production are often followed by a call for innovation such as Pink's (2009) direction to move beyond the visual to other sensory engagement – a new 'latest and greatest' to enter into arguments of critique and defence, which may further and refine our approaches, for we should not accept qualitative techniques at face value and risk research quality, but carefully discern their potentialities (Hammersley 2007). However, at the same time there needs to be an awareness of the inherent dangers of engendering circular quarrels and opposing camps, where we could, more usefully, encourage collaboration.

Arguably, autoethnographic experimental pieces can take the reader into a particular social world and convey phenomenon through depictive techniques and textual devices that foreground lived experience and carnal presence; becoming a form of self-narrative that places the self within a social context (Doloriert and Sambrook 2011; Poulos 2010; Taber 2010). Arguably, interviews can offer insights into the perspectives that govern behaviour and can be a sound source of witness information about what happens in particular settings or in the world more generally (Hammersley 2007). Visual techniques may not be 'a panacea for all ethnography's ills' (Ball and Smith 2001, p. 313), but arguably they too can move beyond the repertoire of preconceived understandings of place and space, unravel the diversity of urban experience and make the familiar strange and interesting again (Mannay 2010).

Value can be found, then, in individual techniques, but is this enough? There is an argument to triangulate and consider plurality; however, as Darbyshire *et al.* (2005) argue, multiple methods in qualitative research are not a guarantee of gaining more insight. Perhaps, then, what is needed is a solid and secure foundation that underpins the research journey and offers the casing for these loose tools so that they become a functional tool kit. For example, in exploring the everyday use of young people's bedroom spaces Lincoln (2012) employs interviews, observations, multisensory ethnography and photo-elicitation. Rather than adopting an orthodox ethnographic approach, Lincoln draws on a family of research tools; however, importantly, it is the security of the ethnographic base and her assurance of being an ethnographer that allows Lincoln to produce valuable qualitative research. In relation to such examples of best practice this section poses the question: when employing visual research methods can we move beyond 'the technique' and draw on wider ethnographic traditions to make the most of our research journeys?

As Hammersley and Atkinson (2007, p. 2) contend, 'ethnography plays a complex and shifting role in the dynamic tapestry that the social sciences has become in the twenty-first century'; and perhaps this intricacy has made it more difficult for researchers to recognise their practice as ethnography and realise their place within an ethnographic base. For Hammersley (2005), in basic terms, ethnography is a form of social research that emphasises the importance of studying at first hand what people do and say in particular contexts; however, a more nuanced understanding can be gained by focusing on what ethnographers actually do. Hammersley and Atkinson (2007, p. 3) offer a parsimonious explanation of the craft of ethnography as involving fairly lengthy contact with people in everyday, rather than experimental, contexts; which involve participant observation and/or relatively open-ended interviews and the analysis of artefacts and documents associated with their lives.

Ethnographic approaches have many forms – classical, natural, interpretative and critical – which have been explored in detail elsewhere (Atkinson *et al.* 2001; Koro-Ljungberg and Greckhamer 2005); however, commonalities can be found. The focus of ethnographic research is generally fairly small scale to engender in-depth study and the analysis of data involves the interpretation of meanings and their relation to local and global context; a process that for Van Maanen (2009, p. 16) attempts to put into writing 'what it is like to be somebody else'. The contemporary ethnographer may find themselves involved in a diverse range of research techniques but the definition of ethnography remains rooted in the first-hand exploration of the research setting; as Atkinson *et al.* (2001, p. 5) contend, it is this sense of social exploration and protracted investigation 'that gives ethnography its abiding and continuing character'.

Ethnographic undertakings, then, are contained in a variety of perspectives; but importantly its researchers are immersed in the field where spaces are never empty – they value the in-between. This immersion engenders the possibility of serendipity not only in relation to the accidental nature of something unexpected, but importantly also the space to draw novel connections and synthesise insights (Fine and Deegan 1996). In contrast, for new researchers, particularly undergraduates, who plan to conduct an interview between 9am and 10am, often there is a tendency to neglect the importance of the in-between. In this way, qualitative research and ethnographic undertakings become reduced to the content of the interview hour in isolation: the transcript tells the tale and the research diary is something that needs to be filled in the night before submission because it is a requirement of dissertation assessment. Ethnographic interviewing could offer so much more and equip our students to become more effective qualitative researchers.

For Delamont (2012, p. 57), what people do seems so much more important than anything they can, or do, say; and she despairs that too much research uses interviews rather than ethnography. Employing interviews rather than ethnography suggests the isolated form of interviewing discussed above but ethnographic interviewing offers an opportunity to use the technique of interviewing within an ethnographic undertaking. As Sherman Heyl (2007, p. 371) argues, ethnographic interviewing challenges the positivistic framework of interviewer as an autonomous 'miner' and she evokes the travel metaphor to position the interview as a 'wandering together with', which is characterised by twists, turns and creativity.

Interviews, visual data production and other creative qualitative techniques are particularly useful when ethnographic fieldwork closes down opportunities for observation. As Lincoln (2012) argues, the home is often seen as a type of sanctuary, which is particularly impervious to forms of anthropological observation and this is why she selected a range of techniques of data production from an ethnographic base. In my visual research, the home has been central and interviews and visual methods have been significant tools of inquiry. However, drawing from Sherman Heyl (2007) I have been careful to acquire a sense of awareness of my role in the construction of meaning within the interview process, to recognise that dialogue offers only partial knowledge and also to centralise the broader social context and the ways in which this affects participants and the interview process. In this way, situating visual techniques within an ethnographic frameworks offers up the potential for engendering a more nuanced understanding of social worlds.

When employing visual and creative methods of data production I have considered the importance of my time in the field 'waiting' to engage in these research techniques. Waiting time in research is neither empty nor without use; and in times of waiting we often learn new things about our participants and ourselves, but the absence of an ethnographic foundation can mean that these opportunities are not always realised. This chapter offers reflections from my research diaries that document this waiting time; and the discoveries of others, and of self, doing ethnography in waiting spaces, which have been conceptualised as the 'waiting field' (Mannay and Morgan 2015). In introducing the 'waiting field', it is important to consider that this is 'old hat' to many ethnographers, and those engaged in other forms of rigorous qualitative practice, who set out on their research with this appreciation as implicit in their craft. However, my own experience in the field, the recent shifts in higher education, and my work with new generations of students and researchers, necessitates a consideration of how to retain the salience of the in-between in contemporary qualitative inquiry.

The 'waiting field' is a space in need of attention and appreciation; and it can act as a compensatory framework to challenge an over-investment in visual and narrative techniques that fail to recognise the holistic process of fieldwork. The 'waiting field' is a framework that seeks to centralise the value of ethnographic approaches so that the visual does not become isolated. If visual techniques of data production are allowed to substitute research methodologies then the researcher risks being blinded by the visual so that more nuanced understandings of the research questions are impaired. It is important to emphasise the 'waiting field' to engender opportunities for rigour in visual qualitative inquiry and the research diary is one space to explore, record and reflect on waiting fields.

The following accounts act to illustrate the 'waiting field' and are taken from my research diaries that were recorded in the *Mothers and Daughters on the Margins: Gender, Generation and Education* project (Mannay 2010, 2012). They are 'spaces previous to' (Mannay and Morgan 2015) because they record the times before the techniques of data production were applied; that is, the spaces before participants engaged in map-making, collage creation, taking photographs, writing narratives or the related elicitation interviews. They are also 'spaces of reflection' (Mannay and Morgan 2015) because they were written up as research diary entries and they informed the analysis of 'the meanings, functions and consequences of human actions' (Hammersley and Atkinson 2007, p. 3).

> *One of the daughters in the study, Carla, had forgotten that I was coming over and was sat in her pyjamas watching 'Under the Hammer' with Patricia (her mother). 'I knew I was supposed to be doing something today but I couldn't remember what' said Carla.*

For ethnographers working in the field applying participant observation (for example Delamont 2006; Hurdley 2013; Renold 2005; Turgo 2012) these everyday encounters are a staple and they generate insights into social and cultural practices. However, as Lincoln (2012) contends, the presence of the researcher in participants' homes breaches the traditional boundaries between the public and the private. For this reason, I could not immerse myself within the territory of mothers' and daughters' homes. The 'waiting field' of 'spaces previous to' then becomes particularly important for it allows an opportunity for a glimpse of the familiar practices of home life; of pyjamas, television and the 'companionate relationship' that has been documented in previous studies of family life in south Wales (Barker 1972, p. 582): such 'spaces previous to' can also be useful in reflecting on the ways wider social issues impact on everyday lives, as demonstrated in the following research diary entry reflecting on a meeting with one of the mothers in the project, Siân.

> *It has been raining and I am waiting for Siân outside her house in the rain and when she arrives we go inside. Before the interview Siân said 'I will have to put the radiators on to dry my shoes as they are soaked through with rain', and she puts her shoes on the radiator. 'I've only got one pair' she explains, 'there is never any money left for me after the kids'. This is the reality of living on low income, having to walk around in wet shoes. When your income gets higher you forget about these things, the everyday inconveniences and the small miseries. I have walked around with holes in the only shoes I've got, wet, cold feet and bronchitis on top. It becomes normal at the time and is forgotten when you have more shoes than you really need.*

For me, observing the routine way in which Siân puts on the radiators to dry her shoes acted as a stark, visual reminder of the everyday inconveniences and the small miseries that make up the reality of living on a low income. Lack of resources and the routines of coping with poverty become normalised and therefore often absent and made invisible in interview talk. In this way 'spaces previous to' again provide an added depth of insight into Siân's everyday life; they provide an opportunity for serendipitous research. 'Spaces of reflection' are also important and writing the research diary acted to reinforce the point that it is all too easy to overlook the materiality of poverty, in fact the mode of writing with pen and paper, as opposed to computer keyboard, elicited a more emotional response to the data: and this 'space of reflection' augmented the possibilities of the data encountered in the fieldwork process; a process also reflected in the following diary entry.

> *I call into see Eleri and her neighbour is there and her friend and friend's sister. The neighbour was going to have a 21st birthday party at one of the local working man's clubs and had been giving her father money each week to pay off the room hire and DJ as he goes to the club. When she had called in to check something out she found there was no booking — her father had spent all the money and never paid anything off so the celebration is cancelled. This led to a conversation about the trouble with the men in these women's lives; about having to watch that sons don't steal out of your purse and how it's good to have a small handbag so you can carry it everywhere with you — to the toilet and you can even sleep with it. Everyone thinks badly of the neighbour's father and the other thieving sons and husbands but the worrying thing is that no one is that shocked or surprised about anything, not even me, it is seen as wrong but still expected, accepted — there is a tacit normalisation that this is what things are like.*

This excerpt represents both 'spaces previous to' and 'spaces of reflection'; and the observation was particularly salient because, as I worked with a small sample of eighteen participants, the charge that I may have based my research on an unrepresentative set of voices was often levied. This brief participant observation, and further experiences with a similar demographic in the area, were consistent with my interviews with participants around their own gendered relationships and those of their wider family and friendship networks.

In this way, 'spaces previous to' and 'spaces of reflection' provided an opportunity to explore the ways in which the data created with participants, rather than being unusual, was representative of some of the wider experiences of mothers and daughters within this urban locale. However, these spaces do not necessitate a form of demarcation where the 'previous to' and 'reflection' become representations of some pure and suspended research space. All spaces are characterised by fluidity and multiplicity (Massey 1994), and for many researchers, they do not need to be named. Consequently, we are not pushing methodological boundaries by simply imposing categorisation on the journeys that already characterise rigorous qualitative inquiry. The naming of spaces, and the apparent demarcation, is a strategy in response to the arguments raised earlier in the chapter in relation to the ways in which these spaces are currently threatened by invisibility in both teaching and research.

Reflecting on the 'waiting field', these types of records were important for capturing aspects of mothers' and daughters' everyday lives and my reactions and reflections. The ethnographic experience is accessible within these 'spaces previous to', the times where lives carry on before they make room for the intrusion of the data production techniques; however, such spaces do not exist in a vacuum, and even with the removal of the technique the intrusive presence of the researcher remains. It is essential then to recognise the dynamic relationship between the researcher and the researched in the 'waiting field'.

Arguably, there is always some form of presentation of self (Goffman 1959) and as Allport (1954, p. 5) maintains 'thoughts, feelings, and behaviours of individuals are influenced by the actual, imagined, or implied presence of other human beings'. In the 'waiting field' notebook and audio recorder may be hidden out of sight but the researcher and research aims, and wider social norms and values are a continuing and constant influence. Enlarging the scope of participant observation cannot eliminate the issue of intrusion but it is important to centralise the 'waiting field' as a salient aspect of the research process, which can be equally important as the time spent applying techniques of data production.

Acknowledging the 'waiting field' offers opportunities to engage with the field in a qualitatively different way that can enable a richer perspective and act to further our understandings. For this reason, 'spaces previous to' and 'spaces of reflection' should not be neglected in research practices that centralise the visual. Visual and creative methods can allow for a nuanced understanding of participants' lives but they are not in themselves a research methodology. Consequently, this chapter emphasises the need for an appreciation of the potential for discoveries of others, and of self, doing quality ethnography and qualitative research in the 'waiting field'.

The salience of the 'waiting field' was illustrated across accounts from the *Mothers and Daughters on the Margins: Gender, Generation and Education* study. The chapter explored the research diary as a reflective and reflexive space; and demonstrated the ways in which empirically and methodologically, it is imperative to acknowledge the ethnographic base and be mindful of 'spaces previous to' and 'spaces of reflection'. Importantly, the chapter has centralised the need to work with a 'family of methods' (Lincoln 2012) from a strong ethnographic base. However, where researchers or students feel that their philosophical principles cannot sit within an ethnographic approach, here perhaps there can be an engagement with the 'waiting field'; as an ideological bridge that allows movement beyond 'the technique' so that researchers can make the most of their visual and creative research journeys.

As discussed in the earlier sections, in engaging with quality qualitative research it is important to consider the micro aspects of the data production design and ensure that the visual techniques adopted resonate with the needs of research participants in relation to their suitability, time commitments and technical proficiencies. It is equally important to explore the meso aspect and consider key processes in visual and narrative data production and the ways in which these need to be embedded into wider frameworks of research practice. Importantly, as discussed in the following section, it also is useful to explore the macro level and see how researchers' work can become constrained by the drive towards perpetual organisational reform, aimed at gaining advantage in the competitive landscape that reflects contemporary social science research.

## Backyards and wider worlds

For contemporary researchers contemplating visual techniques, it is tempting to rush into the field armed with audio recorder and camera and neglect the 'waiting field' (Mannay and Morgan 2015); and this technique-focused approach is something often reported in relation to the research projects of students. For example, Orsini-Jones (2010, p. 3) reflects on how she was 'taken aback by the levels of anxiety expressed by students with reference to their engagement with the planning of their independent piece of research'; and their reluctance to engage in a holistic methodological approach was presented as a product of the lack of epistemic cognition. At the risk of simplifying a complex concept, the term epistemic cognition relates to an understanding of the nature of knowledge and knowing (Avramides and Luckin 2007); and this apprehension about, and disengagement with, ontological and epistemological questions is problematic because rather than demonstrating epistemic cognition, students often engage in strategies to avoid what Orsini-Jones (2010, p. 341) refers to as 'troublesome knowledge'.

Students' epistemic cognition has been explored under a variety of conceptual frameworks, including epistemological beliefs, personal epistemology and epistemic resources (Baxter 2004; Hammer and Elby 2002; Schommer-Aikins 2004); and research suggests that students lack a complex understanding of the nature of knowledge (Hofer and Pintrich 1997). Koro-Ljungberg and Greckhamer (2005, p. 286) contend that they 'cannot envision rigorous qualitative research without any theoretical connections', but in the technique-led approaches, often favoured by emerging researchers, these inadequate foundations are evident. In this chapter, then, there is an argument not only that researchers move beyond 'the technique' of visual data production but that as tutors we are able to enhance the students' learning and scaffold students' epistemic understanding of their qualitative research projects.

There needs to be an opportunity to reflect on where research is located epistemologically and find ways to make 'troublesome knowledge' less troublesome: so that new researchers can engage usefully with projects of qualitative inquiry. Rather than going into the field with 'the technique', students need to be encouraged to practise rigorous qualitative research and an ethnographic base, or at least an acknowledgement of the 'waiting field', can be a good starting ground to reflexively engage with epistemic cognition. However, perhaps it is disingenuous to frame students' epistemic cognition as lacking: much academic teaching and learning comes in the form of 'troublesome knowledge' (Orsini-Jones 2010, p. 3). However, even when topics are difficult and challenging, students work hard to gain mastery of theoretical and conceptual material. That this mastery is not transferred into the active process of individual research projects could be tied to the teaching of research methods in lectures and textbooks, where techniques are divided and the view of conducting a study somewhat compartmentalised. However, there are many excellent research guides, and much topic-based teaching is compartmentalised, but students are still able to successfully make the relevant connections.

Perhaps then we need to refocus our lens of analysis to the wider research setting, exploring what Rogoff (2008) refers to as the community plane, and interrogating the institutional structure and cultural technologies of intellectual activity. As Mills and Ratcliffe (2012, p. 147) argue, 'methods and debates over methods are prisms through which to understand the changing social and economic expectations placed upon qualitative research'; and it is important to explore what has changed in the sociopolitical and economic landscape that could serve to close down ethnographic spaces. Some insights are offered by turning to anthropology and, in particular, the contemporary position of the discipline in the UK.

In her autobiographical reflection, Delamont (2012) cites her training in anthropology as providing a lifelong commitment to ethnography. Similarly for Atkinson (2012, p. 46) there is 'no real intellectual difference between the best of anthropology and the best of sociology': where both engage with an ethnographic imagination. Although the key strengths of ethnographic practice were nurtured in the traditions of anthropology, ethnography is not simply anthropology, and anthropology is not simply ethnography – and I do not make this claim. However, the fate of the anthropological tradition is moulded by complex forces and influences that impact on contemporary higher education and academic research.

Mills and Ratcliffe (2012) provide a sobering insight into the anthropological landscape by reflecting on their interviews conducted with academics trained in anthropology departments between 1990 and 2004. Some anthropologists felt that it was counterproductive to identify as 'an anthropologist' in an academic climate of the knowledge economy. Furthermore, there was a consensus that ethnographic practices were being redefined, with research design moving away from exploratory and long-term fieldwork towards more tightly defined commercial frames, so that the ability to conduct 'real ethnography' was curtailed.

For Mills and Ratcliffe (2012), this reflects the requirements of national and international polities and economies to train knowledge workers within an intense circulation of concepts and commodities. As in business, there is a belief that organisational reform drives development and secures competitive advantage but the push for efficiency potentially narrows the opportunities to engender 'the unpredictable, the tangential and the creative' so that all that remains is 'methodological instrumentalism' (Mills and Ratcliffe 2012, p. 152).

The business model sets out to remove inconsistencies and inefficiencies that cannot feed into the 'instant answers' mode of inquiry and consequently destabilises the position of anthropological approaches. This shift signifies not just a move away from funding ethnographic research and teaching but perhaps also a move away from all forms of in-depth qualitative inquiry and rigorous qualitative research. In this way, students' epistemic cognition can be seen as symptomatic of the wider high-speed, drive-by research climate that has begun to filter into to their educational experience.

We cannot turn back the hands of time but we can try to sustain a methodological commitment to the lessons of an ethnographic imagination; and make space to appreciate the unexpected and unpredictable as key moments of insight: and resist the neatness and control of the economic markets that seek to erode rigorous qualitative inquiry. Ethnography is not simply a research technique but 'an open ended, iterative, non-prescriptive vision for social science, where the researcher is encouraged to acknowledge the complexity and unpredictability of the research encounter' (Mills and Ratcliffe 2012, p. 155).

These external market contingencies continue to stress the business case for research output and often prevent researchers from indulging in 'slow science', which engenders flexibility and serendipity – as a combination of both chance and intuitive reasoning (Salazar and Rivoal 2013). The qualitative researcher is expected to condense their time in the field, be reflective without time for reflexivity; and write and publish at speed to keep their account relevant before it becomes obsolete and void of economic value. Arguably, in research-led teaching such immediacies are communicated to new generations of social scientists. Where the wider socioeconomic and political forces begin to restrict both teaching and research, it is important to guard against the adverse impacts on qualitative inquiry. This is particularly important when engaging with creative and visual techniques that promote a 'slow science' built upon the opportunities for reflection, reflexivity and the aim of better understanding the subjective words of our research participants. Therefore, it is important that researchers understand the market forces that govern their practice and find ways to maintain quality in their research projects and also, where applicable, their involvement with teaching new generations of researchers.

## Conclusion

The everyday practicalities of applying creative techniques of visual data production techniques often become lost in more dominant discourses that are concerned with issues of interpretation and the ethics of recognition. This chapter has worked to address this somewhat neglected area by setting out tales from the field that explore the potentialities and drawbacks of a variety of techniques. The chapter has considered the issues of time, artistic ability, technical proficiency and suitability across the modes of photography, drawing, collage, sandboxing, and the use of artefacts and found materials as tools of elicitation. These reflections on fieldwork have emphasised the need to avoid a 'one size fits all' approach to data production in favour of a more flexible methodology, which centralises the importance of choice for participants.

Moving from a focus on the experience of data production with research participants, the chapter then shifted its lens to explore the research process. It was argued that movements towards new and creative forms of data production can engender a focus on applying 'the technique'; which acts to sideline the importance of ongoing traditional ethnographic and reflective engagement. Consequently, research projects need to be carefully designed to avoid a narrow interpretation of visual methodologies and move beyond the idea of research techniques to a more holistic conceptualisation of the research process and journey. The 'waiting field' was suggested as one way for visual researchers to extend their gaze and gain a more nuanced understanding of their areas of interest.

Lastly, the chapter moved to the macro level to consider the ways in which research practice is guided, governed and restricted by wider changes in the organisation and funding of social sciences research. The move away from 'slow science' to a results-based, 'quick and dirty' form of inquiry was presented as a threat to quality qualitative research, and in particular the use of visual and creative methods. Consequently, researchers have a responsibility to try and maintain flexibility in design for participants, a framework that acknowledges social phenomena beyond the visual, and an approach that prevents a narrow market instrumentalism from detracting from the values of their work. In this way, the practicalities of visual research raise a number of challenges, as do the ethics of creative methodologies, which will be discussed in the following chapter.

## References

Abrahams, J. and Ingram, N. (2013) 'The Chameleon Habitus: Exploring Local Students' Negotiations of Multiple Fields', *Sociological Research Online*, 18 (4): 21.

Allport G. W. (1954) 'The Historical Background of Modern Social Psychology', in G. Lindzey (ed.) *Handbook of Social Psychology*. Reading, MA: Addison-Wesley.

Atkinson, P. (2012) 'Accidental Anthropologist, Sceptical Sociologist, Reluctant Methodologist', *Studies in Symbolic Interaction*, 38: 330–50.

Atkinson, P. and Coffey, A. (2002) 'Revisiting the Relationship between Participant Observation and Interviewing', in J. F. Gubrium and J. A. Holstein (eds) *Handbook of Interview Research*, pp. 801–14. Thousand Oaks, CA: Sage.

Atkinson, P., Coffey, A., Delamont S., Lofland, J. and Lofland, L. (eds) (2001) *Handbook of Ethnography*. London: Sage.

Avramides, K. and Luckin, R. (2007) 'Towards the Design of a Representational Tool to Scaffold Students' Epistemic Understanding of Psychology in Higher Education'. *Proceedings of the Workshop on AIED Applications for Ill-Defined Domains at the 13th International Conference on Artificial Intelligence in Education*, Los Angeles, CA.

Ball, M. S. and Smith, G. W. H. (2001) 'Technologies of Realism? Ethnographic Use of Photography and Film', in P. Atkinson, A. Coffey, S. Delamont, J. Lofland and L. Lofland (eds) *Handbook of Ethnography*, pp. 302–20. London: Sage.

Barker, D. (1972) 'Keeping Close and Spoiling in a South Wales Town', *Sociological Review*, 20 (4): 569–90.

Barker, J. and Weller, S. (2003) 'Is it Fun? Developing Child Centered Research Methods', *The International Journal of Sociology and Social Policy*, 23 (1–2): 33–58.

Baxter, M. B. (2004) 'Evolution of a Constructivist Conceptualization of Epistemological Reflection', *Educational Psychologist*, 39 (1): 31–42.

Cook, T. and Hess, E. (2007) 'What the Camera Sees and From Whose Perspective: Fun Methodologies for Engaging Children in Enlightening Adults', *Childhood*, 14: 29–45.

Damon, F. H. (2000) 'To Restore the Events? On the Ethnography of Malinowski's Photography', *Visual Anthropology Review*, 16 (1): 71–7.

Darbyshire, P., MacDougall, C. and Schiller, W. (2005) 'Multiple Methods in Qualitative Research with Children: More Insight or Just More?', *Qualitative Research*, 5 (4): 417–36.

Delamont, S. (2006) 'The Smell of Sweat and Rum: Teacher Authority in Capoeira Classes', *Ethnography and Education*, 1(2): 161–75.

Delamont, S. (2007) 'Arguments against Autoethnography', *Qualitative Researcher*, 4: 2–4.

Delamont, S. (2009) 'The Only Honest Thing', *Ethnography and Education*, 4 (1): 51–64.

Delamont, S. (2012) 'Milkshakes and Convertibles: An Autobiographical Reflection', *Studies in Symbolic Interaction*, 39: 51–69.

Doloriert, C. H. and Sambrook, S. (2011) 'Accommodating an Autoethnographic PhD: The Tale of the Thesis, the Viva Voce and the Traditional Business School', *Journal of Contemporary Ethnography*, 4 (4): 582–615.

Fine, G. A. and Deegan. J. (1996) 'Three Principles of Serendip: Insight, Chance, and Discovery in Qualitative Research', *Qualitative Studies in Education*, 9 (4): 434–47.

Goffman, E. (1959) *The Presentation of Self on Everyday Life*. Harmondsworth: Pelican.

Goldstein, B. (2007) 'All Photos Lie: Images and Data' in G. C. Stanczak (ed.) *Visual Research Methods: Image, Society and Representation*, pp. 61–82. London: Sage.

Gurevitch, Z.D. (1998) 'The Other Side of Dialogue: On Making the Other Strange and the Experience of Otherness', *American Journal of Sociology*, 93 (5): 1179–99.

Hammer, D. and Elby, A. (2002) 'On the Form of a Personal Epistemology', in B. K. Hofer and P. R. Pintrich (eds) *Personal Epistemology: The Psychology of Beliefs about Knowledge and Knowing*, pp. 169–90. Mahwah, NJ: Lawrence Erlbaum.

Hammersley, M. (2005) 'Ethnography: Potential, Practice, and Problems'. *Qualitative Research Methodology Seminar Series*. ESRC National Centre for Research Methods, University of Southampton.

Hammersley, M. (2007) 'The Issue of Quality in Qualitative Research', *International Journal of Research & Method in Education*, 30 (3): 287–305.

Hammersley, M. (2008) *Questioning Qualitative Inquiry*. London: Sage.

Hammersley, M. and Atkinson, P. (2007) *Ethnography: Principles in Practice* (3rd edn). London: Taylor and Francis.

Health and Social Care Information Centre (2010) *Infant Feeding Survey 2010*. http://www.hscic.gov.uk/catalogue/PUB08694 Accessed 04.06.2014.

Henwood, K., Finn, M., and Shirani, F. (2008) 'Use of Visual Methods to Explore Parental Identities in Historical Time and Social Change: Reflections from the "Men-as-fathers" Project', *Qualitative Research*, 9: 112–15.

Henwood, K. and Shirani, F. (2012) 'Researching the Temporal' in H. Cooper (ed.) *Handbook of Research Methods in Psychology*. Washington, DC: American Psychological Association.

Hofer, B. K. and Pintrich, P. R. (1997) 'The Development of Epistemological Theories: Beliefs About Knowledge and Knowing and Their Relation to Learning', *Review of Educational Research*, 67 (1): 88–140.

Hurdley, R. (2013) *Home, Materiality, Memory and Belonging: Keeping Culture*. Basingstoke: Palgrave Macmillan.

Johnson, G. A., Pfister, E. A. and Vindrola-Padros, C. (2012) 'Drawings, Photos, and Performances: Using Visual Methods with Children', *Visual Anthropology Review*, 28 (2): 164–77.

Kaomea, J. (2003) 'Reading Erasures and Making the Familiar Strange: Defamiliarising Methods for Research in Formerly Colonized and Historically Oppressed Communities', *Educational Researcher*, 32 (2): 14–25.

Kearney, K. S. and Hyle, A. E. (2004) 'Drawing out Emotions: The Use of Participant-produced Drawings in Qualitative Inquiry', *Qualitative Research*, 4 (3): 361–82.

Koro-Ljungberg, M. and Greckhamer, T. (2005) 'Strategic Turns Labelled "Ethnography": from Description to Openly Ideological Production of Cultures', *Qualitative Research*, 5(3): 285–306.

Lincoln, S. (2012) *Youth Culture and Private Space*. Basingstoke: Palgrave Macmillan.

Lomax, H. (2012) 'Shifting the Focus: Children's Image-Making Practices and their Implications for Analysis', *International Journal of Research and Method in Education* (Special Issue: Problematising Visual Methods), 35 (3): 227–34.

Lomax, H. (2013) 'Troubled Talk and Talk about Troubles: Moral Cultures of Infant Feeding in Professional, Policy and Parenting Discourses' in J. Ribbens McCarthy, C.A. Hooper and V. Gillies (eds) *Family Troubles? Exploring Changes and Challenges in the Family Lives of Children and Young People*, pp. 97–106. Bristol: Policy Press.

Lomax, H. and Fink, J. (2014) 'Challenging Images? Dominant, Residual and Emergent Meanings in On-line Media Representations of Child Poverty', *Journal for the Study of British Cultures*, 21 (1): 79–95.

Lowenfeld, M. (1939) 'The World Pictures of Children', *British Journal of Medical Psychology*, 18: 65–101.

Luttrell, W. and Chalfen, R. (2010) 'Lifting up the Voices of Participatory Research', *Visual Studies*, 25 (3): 197–200.

Mannay, D. (2010) 'Making the Familiar Strange: Can Visual Research Methods Render the Familiar Setting more Perceptible?', *Qualitative Research*, 10 (1): 91–111.

Mannay, D. (2012) *Mothers and Daughters on the Margins: Gender, Generation and Education*. PhD Thesis, Cardiff University.

Mannay. D. (2013a) '"Who put that on there … why why why?" Power Games and Participatory Techniques of Visual Data Production', *Visual Studies*, 28 (2): 136–46.

Mannay, D. (2013b) '"Keeping Close and Spoiling" Revisited: Exploring the Significance of "Home" for Family Relationships and Educational Trajectories in a Marginalised Estate in Urban South Wales', *Gender and Education*, 25 (1): 91–107.

Mannay. D. (2014a) 'Mother and Daughter "Homebirds" and Possible Selves: Generational (Dis)connections to Locality and Spatial Identity in South Wales', in N. Worth and R. Vanderbeck (eds) *Intergenerational Space. Routledge Studies in Human Geography*. London: Routledge.

Mannay, D. (2014b) 'Story Telling Beyond the Academy: Exploring Roles, Responsibilities and Regulations in the Open Access Dissemination of Research Outputs and Visual Data', *The Journal of Corporate Citizenship*, 54: 109–16.

Mannay, D. and Edwards, V. (2013) 'It's Written in the Sand: Employing Sandboxing to Explore the Experiences of Non-traditional, Mature Students in Higher Education'. Presented at: *Society for Research into Higher Education (SRHE) Annual Research Conference 2013*, Celtic Manor, Newport, Wales, UK, 11–13 December 2013.

Mannay, D. and Edwards, V. (2014) 'Coffee, Milk and a Sprinkling of Sand: An Initiative to Assist Non-traditional, Mature Students form Supportive Networks in Higher Education'. Presented at: *2014 FACE Annual Conference*, Salford University, Salford, UK, 2–4 July 2014.

Mannay, D. and Morgan, M. (2015) 'Doing Ethnography or Applying a Qualitative Technique?: Reflections from the "Waiting Field"', *Qualitative Research*, 15 (2): 166–82.

Mannay, D., Grant, A. and Marzella, R. (2014) 'Motherhood, Morality and Infant Feeding'. Presented at: *MeSC – Medicine, Science and Culture Event*, Cardiff University, Cardiff, Wales, UK, 15 October 2014.

Massey, D. (1994) *Class, Place and Gender*. Cambridge: Polity Press.

Mills, D. and Ratcliffe, R. (2012) 'After Method? Ethnography in the Knowledge Economy', *Qualitative Research*, 12 (2): 147–64.

Orsini-Jones, M. (2010) 'Shared Spaces and "Secret Gardens": the Troublesome Journey from Undergraduate Students to Undergraduate Scholars via PebblePad', in J. O'Donoghue (ed.) *Technology Supported Environment for Personalised Learning: Methods and Case Studies*, pp. 341–63. Hershey, PA: IGI Global.

Packard, J. (2008) 'I'm Gonna Show you what it's Really Like out Here: The Power and Limitation of Participatory Visual Methods', *Visual Studies*, 23 (1): 63–76.

Pauwels, L. (2011) 'An Integrated Conceptual Framework for Visual Social Research', in E. Margolis and L. Pauwels (eds) *The Sage Handbook of Visual Research Methods*, pp. 3–23. London: Sage.

Pink, S. (2009) *Doing Sensory Ethnography*. London: Sage.

Poulos, C. N. (2010) 'Transgressions', *International Review of Qualitative Research*, 3 (1): 67–88.

Renold, E. (2005) *Girls, Boys and Junior Sexualities: Exploring Childrens' Gender and Sexual Relations in the Primary School*. London: RoutledgeFalmer.

Rogoff, B. (2008) 'Observing Sociocultural Activity on Three Planes: Participatory Appropriation, Guided Participation, and Apprenticeship', in K. Hall, P. Murphy and J. Soler (eds) *Pedagogy and Practice: Culture and Identities*. London: Sage.

Roth, W. M. (2009) 'Auto/ethnography and the Question of Ethics', *Forum: Qualitative Sozialforschung/Forum: Qualitative Social Research*, 10 (1). Available at: http://nbn-resolving. de/urn:nbn:de:0114-fqs0901381 (Accessed 19 August 2015).

Salazar, N. B. and Rivoal, I. (2013) 'Contemporary Ethnographic Practice and the Value of Serendipity', *Social Anthropology*, 21 (2): 178–85.

Schommer-Aikins, M. (2004) 'Explaining the Epistemological Belief System: Introducing the Embedded Systemic Model and Coordinated Research Approach', *Educational Psychologist*, 39 (1): 19–29.

Sherman Heyl, B. (2007) 'Ethnographic Interviewing', in P. Atkinson, A. Coffey, S. Delamont, J. Lofland and L. Lofland (eds) *Handbook of Ethnography*, pp. 369–83. London: Sage.

Sweetman, P. (2009) 'Just Anybody? Images, Ethics and Recognition', in J. Gillett (ed.) *Just Anybody*, pp. 7–9. University of Southampton: The Winchester Gallery.

Taber, N. (2010) 'Institutional Ethnography, Autoethnography, and Narrative: an Argument for Incorporating Multiple Methodologies', *Qualitative Research*, 10 (5): 5–25.

Turgo, N. N. (2012) 'A "Balikbayan" in the Field: Scaling and (Re)producing Insider's Identity in a Philippine Fishing Community', *Qualitative Research*, 12 (6): 666–85.

Tyler, I. (2008) 'Chav Mum Chav Scum', *Feminist Media Studies*, 8 (1): 17–34.

van Dijck, J. (2014) 'Flickr: Photo Sharing Sites between Collective and Connective Memory', in O. Shevchenko (ed.) *Double Exposure: Memory and Photography*, pp. 211–31. London: Transaction.

Van Maanen, J. (2009) 'Ethnography Then and Now', *Qualitative Research in Organizations and Management: An International Journal*, 1 (1): 13–21.

Wagner, J. (2007) 'Observing Culture and Social Life', in G. C. Stanczak (ed.) *Visual Research Methods: Image, Society and Representation*, pp. 23–59. London: Sage.

Wall, K., Hall, E. and Woolner, P. (2012) 'Visual Methodology: Previously, Now and in the Future', *International Journal of Research and Method in Education* (Special Issue: Problematising Visual Methods), 35 (3): 223–6.

Wiles, R., Clark, A. and Prosser, J. (2011) 'Visual Research Ethics at the Crossroads', in E. Margolis and L. Pauwels (eds) *The Sage Handbook of Visual Research Methods*, pp. 685–706. London: Sage.

World Health Organisation (2014) *Comprehensive Implementation Plan on Maternal, Infant and Young Child Nutrition*. Switzerland: World Health Organisation.

# 7

# ETHICAL CONCERNS

## Answers to questions we did not want to ask

## Introduction

The difficulties of anonymising place and person are complex even when research data is collected without the facet of visual imagery as illustrated by the cautionary tale of Vidich and Bensman's (1958) study 'Small Town in Mass Society'. The publication of the study was met with an angry response from the participants who could recognise themselves and others in the research despite the use of obligatory pseudonyms (Clarke 2006); and these problems still have resonance in contemporary social research.

The visual offers a range of exciting possibilities for social research but it also brings an array of challenges and ethical difficulties. Visual ethics can now be regarded as a specialist area within visual methodologies (Mitchell 2011) and the attractiveness of the visual has moved to a post-popular juncture where researchers and practitioners are discussing the limitations of participatory visual methods (Packard 2008); and critiquing the related philosophies, ethics and methodologies in special issues such as the *International Journal of Research and Method in Education* recent edition '*Problematising Visual Methods*' (Lomax 2012; Wall *et al.* 2012).

Much mainstream engagement with the ethics of visual ethnography focuses on issues of anonymity of place and participants so that the focus is on who is taking the picture, who is in the picture; and what else can be known from the geography or materiality of the image. Thus, the 'moral maze of image ethics' (Prosser 2000) has been centrally concerned with the creator of images in relation to informed consent and the tension between revealing and concealing the contents of visual images (Cox *et al.* 2014; Lomax *et al.* 2011; Renold *et al.* 2008; Wiles *et al.* 2008); and who has 'the right' to claim ownership of images to in turn edit their content and show them to others (Lomax 2015).

However, despite the increased use of visual techniques and the accompanying interest in visual ethics, the ethical guidelines available for researchers do not always provide sufficient reference to the creation and use of imagery; and the key issues of informed consent, confidentiality and ownership (Cox *et al.* 2014). Payne (1996, p. 19) argues that 'humans see as well as hear and think. If the locality is relevant, then it is even more important than in other walks of sociology to *see* what it looks like' [author's own emphasis]. Although I appreciate Payne's position, the visual image is a powerful medium of communication and including photographs of participants homes, schools, streets and families in a publication would require far more of the researcher than a mere change of name.

As Sweetman (2009) argues, in visual research, anonymity and confidentiality are almost impossible to guarantee. Consequently, there have been calls for informed consent to be reconceptualised as something that is not fixed but fluid so that the use of images and interview data is continually negotiated with research participants (Cox *et al.* 2014); such participatory practice aims to rebalance the issue of unequal power in the research relationship (Wiles *et al.* 2008). However, once a visual image is created it becomes very difficult to control its use or remove it from the public arena if participants decide that they no longer want to be represented in a fixed visual trope for 'time immemorial' (Brady and Brown 2013, p. 102).

Even if images are successfully anonymised, acts to disguise images can be seen as tantamount to silencing the voice of research participants. This is particularly problematic where researchers invest in the epistemological aims of participatory approaches predicated on giving 'voice' (Kallio 2008; Thompson 2008). In contrast to an emphasis on 'protection' through anonymisation, Sweetman's (2009) 'politics of recognition', argues that collaborative projects in which participants are visible and recognisable is an alternative approach to ethical social research. Nevertheless, some participants may want some level of anonymity, and some topics may be particularly sensitive (Lomax 2015); and in such cases being visible and recognisable may not be practical, possible or ethical. These discourses around the ethics of visibility and invisibility, have led to an impasse or 'crossroads' in visual research whereby researchers are increasingly troubled by their ethical and moral obligations as visual researchers (Wiles *et al.* 2011).

In response, this chapter focuses on the potentialities and challenges associated with visual methodologies, dealing with some of the common issues associated with the use of visual images such as the use of photographs in conferences presentations and papers, and issues of recognition, confidentiality and anonymity. However, these issue have been widely discussed across academic disciplines and for this reason the main focus of the chapter will be on the neglected area of the unforeseen consequences of visual and narrative data production. Engaging in creative representations of their lives often engenders a reflective and emotional response in participants. In this way, their response to visual and narrative methods of data production can move away from the initial remit of the research and can open up sensitive areas of discussion such as domestic violence or child abuse.

Arguably, this is a feature of qualitative research in general (Gabb 2008), but the chapter argues that researchers applying visual and narrative methodologies need to be particularly sensitive to the affective impacts of their work, as artistic creation can be experienced an emotive process; engendering wider ethical concerns. Such accounts can problematised in relation to the ethics of visibility, and the need to explore creative ways to communicate the meanings of visual images without pictures. The chapter discusses the ways in which creative forms of writing, such as theatre and poetry, can be used to offer participants' accounts further de-contextualisation and anonymity, but can, at the same time, be applied to a form that can increase understanding and motivate and compel the viewer to take action against injustice. Importantly, the chapter also moves beyond the focus on partici-pant and researcher to consider the neglected area of those who are not in the picture, both in the respect that they do not form part of the research imagery (or can be easily deleted) and because of the point that they remain unaware that they have become part of the data set.

## Pandora's memories

As Gabb (2008) argues, in empirical qualitative studies of family life, the researcher inevitably becomes embedded in the personal worlds of those being researched; and within these personal worlds the future is often haunted by phantoms of the past, which impact upon the present (de Beauvoir 1949). These concerns can be accentuated when visual techniques of data production are centralised in ethno-graphic approaches; as the act of creating a visual image engenders techniques of 'defamiliarization' (Gurevitch 1998). As discussed in Chapter 3, a strength of visual and creative methods is they can be an element that can overcome the confines of language and open up experience. However, importantly, in this process of defamil-iarisation participants, and indeed researchers, may be confronted with elements of their lives that they manage to defend from consciousness in their everyday existence.

Accessing 'what lies beneath' is a central tenet of Hollway and Jefferson's (2000) Free Association Narrative Interview technique, in which there is a remit to secure access to concerns not visible in traditional interviewing; and elicit unconscious logic not conscious logic and emotional motivations not rational intentions. I have drawn on psychosocial analysis in previous work (Mannay 2013a) and I would argue that this psychoanalytically informed psychosocial approach can be linked with visual and creative data production as such techniques can engender processes of creative free association and generate an engagement with unconscious conflict.

There are strong objections to taking the tools of psychoanalysis, such as free association, outside of the clinical situation of the 'consulting room' (Frosh 2010; Frosh and Emerson 2005). However, in their more recent work, Hollway and Jefferson (2013) refute such challenges and argue that their work is psychoanalyti-cally informed rather than psychoanalytical; and that there are similarities with qualitative research interviewing, which is characterised by a largely uninterrupted flow of talk with an attentive listener whose role it is to try and understand what is being said. Such techniques then can be seen as effective but there remain ethical considerations that engender a level of reflexivity.

Creating visual data can be accompanied by both defamiliarisation (Gurevitch 1998), where participants slow down and re-evaluate their lives, and a form of free association where unconscious content is triggered; in this way visual creativity contributes to a 'slow science', which engenders flexibility and serendipity (Rivoal and Salazar 2013). Returning to the discussions in Chapter 3, this opens up opportunities to make 'the familiar strange and interesting again' (Vrasidas 2001, p. 81) for both researcher and researched. For example, as discussed in Chapter 5, when Tina reflects on her drawing in Figure 5.1 (see page 66), she tells me how drawing her two daughters acted to clarify aspects of the maternal relationship; and that she had not fully realised the imbalance in the family dynamic until drawing her pictures. Such discoveries of self were common across participants' accounts (Mannay 2010) and they illustrate the ways in which creative methods open up new ideas and realisations for participants.

Importantly, the nature of such creative work not only engendered a reflection on neglected aspects of the present but was also linked to Henriques et al.'s (1998) contention that the question of who we are is tied to the memory of who we have been and the imagination of what we might become. In my work with mothers, such creative engagement surfaced memory work that was often characterised by experiences of domestic and familial violence and abuse (Mannay 2011, 2013b). As Gabb (2010, p. 461) contends, 'unsettling stories on emotional social worlds redefine our understandings of harm and distress and reconfigure ideas of responsible knowing'; therefore, there is an important responsibility to connect wider audiences with the emotional weight of empirical evidence in such recollections. However, the ways in which these connections are made should always be based on a reflexive engagement with the ethics of representation and the potential, ongoing impacts of visual images.

## Ethical dissemination

Brannan et al. (2007, p. 401) argue that 'ethnography can place researchers in a position to affect change within their fields of enquiry' for this reason, as researchers we need to disseminate our findings in ways that not only contribute to policy debates, offer innovative methodological techniques and further theoretical dialogue, but also connect with readers at an affective level. The visual can be an effective vehicle for accessing emotion and disseminating the power of participants' accounts. In this way, a 'politics of recognition' (Sweetman 2009) may well engender more impact.

For example, Sweetman and Hensser's (2010) project, *City Portraits*, worked with residents of Southampton and represented the participants in life-sized images in a street-based exhibition. Participants reported that the project fostered a sense of belonging and community involvement; and the act of being seen was regarded by many participants as a transforming process that provided pleasure in seeing the photograph, a new perception of self, the seizing of opportunities and the affirmation of greater ownership of Southampton. For Sweetman and Hensser (2010) a preoccupation with anonymity acts as a resistance to discourses of participant visibility, but, as their project testifies, visibility can engender a potential for advantage.

A 'politics of recognition' (Sweetman 2009) was also engendered in the work of Brady and Brown (2013, p. 99) who attempted to move beyond the pervasive political discourse, which 'authoritatively places teenage parents' experiences outside of the norm, constructing teenage pregnancy as negative for young women, their children and wider society'. Brady and Brown (2013) worked with young mothers to produce visual resources including storyboards, story booklets and film, featuring young mothers and their children, which served to challenge this dominant discourse. As Wiles *et al.* (2008) argue, the concept of anonymity is complicated further by the fact that individuals commonly to want to be identified in their visual images and participants in this study wanted to be both active and visible in reframing discourses of young parenthood.

The visual is a powerful way to question dominant, essentialising stereotypes (Fink and Lomax 2011). In Brady and Brown's work these visual resources have been used in training and cascaded to health and social care professionals to provide a more holistic picture of the lives of young parents, which have influenced positive changes in professional practice. Overall, the creative and visual-based methods created a space for young women to offer alternative narratives, generating different kinds of talk. The techniques also encouraged participation; and importantly they influenced changes in public policy and professional practice. The success of these projects of visibility, suggest that one answer to the 'crossroads' in visual research (Wiles *et al.* 2011) could be to follow an approach now favoured by some researchers, such as Back (2004), who present visual data and text in its entirety with consent based on the premise that data will not be anonymised.

However, despite the impact of the project and the participants' desire to be recognised, this 'politics of recognition' (Sweetman 2009) is further complicated by the problematic nature of 'time immemorial' (Brady and Brown 2013, p. 102). Reflecting on their projects, spanning over a decade of research and development projects with pregnant teenagers and young mothers, Brady and Brown have become increasingly concerned about the ongoing impact of images of mothers and their children placed in the public domain.

In participatory visual approaches, it is important 'to talk about what has worked well, where we have not been so successful and where hindsight has afforded the opportunity to reflect' (Brady and Brown 2013, p. 100). In their reflection, Brady and Brown (2013) focus on the ethical handling of project outputs and their use and availability beyond the lifetime of the study. Focusing on the 'time immemorial' they explore how a 'teenage parent' will not remain a 'teenage parent' but that in assigning a fixed identity to the young mothers who have worked alongside the researchers to produce these visual materials they remain attached to this discourse. Importantly, methods which serve to capture personal images, artefacts, art work, video footage and visual stories will fix the participants within these creations for time immemorial. Therefore, even where participants want to be recognised and attached to research projects (Wiles *et al.* 2008), their decision is based in the present. Researchers can rethink informed consent as ongoing and negotiated rather than fixed, but it is not possible to undo or take back images once they enter the public realm.

Consequently, where topics are particularly sensitive and where visual images act to represent, and fix, participants for 'time immemorial' (Brady and Brown 2013, p. 102), researchers need to think carefully about whether this recognition is ethical, both in the moment and beyond the lifetime of the study. When considering the ethics of recognition it is also important to think about the intended audiences and how they will interpret the presentation of other people's lives. This can be difficult where participatory principles encourage researchers to 'give voice' and control to young people who may not always appreciate the role, and judgements, of an unseen and unknown audience. This raises contradictions about the role of the researcher in the production of knowledge and whether participatory projects should simply be concerned with 'giving voice' or if they need to consider how these voices will be received and who will listen.

This problem is discussed by Lomax (2015) in relation to her work with children creating participatory videos where the children themselves acted as editors to select the content for a presentation of the film. Lomax (2015) had envisaged a short but impactful segment of film, cinematically capturing the importance of arts and community projects; however, the children in the study had other ideas, insisting that the sequence be included in its original unedited form to recognise their individual contributions, as artists and narrators. The editing process was guided by the participants and prioritised the individual children's voices. However, this participatory undertaking was antithetical to the dialogue that the researcher was attempting to disseminate. In this way, simply enabling 'voice' without paying sufficient attention to how voices may (or may not) be heard, may diminish the efficacy of the message. This example further suggests the need to think carefully about how to balance voice and what is being heard, its 'audiencing' (Lomax and Fink 2010) and researchers' responsibilities to their participants but also the wider communities with whom they work.

Arguably, the problematic nature of ethical presentation and the visual is intensified by the move toward Open Access publication and the archiving of data sets. The Berlin Declaration on Open Access to Knowledge in the Sciences and Humanities (2003) set out a vision of a global and accessible representation of knowledge. This vision was to be facilitated by encouraging researchers and grant recipients to support Open Access by providing their resources on the internet according to the principles of the Open Access paradigm. By 2006 there were 77 Open Access UK-based archives and several of the UK Research Councils required their grant-holders to deposit a copy of any publications resulting from the research they fund in an appropriate Open Access repository as soon as possible after publication (Hassen 2006).

More recently, the Research Councils UK *Policy on Access to Research* (2012) has provided a set of Open Access requirements for all outputs published after 1 April 2013, although it suggested that earlier compliance was preferable. The policy also discusses extending existing mechanisms to include compliance monitoring for this policy as well as to track the shift to Open Access and the anticipated changes for the wider academic and political community. In this way, compliance with unrestricted, online access to peer-reviewed and published scholarly research papers becomes a proviso of securing research funding, and this is to be extended to data sets. The Open

Access argument is presented as an ethical one: all knowledge should be freely available to everybody. This view, often phrased in all-or-nothing idealistic terms, has been taken up by governments with the added argument that publicly funded work should be available to any interested reader, anywhere (Wickham and Vincent 2013).

The ethos of Open Access is appealing; however, institutional interpretations of the Open Access movement can inadvertently act to close down the opportunity for ongoing and evolving ethical relationship between researchers and the researched that has been positioned as the gold standard in visual research (Cox *et al.* 2014). This is particularly problematic when researchers themselves are unsure about how the openness of an online repository will not only disseminate but also reformulate their original work. For example, the thesis publication form provided for submission of my earlier research (Mannay 2012) states 'Cardiff University is not under any obligation to reproduce or display the Work in the same formats or resolutions in which it was originally deposited' (Cardiff University 2013).

Therefore, in the institutional regulations the initial reformat, followed by further use of the image, perhaps de-contextualised from the accompanying text, raises additional issues of representation. The issue of (mis)representation can be seen commonly in media images (Wright 2011; Fink and Lomax 2014) and as Sontag (1977, p. 4) contends, 'Photographs that fiddle with the scale of the world, themselves get reduced, blown up, cropped, retouched, doctored, tricked out'. Thus, images are reinvented and mediate new messages depending on context and it is this reinvention and the mediating of new messages that can become problematic when applied to exploring visual productions in qualitative research.

Open Access can act to threaten images produced in visual fieldwork, which can then be shaded, cropped and perhaps be employed by an individual accessing this data to represent a stereotype of particular places, people or groups, in ways that no longer represent the original creation. Importantly, the fragmentation and misquoting of textual information is also something that requires consideration. In relation to my doctoral work (Mannay 2012), I was able to resist the archiving of participants' images in a digital repository by arguing that the process of participant consent did not allow for this form of digital storage (see Mannay 2014a). However, the momentum for Open Access is building and researchers are expected to embrace shared ownership of data sets with invisible others who can download, consume, rework, edit and disseminate new versions of images and text that may be unrecognisable as, and antithetical to, the original study and its purpose. Electronic digital storage systems then enable the reuse of primary research data by others not involved in the original data-generation activities; however, as Dicks (2012) contends, since qualitative data, unlike many forms of quantitative data, are heavily contextual and contingent, questions have been raised as to whether reuse is appropriate or ethical.

## Creative dissemination

In light of the points raised in the previous section, it is evident that the responsibility of maintaining participant confidentiality must remain central when researchers are working with 'unsettling stories on emotional social worlds' (Gabb 2010, p. 461); and this can mean that the visual materials, narratives and interview accounts are not appropriate forms of dissemination. 'Time immemorial' (Brady and Brown, 2013, p. 102) reminds us of the afterlife of images and the ways in which even though participants may want their images and accounts to be shared at the point of the research, in the following years and decades they may not want to be forever associated with a particular representation in future 'audiencing' (Lomax and Fink 2010): a point accentuated in relation to the move towards Open Access archiving and publication. In response to these issues, researchers have been interested in finding new ways to communicate the findings of their research without visual images of textual references that could compromise their relationships with participants, while still retaining the impact of these accounts.

Leavy argues that 'perhaps more than anything else, performance-based methods can bring research findings to life, adding dimensionality and exposing that which is otherwise impossible to authentically (re)present' (2009, p. 135). However, research inquiry is always a moral enterprise and when we apply qualitative methods ethical issues can be amplified not least because the researcher is delving into people's private lives with the intention of placing a version of these accounts in a public arena (Kvale and Brinkman 2009). Therefore, when considering performance-based methods it is important to explore the ways in which authentic representation can employ 'theatre as a safe space' (Richardson 2015a) and to what extent the artist or performer can effectively (re)present the accounts of participants who engaged with research projects to have 'their story' heard.

Chapter 3 introduced the work of Richardson (2015b) who worked with thirty-eight men from Tyneside, in the North East of England, across three generations within nineteen families of Irish descent to explore the concepts of masculinity, inter-generationality and place through interviews and drawings. Chapter 3 was interested in how the drawings completed in the project allowed Richardson and his participants to move beyond the everyday commonalities of their connections and acted to fight familiarity, engendering a space of defamiliarisation, where issues of identity, masculinity and emotion could be articulated in a form that moved beyond the purely verbal communication of the mundane. This chapter revisits Richardson's work to examine the ethical journey he negotiated in organising a theatre commission, which focused on taking the stories back to the participants they derived from 'beyond the confines of the 'Ivory Tower', outside the bounded walls of words in books and texts – and through spoken word and performance' (Richardson 2015a, p. 7).

Like many researchers employing narrative and visual approaches, when reflecting on his study Richardson (2015a) was concerned with how the issue of anonymity creates tensions. Anonymity can make participants feel uncomfortable, there can be less accountability from the researcher; and the possibilities for exploitation are arguably greater with less transparent ties to the participant. However, anonymity may also be a necessary, important and essential component of social science research. In thinking through these debates, Richardson began to question the ability of traditional academic dissemination as a mode of ethical representation;

and Mattingly's (2001, p. 449) argument that theatre offers possibilities for transcending the representational limits of academic discourse by both offering subjects more authority over the representation of their voices and speaking to audiences outside of academia.

The play, developed by Richardson, was named *Under Us All*, which reflected the common ground participants' stories shared with respect to issues of ageing, identity and belonging. The play was envisaged as part of the geography's cultural turn, in which 'a form of place-based performance and public engagement storytelling is being deployed as a practice to propel cross-generational interest in local, community-centred initiatives' (Daniels and Lorimer 2012, p. 5). The play built on the stories and testimonies of three of the participants, exploring the ways in which notions of masculinity, Irishness, religion, family, health, music, life and death have changed and shifted over the years and from individual to individual.

In line with the ethical guidelines around confidentiality and anonymity, Richardson employed fictional names for these three men, Victor, Peter and Simon. However, importantly the verbatim nature of the play meant that their stories were derived from the exact words generated in the interviews, *Under Us All* was 'word for word'. Richardson (2015a) argues that verbatim theatre can do different things with narratives than is possible within academic journal articles and books. Participants were partners in the co-creation of the play and although they were not actors themselves, they provided input to the script during the creative process.

Prior to the debut performance of *Under Us All*, Richardson invited research participants to a 'behind closed doors' run through of the play. At this debut and throughout the process, the participants had been encouraged to comment on aspects of the script; and they did with some changes being made in response. This ongoing collaborative is rarely featured in traditional academic publications and the play engendered a political stance in that 'it seeks to work collaboratively with the public, to provide a catalyst for social change, and to give voice to those silenced and marginalised by mainstream public culture' (Mattingly 2001, p. 450).

In reflecting on the research journey of this study, Richardson (2015a) suggests that in conducting research ethically we need to move beyond prescriptive notions of anonymity in striving towards participant 'protection'. Rather, he calls for the move towards research reciprocity and argues that while anonymity remains an important, and essential, component of social science research, the rationale behind this participant protection should be revised. For Richardson (2015a, p. 15), 'to simply change the names of people and places does not do justice to the involvement of those we work with'. The pursuit of different forms of dissemination, such as the verbatim theatre *Under Us All*, can, however, help to voice participant stories by recognising their narrative authority while at the same time addressing ethical concerns around maintaining confidentiality.

The tensions between anonymity and ethical, but impactful, dissemination were also an evolving issue of concern in my own research projects; this was particularly salient in respect of accounts that raised sensitive issues such as domestic abuse, child neglect and familial violence. Violence was not my initial research focus; nonetheless, as Rock (2007, p. 30) contends, there is a 'need to remain open to the features that cannot be listed in advance of the study', and this family trouble was an invasive element in the construction of femininity (see Mannay 2013b). If we consider visual methods of data production as both techniques of defamiliarisation and tools of free association then we must also realise that they may act to unlock Pandora's memories. In response, as researchers, we must be ready to meet the challenge of hearing unsettling stories and to negotiate landscapes of trust and confidentiality; while still communicating the salience of participants' accounts, which may well mean making the visual invisible but instead employing creative forms of dissemination to retain affective engagement.

As outlined in earlier chapters, in the *Mother and Daughters on the Margins* project, I had drawn on the concept of 'possible selves' (Markus and Nurius 1986; Lobenstine *et al.* 2004; King and Hicks 2007; Casey 2008; Susinos *et al.* 2009). Participants were asked to produce narratives from the retrospective perspective of their childhood self, describing who they wanted to become (positive possible self) and who they feared becoming (negative possible self), and this activity was repeated from the perspective of the present. These narratives often explored the centrality of 'trouble' in family life and the ways in which family troubles are both normalised and pathologised.

The traditional academic format has been a useful platform from which to communicate my research findings; not least in terms of the darker side of family life (Mannay 2013b). Nevertheless, it remains important to act, react and enact, in our writing, teaching and the everyday conversations and actions with others, disseminating in a wider sense, to engender channels through which change becomes possible; at the same time retaining the anonymity of participants and respecting their narrative authorship. Consequently, I have explored the fields of alternative presentation; mediating vigorous research through a creative format to increase impact yet engender some level of protection.

There were life stories produced in the participants' narratives that were important to tell but also complicated by their detail and, as the research was intergenerational, the connections and relationships between mothers and their daughters. The narratives demonstrated the subtle ways in which violence actively contributes to the real and symbolic subordination of women and girls, and often clouds new horizons across the life course. In this way, individual biographies can be useful to examine the ways in which women negotiate the darker side of family life, but this level of contextualisation and detail can also act as a mechanism of identification. For this reason, in presenting some of the themes from these narratives, and their accompanying interviews, I constructed a poem. The poem was constructed long after the interviews and in this way it was not a collaborative activity, rather, it is a poem that hopes to communicate the ways in which violence casts a shadow across future possibilities and ongoing familial relationships.

The excerpt below, is drawn from a poem published previously (see Mannay 2013c) and also read at different conferences, workshops and community-based events, which conveys some of the emotion communicated by participants and their experiences and feelings around being both trapped and silenced by the men in their lives. The poem is an edited version of the possible selves and interview data but one that attempts to communicate the experience of the participants, drawing on their writing and dialogue, while at the same time freeing their accounts from the contextuality that would act to reveal their identities.

*I like rough pubs*
*Words do not have to be measured*
*I have escaped from the waiting gaze on my face*
*I have escaped from the waiting game in this place*
*There will be no injury, no accusations, nothing to fear; here*
*I like rough pubs*

*I like rough pubs*
*The rules are easy to follow*
*Even the drunks have a certain predictability*
*And the toilets are safe; 'Ladies' with locks on doors*
*No one has ever punched my face; when sat and trapped*
*I like rough pubs* (Mannay 2013c)

It is difficult to get a sense of the whole poem from a short extract and there are issues of ownership and voice as participants were not partners in the co-creation of the poem. Nevertheless, this form of dissemination can be positioned as a move towards research reciprocity (Richardson 2015a) in that the poem has acted to engage with audiences beyond the space of academia, engage audiences at an affective level; and raise the issues presented by participants in a manner that does not complicate the requirements of confidentiality. As discussed in the opening sections, visual images can be particularly problematic in relation to the ethics of representation (Mannay 2014a; Brady and Brown 2013); and I have also employed poetic forms to disseminate participants' accounts around the images created in research fieldwork. For example, the following extract is taken from a poem created from the exact words generated in photo-elicitation interviews, with one participant from the *Mothers and Daughters on the Margins* study, Nina.

*I lost the baby, and I was only a couple of months pregnant and, and I lost the baby*
*I just didn't want to marry him*
*I just felt*
*It's too soon*
*The baby was gone*
*We were only doing it to please my father*
*I lost the baby, and I can remember being on the phone to my Dad*
*He said well I've put the hundred pound on the reception*
*I can remember feeling gutted*
*I thought I can't let him down for hundred quid*
*I married him*

*I got Roxanne out of it, that's right,*
*But I can always remember thinking*
*I was so upset*
*Thinking well my Dad's put hundred pound down*
*Hundred pounds in those days was a lot of money*
*Hundred pounds*

*Well really he should never have said it*
*And I could have made my own choice*
*My Dad could have hid it from me*
*And I think that's what he should have done*
*But as it was he made an issue of it*
*And I felt,*
*And I was emotional,*
*After losing the baby*
*I couldn't make my own choice* (Mannay 2014b)

The poem, in its entirety (see Mannay 2014b), was edited from the 'word for word', verbatim accounts from Nina's photographs, narratives and the accompanying interview dialogue. The editing process was undertaken by me; however, I was careful to retain the meaning while at the same time reflecting on issues of anonymity. In this way, the poem acts to disseminate Nina's story, as part of a decolonising methodology (Smith 1999), in an ethical form that retains her anonymity; while also retaining the affective power of the account: moving beyond the dense, dry, flat prose that form a 'linguistic armour' in much academic writing (Lerum 2001). I have engaged with alternative and experimental forms of dissemination, which attempt to retain the impact of participants' data without compromising their anonymity and this mode of representation is one form of alternative dissemination that researchers could consider.

In working with participants across the *Mothers and Daughters on the Margins* study, I was constantly reminded of the ways in which the immersion in the lives of others cannot be easily forgotten; rather, 'it engenders a sense of responsibility, to react, to act and to find a way for what has been shared to translate into something worthwhile' (Mannay 2013c, p. 134). As Mills and Ratcliffe (2012, p. 155) argue, the ethnographer should be 'encouraged to acknowledge the complexity and unpredictability of the research encounter' and to meet this challenge in ethically responsible ways. As the next section documents, such responsibilities lie beyond the immediacy of the research participants and it is important to consider individuals who enter the research data without knowledge, let alone the opportunity to agree to any nature of informed consent.

## The unseen voyeur

As the chapter has demonstrated, immediate concerns of anonymity and consent are a topic of continued debate in social research; however, they often fail to encompass a wider application that appreciates the position of research participants, the researcher, and that of individuals who are unaware that they are a focus of research. Lives are not lived in isolation and participants' accounts often include a range of characters who are enlisted in the staging of their life story. In the process of fieldwork, researchers are offered subjective perspectives of these other lives without their owners' informed consent; and this is particularly problematic when the researcher is indigenous and may know these 'unknowing others' (Mannay 2011).

Consequently, it is important to think about those who are not in the picture, both in the respect that they do not form part of the research imagery (or can be easily deleted) and because of the point that they remain unaware that they have become part of the data set. Richardson (2015a) recognises that issues of consent go beyond the research participants, arguing that even when participants' consent is readily given, their friends, family or indeed anyone who knows them may not give theirs. In this way, those connected to participants' accounts are not consulted, nor can they be, in the giving of individual consent. However, although Richardson acknowledges this difficulty, an appreciation of these un-consenting others is often absent from reflexive accounts of the research process.

To work towards addressing this absence, in previous work (Mannay 2011), I explored these ethical and affective elements of ethnographic research to encompass a wider consideration of informed consent. In this article, again I employed a poetic form, resonant of the work presented in the preceding section, to communicate a sense of the emotional cost of maintaining confidentiality and the disempowering force of surreptitious knowledge; acknowledging the problematic nature of unknowing others as relational, with impacts on the researcher and the unknowing 'researched'. Here, I will discuss these issues in more depth, in a more traditional academic format, but, as in the original article, I will draws on the analogy of the character Sampath Chawla, from Kiran Desai's novel *Hullabaloo in the Orchard Garden*.

Desai's (1998) fictional novel *Hullabaloo in the Orchard Garden* is a satire on provincial India featuring the story of Sampath Chawla. Desai presents Sampath as a disappointment to his family, who after losing his job at the local post office, runs away from home to take refuge in the branches of a guava tree. Initial interest from the town's residents is in Sampath, the man who has lost his mind and become a hermit. However, when Sampath, drawing from many idle hours at the post office illicitly reading other people's letters, reveals intimate secrets to his audience beneath the guava tree their perception is altered; Sampath is transformed into a holy man and a seer.

The writers of the letters are oblivious to his intrusion and the individuals discussed by the letter writers are perhaps unaware that their personal lives were ever the subject of a letter. In reading this novel, I immediately recognised an uneasy parallel between Sampath's misdemeanour and the data produced in my ethnographic research. Visual images are widely recognised as having the potential to evoke emphatic understanding of the ways in which other people experience their worlds (Belin 2005; Mizen 2005; Pink 2004; Rose 2010); and as discussed previously in the chapter, the creativity of art-based and narrative data production has the potential to open up experiences, offer new ways of knowing and make the familiar strange. However, images and the talk around the images are not simply representative of the individual participant, as through their stories researchers learn about the cast of participants' lives through many characters: sisters, brothers, fathers, mothers, lovers, enemies and friends.

The presence of non-consenting others in the visual image is often seen as technically unproblematic as they can be deleted, blacked out or fragmented through digital pixellation (Wiles 2013). However, as Rose (2010) argues, family photographs are rarely thrown away because they are a material trace of the person photographed; and in the same way non-consenting others who appear in visual images will leave a trace even if they are visually masked. Focusing on applying a visual technique can act to side-line the importance of ongoing traditional ethnographic and reflective engagement; however, shifting the focus will not overcome the problem and even when the associations are not visual in nature, detailed qualitative accounts produce detailed narratives of non-consenting others.

In my research, the unintended consequences of being privy to recollections which mapped out in detail the lives of non-consenting others characterised me so that 'I am Sampath Chawla' (Desai 1998). The nature of the creative process of visual and narrative data production had engaged participants on an affective level; and as Richardson (2005) argues, reflections on childhood experience can confront us with the past self, often painfully. My questions were never quite prepared for the answers; for the stories elicited by the visual projects that were shared featuring the villains of the plot who could not simply be pixellated out of the picture or erased from the biographical narrative – and during these interviews I often felt that 'I know too much' (Mannay 2011, p. 963).

The non-consenting others remain completely unaware that their personal lives were ever subject to such qualitative scrutiny; and this can be seen as unethical in itself. In writing up and presenting findings, researchers tell the stories of non-consenting others as told by the participants with no opportunity to consent, withdraw or contribute an alternative perspective. However, a further concern arises when researchers are indigenous or undertaking long-term ethnographic research within a small community. Unlike Sampath, who has the freedom to take refuge in the guava tree, researchers active in the field may meet storied individuals who are unaware the consequences of their past actions have been explored. In order to maintain the confidentiality of participants this knowledge must remain silenced; and the researcher must remain neutral and resist any desire to confront or question the non-consenting other.

As Denzin (2009) contends, inquiry is, at all times, political and moral; and as a researcher what I learnt acted to compromise my relationships with others in ways that I did not envisage at the beginning of the ethnographic journey. Knowledge is often conceptualised as power but in these circumstances it also becomes disempowering. Lives are never lived in isolation, for we are linked in a complex web of connections so that when we ask our consenting participants about their own lives we also learn about the lives of non-consenting others; this can be particularly difficult when creative techniques draw out defended memories into consciousness;

and also when ethnographers have prior and/or ongoing sets of wider relations within the field. It is also important to consider that when we make our participants visible, by publishing their visual images and detailed biographical accounts, we can also make their family, friends and the actual people who form the characters in their accounts visible through association.

## Concluding remarks

In the mediated world of contemporary academia, social scientists are invited to reinvent their methodological approaches, defying restrictive views on disciplinary boundaries and engaging with the 'latest and greatest' techniques. As Margolis and Pauwels (2011) contend, 'the future of visual research will depend on the continued effort to cross disciplinary boundaries and engage in a constructive dialogue with different schools of thought'; however, as researchers it is important to locate ourselves within longstanding research traditions so that we can benefit from this experience rather than re-learning old lessons, particularly in relation to the ethics of social science research. This book has demonstrated how working creatively can contributes to a 'slow science', which engenders flexibility and serendipity in the field (Rivoal and Salazar 2013); eliciting processes of free association, encouraging reflexivity and connecting with participants at the level of affect; however, these attributes act as both a strength and an ethical challenge in visual and creative studies.

The 'slow science' (Rivoal and Salazar 2013) of visual research can engender unsettling stories and facilitate a level of emotional access to participants' social worlds, which the researcher is not always adequately prepared to encounter (Mannay and Morgan 2015). For Rock (2007, p. 30) there is a 'need to remain open to the features that cannot be listed in advance of the study' and for Mills and Ratcliffe (2012, p. 155), researchers must 'acknowledge the complexity and unpredictability of the research encounter'. This is useful guidance for the researcher; and it remains essential to disseminate ethical learning journeys and be reflexive about our own and others' cautionary tales from the field. The chapter has demonstrated that, importantly, in relation to harm and distress, in both modes of data production and dissemination 'ideas of responsible knowing' (Gabb 2010, p. 461) must continually be centralised.

Reflecting on the ethnographic journeys presented in this chapter, in and beyond the field, visual and creative engagement can be advantageous yet also complex and challenging; and as Brannan et al. (2012, p .7) argue, critique is 'key to progressing the aims and promoting the merits of any research tradition'. Therefore, learning to work ethically is an ongoing process, no method is a panacea and we will not always foresee the unintended consequences of our fieldwork; but by accepting this we can refine our craft and move beyond the 'indignity of speaking for others' (Spencer 2011, p. 15) to working and speaking with our participants.

For these reasons, visual and creative researchers themselves need to remain ardent critics of the research process, to be aware of the possible difficulties, and to continue to explore landscapes of representation, interpretation, voice, trust, confidentiality, silence; and the intended and unintended consequences of research with narratives and visual images. It is also useful to consider the ways in which creative narrative forms can replace visual images and detailed, identifying, biographical accounts, yet still retain impact; and ethically, yet powerfully, communicate the stories that participants have shared in the research process. These tensions will be revisited in the following chapter, which summarises the main themes raised in the book and considers the future of visual and creative research.

# References

Back, L. (2004) 'Listening With our Eyes: Portraiture as Urban Encounter', in C. Knowles and P. Sweetman (eds) *Picturing the Social Landscape: Visual Methods and the Sociological Imagination*. London: Routledge.

Belin, R. (2005) 'Photo-elicitation and the Agricultural Landscape: "Seeing" and "Telling" about Farming, Community and Place', *Visual Studies*, 20 (1): 56–68.

Berlin Declaration on Open Access to Knowledge in the Sciences and Humanities (2003) Berlin 22 October 2003.

Brady, G. and Brown, G. (2013) 'Rewarding but Let's Talk About the Challenges: Using Arts Based Methods in Research with Young Mothers', *Methodological Innovations Online*, 8 (1): 99–112.

Brannan, M., Pearson, G. and Worthington, F. (2007) 'Ethnographies of Work and the Work of Ethnography', *Ethnography*, 8 (4): 395–402.

Brannan, M., Rowe, M. and Worthington, F. (2012) 'Editorial for the Journal of Organizational Ethnography: Time for a New Journal, a Journal for New Times', *Journal of Organizational Ethnography*, 1 (1): 5–14.

Cardiff University (2013) *Cardiff University Electronic Theses and Dissertations Publication Form*. Cardiff: Cardiff University.

Casey, E. (2008) 'Working Class Women, Gambling and the Dream of Happiness', *Feminist Review*, 89: 122–37.

Clarke, A. (2006) 'Anonymising Research Data'. ESRC National Centre for Research Methods NCRM Working Paper Series 7/06.

Cox, S., Drew, S., Guillemin, M., Howell, C., Warr, D. and Waycott, J. (2014) *Guidelines for Ethical Visual Research Methods*. The University of Melbourne: Melbourne.

de Beauvoir, S. (1949) *The Second Sex*. Penguin: London.

Daniels, S. and Lorimer, H. (2012) 'Until the End of Days: Narrating Landscape and Environment', *Cultural Geographies*, 19: 3–9.

Denzin, N. (2009) 'The Elephant in the Living Room: Or Extending the Conversation about the Politics of Evidence', *Qualitative Research*, 9 (2): 136–60.

Desai, K. (1998) *Hullabaloo in the Guava Orchard*. Faber and Faber: London.

Dicks, B. (2012) *Digital Qualitative Research Methods*. London: Sage.

Fink, J. and Lomax, H. (2011) 'Introduction: Inequalities, Images and Insights for Policy and Research', *Critical Social Policy*, 6 December 2011.

Fink, J. and Lomax, H. (2014) 'Challenging Images? Dominant, Residual and Emergent Meanings in On-line Media Representations of Child Poverty', *Journal for the Study of British Cultures*, 1 (21): 79–95.

Frosh, S. (2010) *Psychoanalysis Outside the Clinic: Interventions in Psychosocial Studies*. Macmillan: Basingstoke.

Frosh, S. and Emerson, P. (2005) 'Interpretation and Over-interpretation: Disrupting the Meaning of Texts', *Qualitative Research*, 5 (5): 307–24.

Gabb, J. (2008) *Researching Intimacy in Families*. Basingstoke: Palgrave Macmillan.

Gabb, J. (2010) 'Home Truths: Ethical Issues in Family Research', *Qualitative Research*, 10 (4): 461–78.

Gurevitch, Z. D. (1998) 'The Other Side of Dialogue: On Making the Other Strange and the Experience of Otherness', *American Journal of Sociology*, 93 (5): 1179–99.

Hassen, S. (ed.) (2006) *Open Access: JISC Briefing Paper*. JISC: London.

Henriques, J., Holloway, W., Urwin, C., Venn, C. and Walkerdine, V. (1998) *Changing the Subject*. Routledge: London.

Hollway, W. and Jefferson, T. (2000) *Doing Qualitative Research Differently*. Sage: London.

Hollway, W. and Jefferson, T. (2013) *Doing Qualitative Research Differently* (2nd edn). Sage: London.

Kallio, K.P. (2008) 'The Body as a Battlefield: Approaching Children's Politics', *Geografiska Annaler/Human Geography*, 90 (3): 285–97.

King, L. A. and Hicks, J. A. (2007) 'Lost and Found Possible Selves: Goals, Development and Well-being', *New Directions for Adult and Continuing Education*, 114: 27–37.

Kvale, S. and Brinkman, S. (2009) *Learning the Craft of Qualitative Research Interviewing* (2nd edn). London: Sage.

Leavy, P. (2009) *Method Meets Art: Arts-based Research Practices*. New York, NY: The Guildford Press.

Lerum, K. (2001) 'Subjects of Desire: Academic Armor, Intimate Ethnography and the Production of Critical Knowledge', *Qualitative Inquiry*, 7 (4): 466–83.

Lobenstine, L., Pereira, Y., Whitley, J., Robles, J., Soto, Y., Sergeant, J., Jimenez. D., Jimenez, E., Ortiz, J. and Cirino, S. (2004) 'Possible Selves and Pastels: How a Group of Mothers and Daughters took a London conference by Storm', in A. Harris (ed.) *All About the Girl: Culture, Power, and Identity*, pp. 255–64. New York: Routledge.

Lomax. H. (2012) 'Shifting the Focus: Children's Image-making Practices and their Implications for Analysis', *International Journal of Research & Method in Education* 35 (3): 227–234.

Lomax, H. (2015) (forthcoming) 'Seen and Heard? Ethics and Agency in Participatory Visual Research with Children, Young People and Families', *Families, Relationships and Societies*.

Lomax, H. and Fink, J. (2010) 'Interpreting Images of Motherhood: The Contexts and Dynamics of Collective Viewing', *Sociological Research Online*, 15 (3).

Lomax, H., Fink, J., Singh, N and High, C. (2011) 'The Politics of Performance: Methodological Challenges of Researching Children's Experiences of Childhood through the Lens of Participatory Video', *International Journal of Social Research Methodology*, 14 (3): 231–43.

Mannay, D. (2010) 'Making the Familiar Strange: Can Visual Research Methods Render the Familiar Setting more Perceptible?', *Qualitative Research*, 10 (1): 91–111.

Mannay, D. (2011) 'Taking Refuge in the Branches of a Guava Tree: The Difficulty of Retaining Consenting and Non-consenting Participants' Confidentiality as an Indigenous Researcher', *Qualitative Inquiry*, 17 (10): 962–4.

Mannay, D. (2012) *Mothers and Daughters on the Margins: Gender, Generation and Education*. PhD Thesis, Cardiff University.

Mannay, D. (2013a) '"Keeping Close and Spoiling" Revisited: Exploring the Significance of "Home" for Family Relationships and Educational Trajectories in a Marginalised Estate in Urban South Wales', *Gender and Education*, 25 (1): 91–107.

Mannay, D. (2013b) 'The Permeating Presence of Past Domestic and Familial Violence: So Like I'd Never Let Anyone Hit me but I've Hit them, and I Shouldn't have Done' in J. Ribbens McCarthy, C. Hooper and V. Gillies (eds) *Family Troubles? Exploring Changes and Challenges in the Family Lives of Children and Young People*, pp. 151–62. Bristol: Policy Press.

Mannay, D. (2013c) '"I Like Rough Pubs": Exploring Places of Safety and Danger in Violent and Abusive Relationships', *Families, Relationships and Societies*, 2 (1): 131–7.

Mannay, D. (2014a) 'Storytelling Beyond the Academy: Exploring Roles, Responsibilities and Regulations in the Open Access Dissemination of Research Data', *Journal of Corporate Citizenship*, 54: 109–16.

Mannay, D. (2014b) 'Achieving Respectable Motherhood? Exploring the Impossibility of Feminist and Egalitarian Ideologies against the Everyday Realities of Lived Welsh Working-class Femininities', *Women's Studies International Forum* ifirst edition. Available at: http://dx.doi.org/10.1016/j.wsif.2014.10.020 (Accessed 19 August 2015).

Mannay, D. and Morgan, M. (2015) 'Doing Ethnography or Applying a Qualitative Technique?: Reflections from the "Waiting Field"', *Qualitative Research*, 15 (2): 166–82.

Margolis, E. and Pauwels, L. (2011) 'Introduction', in E. Margolis and L. Pauwels (eds) *The Sage Handbook of Visual Research Methods*, pp. 3–23. London: Sage.

Markus, H. and Nurius, P. (1986) 'Possible Selves', *American Psychologist*, 41 (9): 954–69.

Mattingly, D. (2001) 'Place, Teenagers and Representations: Lessons from a Community Theatre Project', *Social and Cultural Geography*, 2: 445–59.

Mills, D. and Ratcliffe, R. (2012) 'After Method? Ethnography in the Knowledge Economy', *Qualitative Research*, 12 (2): 147–64.

Mitchell, C. (2011) *Doing Visual Research*. Sage: London.

Mizen, P. (2005) 'A Little "Light Work"? Children's Images of their Labour', *Visual Studies*, 20 (2): 124–39.

Packard, J. (2008) '"I'm Gonna Show you What it's Really Like Out Here": The Power and Limitation of Participatory Visual Methods', *Visual Studies*, 23 (1): 63–76.

Payne, G. (1996) 'Imagining the Community', in E. S. Lyon and J. Busfield (eds) *Methodological Imaginations*, pp. 17–33. Basingstoke: Macmillan.

Pink, S. (2004) 'Applied Visual Anthropology Social Intervention, Visual Methodologies and Anthropology Theory', *Visual Anthropology Review*, 20 (1): 3–16.

Prosser, J. (2000) 'The Moral Maze of Image Ethics', in H. Simons and R. Usher (eds) *Situated Ethics in Educational Research*, pp. 116–32. London: RoutledgeFalmer..

Renold, E., Holland, S., Ross, N. and Hillman, A. (2008) 'Becoming Participant: Problematizing Informed Consent in Participatory Research with Young People in Care', *Qualitative Social Work*, 7 (4): 427–47.

Research Councils UK (2012) *Policy on Access to Research*. Swindon: Research Councils UK.

Richardson, L. (2005) 'Sticks and Stones: An Exploration of the Embodiment of Social Classism', *Qualitative Inquiry*, 11 (4): 485–91.

Richardson, M. (2015a) 'Theatre as Safe Space? Performing Intergenerational Narratives with Men of Irish Descent', *Social and Cultural Geography*, ifirst edition. Available at: http://dx.doi.org/10.1080/14649365.2014.998269 (Accessed 19 August 2015).

Richardson, M. (2015b) 'Embodied Intergenerational: Family Position, Place and Masculinity', *Gender, Place and Culture*, 22 (2): 157–71.

Rivoal, I. and Salazar, N. B. (2013) 'Contemporary Ethnographic Practice and the Value of Serendipity', *Social Anthropology*, 21 (2): 178–85.

Rock, P. (2007) 'Symbolic Interactionism and Ethnography', in P. Atkinson, A. Coffey, S. Delamont, J. Lofland and L. Lofland, *Handbook of Ethnography*, pp. 26–39. London: Sage.

Rose, G. (2010) *Doing Family Photography: The Domestic, the Public and the Politics of Sentiment*. Farnham: Ashgate.

Smith, L. T. (1999) *Decolonizing Methodologies: Research and Indigenous Peoples*. London: Zed Books.

Sontag, S. (1977) *On Photography*. London: Penguin.

Spencer, S. (2011) *Visual Research Methods in the Social Sciences: Awakening Visions*. Routledge: London.

Susinos, T., Calvo, A. and Rojas, S. (2009) 'Becoming a Woman: The Construction of Female Subjectivities and its Relationship with School', *Gender and Education*, 21 (1): 97–110.

Sweetman, P. (2009) 'Just Anybody? Images, Ethics and Recognition', in John Gillett (ed.) *Just Anybody. Renja Leino*, pp. 7–9. Winchester: Fotonet/The Winchester Gallery.

Sweetman, P. and Hensser, L. (2010) *City Portraits* - Research output: Non-textual form › Exhibition https://www.southampton.ac.uk/mediacentre/news/2010/jul/10_78.shtml (Accessed 19 August 2015).

Thompson, P. (2008) *Doing Visual Research with Children and Young People*. Abingdon: Routledge.

Vidich, A. J. and Bensman, J. (1958) *Small Town in Mass Society: Class Power and Religion in a Rural Community*. Princeton: Princeton University Press.

Vrasidas, C. (2001) 'Interpretivism and Symbolic Interactionism: "Making the Familiar Strange and Interesting Again" in Educational Technology Research', in W. Heinecke and J. Willis (eds) *Research Methods in Educational Technology*, pp. 81–99. Charlotte, NC: Information Age Publishing.

Wall, K., Hall, E. and Woolner, P. (2012) 'Visual Methodology: Previously, Now and in the Future', *International Journal of Research and Method in Education* (Special Issue – Problematising Visual Methods), 35 (3): 223–6.

Wickham, C. and Vincent, N. (2013) 'Debating Open Access: Introduction', in C. Wickham and N. Vincent (eds) *Debating Open Access*. London: The British Academy.

Wiles, R. (2013) *What are Qualitative Research Ethics?* Bloomsbury: London.

Wiles, R., Clark, A and Prosser, J. (2011) 'Visual Research Ethics at the Crossroads', in E. Margolis and L. Pauwels (eds) *The Sage Handbook of Visual Research Methods*. Sage: London.

Wiles, R., Prosser, J., Bagnoli, A., Clarke, A., Davies, K., Holland, S. and Renold, E. (2008) 'Visual Ethics: Ethical Issues in Visual Research'. ESRC National Centre for Research Methods Review Paper NCRM/011. ESRC National Centre for Research Methods, University of Southampton. Available at: http://eprints.ncrm.ac.uk/421/1/MethodsReviewPaperNCRM-011.pdf (Accessed 19 August 2015).

Wright, T. (2011) 'Press Photography and Visual Rhetoric', in E. Margolis and L. Pauwels (eds) *The Sage Handbook of Visual Research Methods*, pp. 317–36. London: Sage.

# 8

# CONCLUSION

## Looking back and moving forward

This final chapter revisits some of the main points raised across the book and reflects on lessons learnt and further opportunities for, and threats to, visual techniques as a qualitative research tool; in terms of data production, dissemination and the wider field of ethnographic research. The chapter will explore the barriers to progression in the field of visual studies and how we can resist the urge to keep reinventing the wheel by crossing disciplinary boundaries and sharing best practice. It will also focus on emergent writing methodologies and recent debates around the personal, subjective and transformative dimensions of writing up and disseminating research findings; as well as considering how moves towards Open Access in publishing can raise new ethical dilemmas for visual researchers. In this way, the discussions will be both reflexive and progressive, looking back and moving forward, by consolidating the arguments presented so far and exploring new developments in visual and creative research; focusing on threats, challenges and opportunities in visual studies.

### Crossing disciplinary boundaries

In writing this book, I began with an appreciation that visual, narrative and creative research are not held within a single discipline, rather they are within and beyond all disciplines. However, as the references sections in each chapter indicate, the disciplinary spread is wide and vast; and I have been surprised by how far away from my home School of Social Sciences I have travelled in bringing together this volume. For Nicolescu (2011, p. 1), many researchers actively avoid any movement between disciplines as 'for them, the boundaries between disciplines are like boundaries between countries, continents and oceans on the surface of the Earth'. These boundaries may have temporal fluctuations but an assumed property remains unchanged, the continuity between territories; and such clear demarcations act as a challenge to conducting and progressing visual studies.

Anderson (1983) discusses nations as 'imagined communities' constructed with symbolism and linguistic forms through which a common identity is assumed, where cultural products come to stand for or symbolise nationality; and we can apply this framework to consider academic identity. Billig's (1995) concept of 'banal nationalism' illustrates how small everyday actions reinforce the imagined community of nation and the performance of national identity; and in academic disciplines we continually demarcate and affirm identity through our associations, publications, conferences and reading materials. These demarcations are illustrated in visual studies texts that clearly situate themselves in a particular discipline, for example, 'visual sociology' (Harper 2012), 'visual methods in psychology' (Reavey 2011), and, the slightly wider, 'visual research methods in the social sciences' (Spencer 2011).

This is not to say that these texts are not valuable, they have been invaluable in writing this book; however, although it is useful to think about the visual as it applies to particular disciplines, it is also advantageous to reclaim the spaces in-between and consider the fusion of disciplinary boundaries. For Nicolescu (2006), disciplines create windows to look through at very specific aspects of reality but looking through multiple windows engenders the beginnings of transdisciplinarity; and in working with visual, narrative and creative forms, it is useful to look through many windows. As I argued in Chapter 2, the fixing of the gaze within specific disciplines has contributed to a reinventing of the wheel, where visual methodologies are reinvented over and over again, often with little consideration of what went before or of what is going on in the parallel worlds of neighbouring approaches.

As Pauwels (2011, p. 4) contends, ahistorical and highly dispersed approaches are 'detrimental to advancing a more mature methodology' and it is important to embrace both the wisdom of classic studies of the visual and the creative practices of a wide range of research fields. In order to achieve this, it is important to establish a dialogue between disciplines, and events such as the bi-annual *International Visual Methods Conference* (IVMC) are key opportunities for opening up communication and learning about the wider field. At these cross-disciplinary events, such as the third IVMC in New Zealand, I have had the opportunity to make connections with artists, historians, curators, social scientists, human geographers, health practitioners and a range of other visualistas[1]; and listening to these diverse presentations, and the following conversations, have helped me to both refine my knowledge and craft my research practice.

In Chapter 2, the problem of disciplinary distance was discussed in relation to the time delay of the photovoice approach moving from health-based research to visual sociology (Harper 2012); and these temporal gaps are sustained by a lack of interdisciplinary dialogue. Arguably, there are a range of interdisciplinary texts, particularly edited collections, around the visual (Margolis and Pauwels 2011; Pink 2012; Stanczak 2007) and a range of leading qualitative and visual research journals, such as *Qualitative Inquiry, Qualitative Research, Visual Studies* and *Visual Methodologies*; but the tendency to select the frames that are most closely aligned with our background and interests remains. Consequently, it may be much less challenging for a visual sociologist to venture across the street to cultural studies, than to take the continental leap of engaging with readings in archeology. As sociologist Burton R. Clark commented 'Men of the sociological tribe rarely visit the lands of the physicists and have little idea of what they do over there. If the sociologists were to step into the building occupied by the English department, they would encounter the cold stares if not the slingshots of the hostile natives' (cited in Becher and Trowler 2001, p. 45).

Interdisciplinarity is conceptualised with a range of terms, including crossdisciplinarity, multidisciplinarity, supradisciplinarity or transdisciplinarity; but at a basic level it refers to 'any form of dialogue or interaction between two or more disciplines' (Moran 2001, p. 16). In this chapter, I am not arguing that we abandon disciplinary positions, rather that we actively pursue useful interdisciplinary dialogues. Thompson Klein (1996, p. 51) discusses 'trading zones' at the fringes of disciplines in which 'interlanguages' like pidgins and creoles can emerge; and visual and creative approaches can be positioned as a 'trading zone'. To make the most of creative approaches, then, 'disciplines have to make a greater effort in understanding and appreciating each other's work without abandoning their own distinct identities' (Krishnan 2009, p. 51), embracing interdisciplinarity, while at the same time respecting and nurturing individual disciplines.

Practically, this engagement can be fostered in our reading and interdisciplinary conferences with a focus on visual and creative practice, as discussed. However, it is also important to consider how a willingness to work in an interdisciplinary way can be fostered in students, in preparation for their own research projects and future careers. As Krishnan (2009, p. 45) argues, 'disciplinary instruction does make a lot of sense at an undergraduate level' not least because an academic degree acts as corporate certification of accomplishment in a field of knowledge, which allows potential employers to have some idea of the particular training a graduate has undergone and their skills and knowledge. Therefore, teaching the groundings of disciplines remains central but there can still be opportunities to present cross-disciplinary theory and empirical work in relation to visual, narrative and creative practice.

As discussed in the opening chapter, my own teaching has influenced the writing of this book and in my third year undergraduate module, located within social and cultural psychology, I have been careful to introduce visual studies within their historical traditions and cross-disciplinary settings. By their final year of study, students have an understanding of their particular fields, in this case, Education, Psychology, Criminology and Sociology, and they are also conducting research for their dissertations. Arguably, then, this is a key time for both consolidation of discipline-specific knowledge and drawing on wider paradigms. The workshops that I run for doctoral students and new researchers also adopt an interdisciplinary focus. Importantly, it is also useful to work directly with other academic schools and scholars where possible and a new series of workshops I am involved with reflects this collaborative approach.

For example, in conjunction with the co-conveners of the Families, Identity and Gender Research Network[2], I am organising workshops around the theme of *Constructing and Deconstructing Selfhood* aimed at providing training for doctoral students. Visual, creative and narrative methodologies are centralised in the workshops and the sessions are presented by scholars from Psychology, History, English Literature, Sociology, Health and Social Care, and Media and Communication Studies. The Economic and Social Research Council-funded Wales Doctoral Training Centre provided the grant to run these workshops specifically because of their potential to engender interdisciplinary and collaborative activities. These workshops will explore different disciplinary techniques for researching identity and expose delegates to radically different quantitative and qualitative methodological approaches. Importantly, the workshops will engender opportunities for students, lecturers and researchers to be introduced to diverse, multi-modal and multi-disciplinary research methods so that they can reflect on how these might apply to their own studies.

Temporal and disciplinary demarcations do act as a challenge for progressing visual and creative approaches. However, by looking through multiple windows to explore contemporary perspectives, and looking back to acknowledge what has come before and the value of classic work in the field, these challenges can be countered. In the history of the academic disciplines there has been a strong tendency towards hyperspecialisation and insularity (Bicchieri 2006); and it is important to maintain distinctions. However, for visual and creative methods to be productive there must be moves beyond insularity and towards collaborative understandings, not simply turning inwards but looking outwards. The future of visual studies then needs to be one in which we no longer keep reinventing the wheel but, instead, consider the ways in which these wheels can be modified, improved, tweaked and applied in radically different frameworks; and find ways to share both existing knowledge and emerging concepts.

## Creative data analysis, production and dissemination

The potentialities of moving between or drawing from different disciplines, in relation to data analysis, production and dissemination, have been illustrated with the case studies presented throughout the book. In regard to found materials, there was a consideration of the ways in which audiences bring their own ways of seeing and other knowledges to bear on an image (Rose 2001); and these audiences are both public and academic. In reading the image then we need to consider perspective and draw on frameworks of interpretation to guide the reading of images and narrative forms. This analysis can draw on the art historian's technique of 'performing the art' (Belton 2002), the tools of archeology and interpretive frameworks from the social sciences such as 'breaking the frame', cultural studies, social representations theory and semiotics, which were discussed in Chapter 5. However, in all these approaches there needs to be an appreciation that academics can be seduced by their own commitment to a symbolic way of seeing, academics cannot necessarily read a truer account of the meanings intended by visual images than other audiences; and all theories and applications of interpretation are bounded within these limitations.

As Rose (2010, p. 26) contends, 'visual imagery is never innocent' and neither is its viewing; and as well as analysing the image it is useful to engage with the image-creator. In Chapter 5, auteur theory was introduced in relation to its premise that to gain an understanding of the internal narrative of the image it is imperative to acknowledge the role of the image-maker (Rose 2001; Mannay 2010); but with found materials this can be difficult when we have no access to the image-maker. In relation to family photographs and home artefacts, in Chapter 2 we considered the opportunities to move these 'found' materials to more participatory frameworks to involve the image-maker and consider how images are involved in processes of 'doing' not simply being (Rose 2010); and the ways in which 'narratives and objects inhabit the intersection of the personal and the social' (Hurdley 2006, p. 717). The creators of art and photography were also explored with the analysis of historical accounts (Chadwick 1990) and contemporary interpretations from press and documentary photographers (Wright 2011; Meltzer 2000).

It is also important to explore the audiencing of images and their wider interpretations with different publics, beyond the voice of the image-creator and academic viewer. In Chapter 2, there was an exploration of how the readers of the newspapers are positioned and what they were invited to feel, through the use of imagery (Rose 2010). Chapter 5 revisited the complexity and multiplicity of connotation in the situated act of viewing; and interpretation was explored through a cultural lens, where the geographical context of viewing created diverse and competing understanding of images in advertising (Harper and Faccioli 2000). In relation to ethics and voice, Chapter 7 also focused on public audiences and considered the need to think carefully about how to balance voice and what is being heard, its 'audiencing' (Lomax and Fink 2010). In all these accounts the power of the image and its emotional impact on audiences was centralised, aligning with Barthes' (1981) 'punctum' as a piercing or bruising of the viewing subject. The emotionality of audience and the affective elements of the image, may speak of subjectivities but their exploration is of central importance.

In teaching about found images and their analysis, I am always concerned with their wider contextualisation of objects of inquiry and my students' reflexivity, encouraging them to 'resist the universalising claims of academic knowledge and to insist that academic knowledge, like all other knowledge is partial' (Rose 2001, p. 130). In considering the future of visual analysis and the potentiality to make this a more creative and reflexive process, which seeks multiple perspectives and appreciates differential contexts for interpretation, I am most interested in studies that can locate interpretation in creators, academic viewers and public audiences. It is not always possible to contextualise a found image to this extent; but it is useful to consider how this form of creative interpretation can be achieved in the movement between found, researcher-initiated and participatory productions.

For example, Blinn-pike et al. (2012) explored the affective power of images in relation to the *Winged Victory: Altered Images: Transcending Breast Cancer* (Myers and Marrocchino 2009). The book is a collection of photographic portraits of women who have undergone treatment for breast cancer. Importantly, the book itself offers contextualisation by offering the accounts of the subjects of the photograph themselves, a narrative account that is often absent from fine art and portrait photography. Each of the portraits are accompanied by vignettes written by the women subjects relating a brief story of their breast cancer experience; and for some portraits the women's husbands, family members, or significant others also share their stories and are photographed.

The study that followed, and drew from this portrait collection, worked with fifteen women who had been diagnosed with breast cancer at least a year prior to the study. Disease, pain, death and sensory experiences often do not easily lend themselves to language and the centralisation of these images hoped to overcome the difficulties of representing bodily experiences adequately with only words. Elicitation interviews were conducted around these images, which were provided to participants in advance of the interviews and the elicitation approach was selected as a potential vehicle of empowerment. The study drew on Art Myers' photographs, but they were not simply discussed as found materials – Myers was part of the research team. In this way, although the images were not created for social science research, the photographer became a researcher who initiated and created the images discussed. This arrangement enabled a discourse with the photographer, allowing an application of auteur theory and the elicitation interviews positioned participants as experts in the subject matter, women with breast cancer who could articulate their interpretations of Myers' work, their affective properties and the differential impacts on individuals, the effects of audiencing.

This study illustrates the ways in which social researchers can work with artists and expert audiences to extend our understanding of the visual, the meaning for the image-creator, how it is interpreted, what it does, and the multiple subjectivities that guide its viewing. Potentially, this form of creative, collaborative work can act to move image-creators, academic researchers and participants beyond their symbolic ways of seeing, enabling the production of more nuanced understandings not only of visual images but the topics they represent. Blinn-pike *et al.*'s (2012) study demonstrates the benefit of working across disciplines discussed in the previous section; but even within our own departments we can creatively engage with an interrogation of our meaning making. Focusing on context, sharing our initial interpretations with colleagues and working across alternative frameworks of analysis can help us consider how the meanings of images, and the intentions of their creators, can become 'lost in translation' (Lomax 2015); and help to guard against one-dimensional, insular readings of visual, narrative and creative data sources.

In the same way that creativity is required in the analysis of images, imaginative, resourceful and innovative practice can be advantageous at the stage of data production. The book has committed the majority of its efforts to exploring the potentialities of visual, narrative and creative forms of data production and discussed multi-modal forms such as photography, drawing, collaging, mapping, modelling, biographical accounts, sandboxing and film. These forms have been beneficial in fighting familiarity and engendering defamiliarisation (Chapter 3), and enabling participatory frameworks (Chapter 4). In data production, we see an enthusiastic borrowing from other disciplines and traditions such as documentary photography, creative arts and psychoanalysis, for example, in relation to the world technique (Lowenfeld 1939) and sandboxing (Mannay and Edwards 2013); and an ever-growing plethora of techniques and approaches.

The focus on data production, then, has not, for me, resulted in the argument that we need to be more creative, rather, the concern here is that before rushing to fight for the paint brushes we need to consider why we want to paint at all. In my supervision of student dissertations, my conversations with other researchers and, admittedly, my own work, I can recognise that in some cases we become over invested in the latest and greatest technique. Therefore, before loading up with the camera, tripod, crayons, canvases and sand, there needs to be careful discussions at the design stage about what the visual can bring, why we need it and what the associated difficulties could be.

In Chapter 4, there was a critique of the idea of an easy marriage between the visual and the participatory (Luttrell and Chalfen 2010); and participatory visual projects have not resolved the goal of 'giving voice', neither should they be conferred the ability to achieve this goal simply because they are 'creative'. Chapter 6 focused specifically on the practicalities of applying creative techniques and questioned the temporal restrictions, the problems of confidence and artistic ability (Kearney and Hyle 2004; Mannay 2010), and the suitability of approaches for different participants (Johnson et al. 2012). There was also a discussion about how we embed the visual in epistemologically sound frameworks and move beyond the idea of research techniques to a more holistic conceptualisation of the research process and journey (Mannay and Morgan 2015). Then in Chapter 7, discussions were embedded in the 'moral maze of image ethics' (Prosser 2000). Consequently, in relation to data production, I am suggesting that although it can be useful to be imaginative and innovative, rather than calling for more creativity, perhaps the appeal should be for more consideration; a more thoughtful engagement with the rationale, the practicalities and the ethics of visual fieldwork.

Moving to reflect on dissemination, this is an area that calls for both high levels of reflexivity and creativity. Chapter 7 focused on the ethical landscapes of representation, interpretation, voice, trust, confidentiality, and the unintended consequences of research with narratives and visual images. Here, I considered the 'politics of recognition' (Sweetman 2009), research reciprocity (Richardson 2015) and 'time immemorial' (Brady and Brown 2013) and how these offer competing accounts about our research outputs and the visibility of places, spaces and participants. The debate around if, when and how participants can and should be seen is yet to be resolved; and the tension between revealing and concealing the contents of visual images is central in visual research ethics (Cox et al. 2014). However, when we decide that participants should not be seen, it is important to seek alternative forms of presentation so that audiences can 'see what it looks like' (Payne 1996, p. 19); and consider a 'seeing' without the necessity for visual images.

The previous chapter introduced creative forms of dissemination, which have attempted to engender these spaces of 'seeing'; for example, Richardson's (2015) conceptualisation of 'theatre as a safe space' and the play Under Us All, which drew on the verbatim accounts of participants' visual elicitation interviews and conversations in his ethnographic fieldwork. There was also a discussion of my own work and the ways in which I have employed poetry as a tool to communicate participants' narratives, retaining the power of these accounts but removing the associated images and wider contextualisation to maintain confidentiality (Mannay 2013, 2014a). These are approaches that have attempted to negotiate the tension between concealing identity and giving participants a voice; and also engaging audiences at an affective level and achieving impact. However, these forms of dissemination may not be practical solutions for all studies or researchers. Richardson's (2015) *Under Us All*, required additional funding for staging, production and actors, and when I have presented and taught about the use of poetry, there is often an understanding of the potential but an anxiety around a prerequisite to write poetry; a common response from social scientists is 'I can't write poetry'.

It is important then to keep thinking about ethical, impactful dissemination that can communicate the depth of identifying visual and narrative productions when these are at risk of being silenced by their absence; and the dialogic epistolary form is worth consideration. Carroll (2015) has employed the epistolary genre to communicate her findings from an ethnographic research project on human milk donation and the use of donated breast milk for hospitalised, preterm infants. Carroll created a series of letters from a donating mother and the recipient mother; although the letters themselves were constructed by Carroll, they act as a representation of the intimate thoughts, affective sentiments, and labours that surround the provision and use of donor milk, generated in the ethnographic fieldwork. The fieldwork generated observations and conversations, which were recorded in textual and visual forms, including video recordings; and the value of representing data in this epistolary form is transferable to multiple modes of ethnographic inquiry.

Carroll (2015, p. 8) argues that use of the epistolary form to share ethnographic findings with a broad audience may seem paradoxical; 'the letter is a private form, and so too are the sentiments expressed by the female correspondents'. However, within the deeply personal form of letter writing, Carroll is able to engage the reader and communicate the 'important subtle, affective moments that were not only conveyed to' her, but also experienced by her during ethnographic fieldwork. The careful crafting of these letters provides a platform to communicate the experiences of the mothers in the study in a way that retains their anonymity but also highlights the emotional impact of connection, disconnection and silencing that is engendered by the formal milk banking sector's anonymous system of donation. In this way, Carroll's work represents and communicates her 'sense of responsibility, to react, to act and to find a way for what has been shared to translate into something worthwhile' (Mannay 2013, p. 134). Where producing theatre and engaging with poetry may seem impracticable, then perhaps, dialogic epistolary form, letter writing with its familiar conventions of dates, salutations, closings, signatures, and addresses, could well prove a useful resource for disseminating the findings of visual data; as it has for the multi-modal data in Carroll's sensitive and powerful examples of representational correspondence.

In considering impactful and ethical dissemination we can also consider the possibility of reframing the ordering from 'visual in textual out', to 'textual in and visual out'. For example, in my forthcoming edited collection, *Our Changing Land: Revisiting*

*Gender, Class and Identity in Contemporary Wales* (Mannay 2016), a group of academics came together to revisit and reflect on seminal Welsh papers written in the 1980s and 1990s, all prior to devolution. The earlier editions that the book reviewed included Welsh poetry, which was not specifically developed in the collection. However, the project was interested in engaging with the discourse of the 'Welsh Bard' but also extending the concept in relation to contemporary Wales. Therefore, funding was secured to work in collaboration with the organisation Ministry of Life[3] to produce original rap poetry with young Welsh artists that then featured in a written form in the text and was linked to audio and visual/audio materials.

Ministry of Life also worked with the Welsh photographer, Ian Homer, to develop a range of visual images to represent the themes of the twelve edited chapters. These themes were discussed and developed in a workshop with young people and represented through the artists' existing work and new bespoke images, which were showcased in the edited collection. A dissemination and display event is also being organised to coincide with the launch of the book, which will include a display of the photographic images and live performance of the rap poetry. This project acted to engage with marginalised young people in Wales and provide the opportunity for their conceptualisations of nation, identity, Welsh culture and social issues to have a voice in the publication and the associated audio, visual and event outputs. These creative outputs were not simply a reflection of the content of the chapters, rather the young people involved took the themes and came back with issues that had not necessarily been considered by the academic authors; but issues that were of central importance to them.

In producing powerful visual and musical accounts, the venture has offered an opportunity for young people to express their ideas and, in doing so, suggest an agenda for further academic research, policy making and projects of social justice. As illustrated in this section then, and at different points across the book, visual and narrative methods can be employed creatively, in relation to data production, analysis and dissemination. Yet, they also need to be applied reflexively, ethically and with a knowledge of previous studies and interdisciplinary contributions. However, researchers are not operating in isolation, rather they are working within wider frameworks of institutional, economic and funding-related boundaries, which can both offer opportunities and present challenges to creative research approaches, as documented in the following section.

## Open Access and closing doors

The Open Access movement and its premise that all funded research should be available to any interested reader, anywhere (Wickham and Vincent 2013), was discussed in the previous chapter in relation to visual images. Arguably, Open Access publishing and the sharing of data, and reuse of data sets, offers a range of opportunities for the progression of knowledge and engenders economic benefits. However, as explored in Chapter 7, calls for Open Access publications and data sets also bring a number of threats and challenges for qualitative researchers, particularly those who work with visual images. Questions have been raised as to whether re-use of primary research is appropriate or ethical (Dicks 2012), and the potential for images to be 'reduced, blown up, cropped, retouched, doctored, tricked out' (Sontag 1977, p. 4) is a central concern now that digital technologies to manipulate images are so readily available.

There is a danger that the images created by researchers and participants will become online commodities, and the circulation of photographs in the visual economy could engender particular kinds of viewing publics, which were not anticipated by the researcher or participants. In this way, new narratives evoked in the re-use of primary research could act to counter and re-represent participants' original accounts as they are taken out of their original context and re-conceptualised to tell a different story. This raises issues about the ethics of visibility and obligations around 'informed consent'; as researchers themselves lose certainty about how their data will be re-used in the future, who may re-work the data, and to what purpose.

As discussed in the previous section, researchers can work creatively to protect the confidentiality of their participants but retain the power of their accounts in projects of ethical dissemination. However, as funding becomes tied to Open Access archiving, researchers lose control of their data sets and the ways that they are communicated. This puts researchers in a difficult position where they are required to secure grants from funding bodies but the conditions of these grants require an agreement to share ownership of data sets with invisible others who can re-work, edit and disseminate new versions of images and text. Researchers will have to make difficult decisions about what funding to apply for and whether it is ethical to work with visual data, with the knowledge that it could potentially be re-used in ways that are antithetical to the original study and its purpose. Therefore, 'in the rush towards Open Access, researchers need to put on the brakes, rock the boat of new conventions and consider what is right, agreed, informed' (Mannay 2014b, p. 111); if not the value of creative and visual approaches could be tainted by its future re-workings.

In cases where individual research councils and academic institutions facilitating the Open Access movement fail to acknowledge the research participant as central in the production of research knowledge and ensure that the obligations of informed consent, and duties of care, are maintained, then it will fall to researchers; however, in a neoliberal educational market researchers occupy an increasingly marginalised position. For Reay (2014), the neoliberal university is one characterised by an insidious privatisation of higher education in which sources of funding are controlled by elite groups and junior lecturers and researchers are employed on short-term, fixed and precarious contracts. Reay suggests that academic institutions are characterised by a process of intellectual extraction in which the labours of research staff are converted into both academic and symbolic capital, which accrue to the project directors rather than the researcher. Arguably, the precarious nature of contemporary academic employment may make it increasingly difficult for researchers to 'rock the boat of new conventions'.

In Chapter 6, there was an exploration of these changes in the sociopolitical and economic landscape in relation to the ways in which they have acted to close down ethnographic spaces, which also threatens creative research. The chapter presented Mills and Ratcliffe's (2012, p. 152) argument that the neoliberal university's push for efficiency has narrowed opportunities to engender 'the unpredictable, the tangential and the creative' so that all that remains is 'methodological instrumentalism'. These external market contingencies stress the business case for research output and often prevent researchers from indulging in 'slow science', which engenders flexibility and serendipity (Salazar and Rivoal, 2013). This is particularly problematic given the argument made in earlier sections of this chapter that in order for visual studies to progress there need to be opportunities for interdisciplinary collaboration, creativity and reflexivity.

## Concluding remarks

This chapter, and the preceding chapters, have explored the practicalities, problematics, opportunities, threats and challenges to visual studies. In doing so, *Visual, Narrative and Creative Research Methods: Application, Reflection and Ethics* has offered an insight into the usefulness of classic studies and interdisciplinary approaches, and considered found materials, researcher-initiated productions and participatory frameworks. The book has engaged with a range of best practice empirical studies and introduced my own work, exploring its potential and reflecting on ways to move forward. In writing this book, I have been reminded of the power of visual and creative approaches and the ways in which they are always intimately connected to and embedded in narrative forms. The writing has also reinforced my positioning as a 'visualista' and confirmed my commitment to creative approaches more widely, and in my current project[4] there is an engagement with clay modelling, sandboxing, craft activities, interviews and the creation of a film, which will be drawn on to gain an understanding of the educational experiences of looked after children and disseminate the findings in an ethical, yet impactful, set of outputs. The book has engaged with issues of theory, methodology, ethics and dissemination, which I hope will be a useful base for readers interested in exploring, studying, applying and extending the field of visual, narrative and creative studies, with their own scholarship and research projects.

## Notes

1 Visualista was a term used by Eric Margolis to address an audience of visual researchers at the 2006 International Visual Sociological Association conference in Urbino.
2 The Families, Identity and Gender Research Network (FIG) is a Cardiff University based interdisciplinary research group. The network was founded in 2010 by scholars working on the rich and complex topics of families, identities and gender from many different disciplinary perspectives. FIG is convened by Cardiff University scholars Dr Tracey Loughran (History), Dr. Katherine Shelton (Psychology), Dr Melanie Bigold (English Literature) and Dr. Dawn Mannay (Social Sciences). The organisation of the Constructing and Deconstructing Selfhood workshops was undertaken by the conveners and Erin Roberts, doctoral student at the School of Social Sciences.
3 Ministry of Life have delivered youth work to disadvantaged and marginalised young people in Wales for six years. During this time they have delivered community events,

youth workshops, and youth clubs, accreditations and artistic outputs, courses and events for young people in Cardiff: http://www.ministryoflife.co.uk/
4 'Understanding the educational experiences and opinions, attainment, achievement and aspirations of looked after children in Wales' was funded by the Department for Education and Skills, (DfES) Welsh Government, and the research was conducted by the Children's Social Care Research and Development Centre, Cardiff University in partnership with Voices from Care, Fostering Network and SPICE.

# References

Anderson, B. (1983) *Imagined Communities*. London: Verso.

Barthes, R. (1981) *Camera Lucida: Reflections on Photography*. New York: Hill and Wang.

Becher, T. and Trowler, P. R. (2001) *Academic Tribes and Territories*. Buckingham: The Society for Research into Higher Education and Open University Press.

Belton, R. (2002) *Art: The World of Art from Aboriginal to American Pop, Renaissance Masters to Postmodernism*. London: Flame Tree.

Billig, M. (1995) *Banal Nationalism*. London: Sage.

Bicchieri, C. (2006) 'Philosophy: What Is to Be Done?', *Topoi*, 25: 21–3.

Blinn-pike, L., Fife, B. and Myers, A. (2012) 'Women with Breast Cancer: Photo-elicitation Interviews Using Photographs of Women with the same Disease', *Visual Methodologies*, 1 (1): 3–24.

Brady, G. and Brown, G. (2013) 'Rewarding but Let's Talk About the Challenges: Using Arts Based Methods in Research with Young Mothers', *Methodological Innovations Online*, 8 (1): 99–112.

Carroll, K. (2015) 'Representing Ethnographic Data through the Epistolary Form: A Correspondence between a Breastmilk Donor and Recipient', *Qualitative Inquiry*, ifirst edition http://qix.sagepub.com/content/early/2015/02/21/1077800414566691.full.pdf+html (Accessed 19 August 2015).

Chadwick, W. (1990) *Women, Art and Society*. London: Thames and Hudson.

Cox, S., Drew, S., Guillemin, M., Howell, C., Warr, D. and Waycott, J. (2014) *Guidelines for Ethical Visual Research Methods*. The University of Melbourne: Melbourne.

Dicks, B. (2012) *Digital Qualitative Research Methods*. London: Sage.

Harper, D. (2012) *Visual Sociology*. London: Routledge.

Harper, D. and Faccioli, P. (2000) 'Small, Silly Insults, Mutual Seduction and Misogyny: the Interpretation of Italian Advertising Signs', *Visual Sociology*, 15 (1): 23–50.

Hurdley, R. (2006) 'Dismantling Mantelpieces: Narrating Identities and Materializing Culture in the Home', *Sociology*, 40 (4): 717–33.

Johnson, G. A., Pfister, E. A. and Vindrola-Padros, C. (2012) 'Drawings, Photos, and Performances: Using Visual Methods with Children', *Visual Anthropology Review*, 28 (2): 164–77.

Kearney, K. S. and Hyle, A. E. (2004) 'Drawing out Emotions: The Use of Participant-produced Drawings in Qualitative Inquiry', *Qualitative Research*, 4 (3): 361–82.

Krishnan, A. (2009) 'What are Academic Disciplines? Some Observations on the Disciplinarity vs. Interdisciplinarity Debate', *ESRC National Centre for Research Methods NCRM Working Paper Series 03/09*. Southampton: University of Southampton.

Lomax, H. (2015) 'Lost in Translation? Images, Audiences and Identities'. Presented at: *Constructing and Deconstructing Selfhood, ESRC Wales DTC Workshop*, Cardiff University, Wales, UK, 30 May 2015.

Lomax, H. and Fink, J. (2010) 'Interpreting Images of Motherhood: The Contexts and Dynamics of Collective Viewing', *Sociological Research Online*, 15 (3).

Lowenfeld, M. (1939) 'The World Pictures of Children', *British Journal of Medical Psychology*, 18: 65–101.

Luttrell, W. and Chalfen, R. (2010) 'Lifting up the Voices of Participatory Research', *Visual Studies*, 25 (3): 197–200.

Mannay, D. (2010) 'Making the Familiar Strange: Can Visual Research Methods Render the Familiar Setting more Perceptible?' *Qualitative Research*, 10 (1): 91–111.

Mannay, D. (2013) '"I Like Rough Pubs": Exploring Places of Safety and Danger in Violent and Abusive Relationships', *Families, Relationships and Societies*, 2 (1): 131–7.

Mannay, D. (2014a) 'Achieving Respectable Motherhood? Exploring the Impossibility of Feminist and Egalitarian Ideologies against the Everyday Realities of Lived Welsh Working-class Femininities', *Women's Studies International Forum* ifirst edition. Available at: http://dx.doi.org/10.1016/j.wsif.2014.10.020 (Accessed 19 August 2015).

Mannay, D. (2014b) 'Storytelling Beyond the Academy: Exploring Roles, Responsibilities and Regulations in the Open Access Dissemination of Research Data', *Journal of Corporate Citizenship*, 54: 109–16.

Mannay, D. (ed.) (2016) *Our Changing Land: Revisiting Gender, Class and Identity in Contemporary Wales*. Cardiff: University of Wales Press.

Mannay, D. and Edwards, V. (2013) 'It's Written in the Sand: Employing Sandboxing to Explore the Experiences of Non-traditional, Mature Students in Higher Education'. Presented at: *Society for Research into Higher Education (SRHE) Annual Research Conference 2013*, Celtic Manor, Newport, Wales, UK, 11–13 December 2013.

Mannay, D. and Morgan, M. (2015) 'Doing Ethnography or Applying a Qualitative Technique?: Reflections from the "Waiting Field"', *Qualitative Research*, 15 (2): 166–82.

Margolis, E. and Pauwels, L. (eds) (2011) *The Sage Handbook of Visual Research Methods*. London: Sage.

Meltzer, M. (2000) *Dorothea Lange: A Photographer's Life*. New York: Syracuse University Press.

Mills, D. and Ratcliffe, R. (2012) 'After Method? Ethnography in the Knowledge Economy', *Qualitative Research*, 12 (2): 147–64.

Moran, J. (2001) *Interdisciplinarity: The New Critical Idiom*. London: Routledge.

Myers, A. and Marrocchino, M. (2009) *Winged Victory: Altered Images: Transcending Breast Cancer* (2nd edn). San Diego, CA: Photographic Gallery of Fine Art Books.

Nicolescu, B. (2006) 'Transdisciplinarity: Past, Present and Future', in B. Haverkort and C. Reijntjes, *Moving Worldviews – Reshaping Sciences, Policies and Practices for Endogenous Sustainable Development*, pp. 142–66. Leusden: Compas.

Nicolescu, B. (2011) 'Disciplinary Boundaries – What Are They and How They Can Be Transgressed?' Available at: http://basarab-nicolescu.fr/Docs_articles/Disciplinary_Boundaries.htm (Accessed 30 March 2015).

Pauwels, L. (2011) 'An Integrated Conceptual Framework for Visual Social Research', in E. Margolis and L. Pauwels (eds) *The Sage Handbook of Visual Research Methods*, pp. 3–23. London: Sage.

Payne, G. (1996) 'Imagining the Community', in E. S. Lyon and J. Busfield (eds) *Methodological Imaginations*, pp. 17–33. Basingstoke: Macmillan.

Pink, S. (ed.) (2012) *Advances in Visual Methodology*. London: Sage.

Prosser, J. (2000) 'The Moral Maze of Image Ethics', in H. Simons and R. Usher (eds) *Situated Ethics in Educational Research*, pp. 116–32. London: RoutledgeFalmer.

Reavey, P. (ed.) (2011) *Visual Methods in Psychology: Using and Interpreting Images in Qualitative Research*. London: Routledge.

Reay, D. (2014) 'From Academic Freedom to Academic Capitalism', *Discover Society*. Available at: http://www.discoversociety.org/2014/02/15/on-the-frontline-from-academic-freedom-to-academic-capitalism/ (Accessed 30 March 2015).

Richardson, M. (2015) 'Theatre as Safe Space? Performing Intergenerational Narratives with Men of Irish Descent', *Social and Cultural Geography*, ifirst edition. Available at: http://dx.doi.org/10.1080/14649365.2014.998269 (Accessed 19 August 2015).

Rose, G. (2001) *Visual Methodologies: An Introduction to Researching with Visual Materials*. London: Sage.

Rose, G. (2010) *Doing Family Photography: The Domestic, the Public and the Politics of Sentiment*. Farnham: Ashgate.

Salazar, N. B. and Rivoal, I. (2013) 'Contemporary Ethnographic Practice and the Value of Serendipity', *Social Anthropology*, 21 (2): 178–85.

Spencer, S. (2011) *Visual Research Methods in the Social Sciences: Awakening Visions*. London: Routledge.

Sontag, S. (1977) *On Photography*. New York: Picador.

Stanczak, G. C. (2007) *Visual Research Methods: Image, Society and Representation*. London: Sage.

Sweetman, P. (2009) 'Just Anybody? Images, Ethics and Recognition', in John Gillett (ed.) *Just Anybody. Renja Leino*, pp. 7–9. Winchester: Fotonet/The Winchester Gallery.

Thompson Klein, J. (1996) *Crossing Boundaries/Knowledge, Disciplinarities, and Interdisciplinarities*. Charlottesville: University of Virginia Press.

Wickham, C. and Vincent, N. (2013) 'Debating Open Access: Introduction', in C. Wickham and N. Vincent (eds) *Debating Open Access*. London: The British Academy.

Wright, T. (2011) 'Press Photography and Visual Rhetoric', in E. Margolis and L. Pauwels (eds) *The Sage Handbook of Visual Research Methods*, pp. 317–36. London: Sage.

# INDEX

For Product Safety Concerns and Information please contact our EU representative GPSR@taylorandfrancis.com Taylor & Francis Verlag GmbH, Kaufingerstraße 24, 80331 München, Germany